Hoo, Hops and Hods: The l  and times of Robert Pateman

John Pateman

Pateran Press
11 Windsor Close
Sleaford
Lincolnshire
NG34 7NL

June 2011

Second edition

ISBN 9781447767336

Acknowledgements

To my partner, Annette Pateman, for encouraging me to research my family history and for putting up with the consequences.

To the 'other Annette Pateman', for working with me on the text and for writing substantial parts of chapters one and two.

To the 'other John Pateman', for sharing with me some of the findings of his one name study into our surname.

And to all those members of the extended Pateman family - especially Irene Colbert, Linda Taylor, Barry Dighton and Bob Collins – who have sent me information, encouragement and support.

I would also like to thank the following who have helped me in the research for this book:

Bob Ogley
Bromley Local Studies Library
Centre for Kentish Studies
Family Record Centre
Gillian Rickard
Kent Family History Society
Medway Archives
Museum of English Rural Life
Public Record Office
Robert Dawson
Romany & Traveller Family History Society
Simon Evans

Dedication

This family history is dedicated to the memory of Robert Pateman and all his fellow Gypsy travellers.

Contents

1. Introduction...1

2. Gypsies or Gorjers?...21
- John Pateman (1742-1803)
- John Pateman (1772-1849)
- Theophilus Pateman (1778-1864)

3. Tanners and Bermondsey..40
- William Pateman (1801-1885)

4. The Hoo Peninsula..60
- George Pateman (1807-1840)
- Jesse Pateman (1816)
- Robert Pateman (c. 1821-1890)
- John Pateman (1821-?)

5. Wimbledon Common...84
- Mary Ann Pateman (1840-1844)
- Alice Pateman (1842-1892)

6. The Dickens Connection...104
- John Pateman (1844-1883)
- James Pateman (1846-1926)

7. Gypsies of Kent..124
- Mary Ann Pateman (1851-1929)
- Elizabeth Pateman (1852-1916)
- Henry Pateman (1856-1858)
- William Pateman (1857-1921)

8. Notting Hill Potteries..149
- Anne Pateman (1858-?)
- Walter Pateman (1859-1943)
- Robert Pateman (1860-?)
- Louisa Pateman (1861-?)
- Thomas Pateman (1861)

9. Mitcham Common..170
- Noah Pateman (1866-?)

10. Chronology..190
11. Family Tree..194
12. Census..196
13. Sources..208

1. Introduction

'No race, not even the Jews, has so successfully maintained its characteristics in the face of a hostile world. And no race has so strongly developed the power of handing on those characteristics. The half-bred Gypsy is invariably more Gypsy than Gorgio in temperament. Even a small drop of Romani blood in the veins is sufficient to colour a whole life A famous Lord Chancellor – F.E.Smith, Earl of Birkenhead (though he had more than a small drop) – is an excellent example. He rose to great eminence in our legal and political life, but he was always more Romani than Giorgio in temperament. Birkenhead was proud of his Gypsy blood. He was no exception. I have yet to meet a man or woman who is not proud of the possession of Gypsy blood' (Vesey-Fitzgerald).

I am proud of my Gypsy blood, but for most of my life I did not know that it coursed through my veins. My grandfather, Noah Pateman (1883-1949), was born in a 'house cart' at Locks Bottom, Farnborough, Kent. He died before I was born. And my father, Arthur Pateman (1916-1966), died when I was nine, without telling me about my rich Gypsy ancestry; perhaps he intended to wait until I was older; perhaps he decided to keep it a secret, because of the strong stigma that society attaches to Gypsies.

My mother, who died in 1988, never told me about my father's side of the family. But she did use Romany words such as 'yog' (fire) to describe both our indoor open fire (which she refused to replace with central heating) and the numerous bonfires which we held in our back garden. She liked nothing better than sitting round a yog! And something very strange happened on the night that she died. I had an overwhelming compulsion to burn all of her belongings – I threw all of her clothes, her shoes, her possessions, everything except her wedding ring, onto the fire. It was years later, after I had discovered my Gypsy blood, that I understood this to be a Romany custom:

'This people have a singular custom of burning all the clothes belonging to any deceased member of their tribe, with the straw and litter of his or her tent. Whether this arises from fear of infection, from superstition, or because it is simply a custom handed down amongst them from generation to generation, we have not been able positively to learn.' (Morwood).

Morwood tells the story of a Gypsy family who witness the death of a farmer's child in November 1873. On being told that the baby's clothes will be kept in remembrance of it, one of the Gypsies says 'That would be very wrong'. When asked what she would do with them the Gypsy replied 'We should burn them. Our people always do, it is our custom; we don't think it right to keep the clothes'. She however assigned no reason for this custom.

Vesey –Fitzgerald tells a similar story. On April 17th 1926, there was buried at Crediton, Devonshire, Mrs. Caroline Penfold, a Gypsy. After the burial the living wagon in which she died, together with all her personal belongings that could be burned, were reduced to ashes, all her crockery was smashed and buried, and all her jewellery, with the exception of one heavy gold ring, was also buried.

The burning of the belongings of the deceased is the best known and most characteristic of all English Gypsy funeral rites. But that is not all. When I selected a plot for my mother's remains at Beckenham cemetery my choice was close to a hedgerow, and I planted a rose bush on her grave. Vesey-Fitzgerald again:

'I think that the occasional preference expressed even today by Gypsies (and expressed much more frequently a few years ago) that they should be buried as close to the hedgerow of a churchyard as possible, and the desire still frequently expressed that a thorn bush should be planted on the grave, is also a relic of wayside burial'.

Coincidence or blood memory, who can say? As a family historian I frequently visit churchyards to study the ancient writing on head stones in the hope that it will reveal information about my ancestors. On these visits I have noticed that holly wreaths have been left on the graves of some of my relatives at Christmas time. This is another Gypsy custom: 'most families visit the graves of their near relations once in the year; generally about the time of Christmas. Then the depository of the dead becomes a rallying spot for the living; there they renew their attachments and sympathies and give and receive assurances of good will' (Vesey-Fitzgerald).

'It is by no means an uncommon thing for Gypsies to have the graves of their deceased friends and relatives kept in good order, and flowers planted on them, for which they often pay five shillings yearly to the sextons of the village churchyards." (Morwood).

Writing this book has renewed my attachments to my family and its history. In the process I have met many members of my family for the first time. One of them, Annette Pateman, has helped me to write this book. I have also learned much about Gypsy culture and the history of nineteenth century Kent.

People

This book tells Robert Pateman's story but I do not know anything about him and his family other than the information found in official documents such as birth, marriage and death certificates, census returns, baptism and burial registers, Settlement Examinations and Removal Orders. In order to fill in these gaps I have used a technique known as history by association – I write about the people, the places and the periods, or historical events, which were associated with Robert and his family.

The historical people in this family history include: Robert Gascoyne Burt, the long time clergyman at St Mary's Hoo, who baptized several Pateman children; William Wyllie, the artist who painted many scenes depicting life on the River Medway; and Henry Pye, a larger than life character who revolutionized farming on the Hoo Peninsula. But this book is dominated by two writers, Charles Dickens and Flora Thompson, whose novels form the perfect backdrop to the life and times of Robert Pateman.

Charles Dickens lived in south London and wrote about areas such as Southwark and Bermondsey, where William Pateman lived in the 1850's. The streets he lived in were those in which Charles Dickens found his muse. As an adult Dickens returned regularly to wander the neighbourhood where his father had been incarcerated in a debtors' prison, the Marshalsea, on Borough High Street, and he fictionalized John Dickens's experience in the stories of William Dorritt and Mr. Micawber.

In *Little Dorrit*, published in 1857 (when William Pateman was living at 12 Wights Buildings, Bermondsey, Southwark), he writes: 'Thirty years ago there stood, a few doors short of the church of Saint George, in the Borough of Southwark, on the left hand side of the way going southward, the Marshalsea Prison. It had stood there many years before, and it remained there some years afterwards; but it is gone now, and the world is none the worse for it.' Charles occupied a nearby attic room, overlooking a lumber yard, during his father's imprisonment. David Copperfield sold his waistcoat to Mr. Dolloby on Kent Street. Little Dorrit was christened and married in the parish church of St George.

Charles Dickens lived at Gads Hill Place, on the Hoo Peninsula, from 1859-1870 and the countryside he described is the same as that which Robert Pateman and his family lived in and traveled through. Charles Dickens and Robert Pateman were contemporaries, living in the same place and at the same time, and it is not inconceivable that Charles could have passed Robert in a Kentish lane, or described him in one of his stories such as 'Tramps' (*The Uncommercial Traveller*).

In *Great Expectations,* Dickens draws heavily on the landscape of the Hoo peninsula. The atmosphere of the marshland, with its isolated churches and remote villages, was well suited to the mysterious events of the book. It is to the damp mound of the Cliffe Battery that Pip makes his tremulous way to carry provisions and a file to the fugitive Magwitch. John Pateman was born in a tent in the parish of Cliffe in 1844.

The thirteen little tombs huddled pathetically in Cooling churchyard indicate the high level of infant mortality on the Hoo peninsula in the eighteenth century. Dickens used this poignant setting when describing the last resting place of Pip's parents and infant brothers. James Pateman was born on Cooling Common in 1846.

References to the Medway towns, both by name and implication, appear throughout Dickens's work. Rochester castle and cathedral are appraised by Mr. Jingle in *The Pickwick Papers*. Although not mentioned by name, Rochester is clearly the market town used as a specific background in *Great Expectations*. One of the *Christmas Stories* – 'The Seven Poor Travellers' - centres on Watts's Charity, a building in Rochester endowed by the sixteenth century MP, Richard Watts, for the purpose of providing one nights free lodging for six poor travelers who were 'neither rogues nor proctors'. Rochester appears as 'Dullborough Town' in *The Uncommercial Traveller* and as Cloisterham in *The Mystery of Edwin Drood*. William Pateman was born in Rochester in 1857.

Charles Dickens had ten children: Charley (1837), Mary (1838), Kate (1839), Walter (1840), Francis (1843), Alfred (1845), Sydney (1847), Henry (1849), Dora (1850) and Edward (1852). Kate Dickens was married at St Mary Hoo. Her brother in law was Wilkie Collins, author of *The Woman in White* and *Moonstone*. Anne Pateman was born at St Mary Hoo in 1858.

Flora Thompson's *Lark Rise to Candleford* is used to illustrate life in the countryside in the 1870s and 1880s. Flora (Laura in the story) portrays her childhood and adolescence in a remote Oxfordshire village, where she later worked in the post office. Laura describes her encounters with Gypsies: 'Many Gypsies frequented the neighbourhood, where there were certain roadside dells which they used as camping grounds. These, for weeks together, would be silent and deserted, with only circles of black ash to show where fires had been and scraps of coloured rag fluttering from bushes. Then one day, towards evening, tents would be raised and fires lighted, horses would be hobbled and turned out to graze, and men with lurchers at their heels would explore the field hedgerows (not after rabbits. Oh, no! Only to cut a nice ash stick with which to make their old pony go), while the women and children around the cooking pots in the dell shouted and squabbled and called out to the men in a different language from that they used for business purposes at cottage doors.

'There's them ole gipos back again,' the villagers would say when they saw the blue smoke drifting over the treetops. 'Time they was routed out o' them places, the ole stinkin' lot of 'em. If a poor man so much as looks at a rabbit he soon finds hisself in quod, but their pot's never empty. Says they eat hedgehogs! Hedgehogs! He ! He ! Hedgehogs wi' soft prickles!'

Laura liked the Gypsies, though she did sometimes wish they would not push with their baskets into the office, three or four at a time. If a village woman happened to be there before them she would sidle out of the door holding her nose, and their atmosphere was, indeed, overpowering, though charged as much with the odours of wood smoke and wet earth as with that of actual uncleanliness.

There was no delivery of letters at their tents or caravans. For those they had to call at the Post Office. 'Any letters for Maria Lee?' or for Mrs. Eli Stanley, or for Christina Boswell, they would say, and, if there were none, and there very often were not, they would say: 'Are you quite sure now, dearie? Do just look again. I've left my youngest in Oxford Infirmary,' or, 'My daughter's expecting an increase,' or 'My boy's walking up from Winchester to join us, and he ought to be here by now.'

All this seemed surprisingly human to Laura, who had hitherto looked upon Gypsies as outcasts, robbers of hen roosts, stealers of children, and wheedlers of pennies from pockets even poorer than their own. Now she met them on a business footing, and they never begged from her and very seldom tried to sell her a comb or a length of lace from their baskets, but one day an old woman for whom she had written a letter offered to tell her fortune. She was perhaps the most striking looking person Laura ever saw in her life: tall for a Gypsy, with flashing black eyes and black hair without a fleck of grey in it, although her cheeks were deeply wrinkled and leathery. Some one had given her a man's brightly coloured paisley patterned dressing gown, which she wore as an outdoor garment with a soft billy-cock hat. Her name was Cinderella Doe and her letters came so addressed, without a prefix.

The fortune was pleasing. Whoever heard of one that was not? There was no fair man or dark man or enemy to beware of in it, and though she promised Laura love, it was not love of the usual kind. 'You're going to be loved,' she said; 'loved by people you've never seen and never will see.' A graceful way of thanking one for writing a letter.'

That prophecy came true when Flora Thompson published her endearing and precise record of country life at the end of the century – a record in which she brilliantly engraves the fast dissolving England of peasant, yeoman and craftsman and tints her picture with the cheerful courage and the rare pleasures that marked a self sufficient world of work and poverty.

Places

Traveling was an essential part of nineteenth century economic and social life, with the various itinerant groups performing important functions both before the development of an efficient communications and trade network and also after, though in a modified form. John Swinstead, writing in the 1890s, identified seven classes of traveler which covered the uncommercial tramps, unemployed artisans, showmen, Gypsies, horse dealers, hawkers and cheap jacks. The range and duration of the Gypsy travellers wanderings were neither carefully planned nor chaotically irregular. Circuits were followed and certain districts were regularly visited, with the exact route and length of stay in any area dependent on the nature of the relationship between the Gypsies and the local community as expressed in terms of the success of the hawking ventures, the response of the local police, local authority officials and local residents, the condition of the camping ground, and the desire for change.

Robert Pateman visited many places and I have used local histories, newspapers and gazetteers to paint a picture of what life would have been like in these localities at the time that Robert was passing through on his travels. I have drawn heavily on contemporary accounts such as *Post Office* and *Kelly's Directories*, and maps such as early *Ordnance Surveys*. These are used to build up a profile of places like the Notting Hill Potteries (where Robert stayed in 1861), which was one of the Great Metropolitan Gypsyries described by George Borrow.

London and the surrounding districts were the undisputed heart of the traveling population throughout the nineteenth century. Even when pushed from the central areas the Gypsies continued to base their varied comings and goings from the fringes of the city into the surrounding counties. Thus it was in and around the metropolis that sizeable numbers of itinerants traveled, and their camps were to be found almost everywhere. When the season arrived for the commencement of traveling large numbers could be seen radiating from this centre, only for the direction to be reversed with the end of hop picking and the onset of wintry weather. London proved to be a convenient and large market for hawking and street trading, and a place where relative anonymity took precedence over conspicuousness. Vagrants, beggars and tramps were a common sight, and camps of people living in tents, in the open or under the arches of the London bridges were a regular feature of the landscape and environment.

In the main the Gypsies camped, during the summer, on the edges of the metropolis in the forests, on the waste ground and on the commons. The winter months saw many of them migrate further inwards to seek alternative sites and lodgings in the mean streets of the city. Camp sites varied from the idyllic surroundings of the woodland and forest to the slum regions of the Notting Hill Potteries, where Louisa and Thomas Pateman were born in February 1861.

Robert Pateman also visited the other Great Metropolitan Gypsyry at Battersea in Surrey. Robert stayed on nearby Wimbledon Common where his daughter Alice was born in 1842. During the late 1850's and early 1860's the 5th Earl Spencer, Lord of the Manors of Putney and Wimbledon, was receiving many letters and petitions from local residents complaining of the Gypsy and vagrant nuisance on Wimbledon Common. The Putney ratepayers even held a meeting on the subject in 1860, drawing up a memorial which highlighted the need to curb the 'problem'. In 1861 Earl Spencer replied thus to one such complainant, a letter showing many signs of anger, frustration and impotence:

'Sir, I regret that the Gypsies on Putney and Wimbledon Manors should again be troublesome. I assure you it is not the first time that this question has been brought before me. It has given me great trouble and annoyance because whatever I do my powers are so limited that I cannot take effectual means to get rid of the nuisance. The defect in my powers lies in the difficulty of conviction, and the facility that exists for the Gypsies to escape wherefore the summons can be executed. The position is an extremely harassing and difficult one for my common keeper.

I assure you it is my earnest wish to do all I can for the neighbourhood in this respect: and my orders are strict to lessen the nuisance as much as possible. I am willing to adopt any effectual way of putting down the Gypsies. It is curious that at this very time last year I annoyed a lady friend of Lady Spencer's by refusing to comply with her request, which was just the contrary to yours, that the Gypsies might be allowed to remain on the Common in order that their children might go to school.'

The problem thus continued unabated, with as many as 130 Gypsies camping in a corner on the Common, until it was decided the only possible effective remedy would be enclosure. Earl Spencer's proposals to sell off Putney Heath, which comprised about a third of the land, and to turn the rest into an enclosed and fenced park, met with much opposition. Such a solution served to annoy the commoners even more than his inability to remove the Gypsies from the common land. Although there was a general desire to preserve order and prevent nuisances on the Common, a Committee was formed in opposition to these specific proposals.

The issues concerned, about the nature and legality of enclosure, were such that a Select Committee was called into existence to consider the arguments. In relation to the specific problem of the Gypsies much contradictory evidence was presented. Generally most of the witnesses provided testimony to the Gypsy nuisance, though there then followed great differences in the assessments of the menace posed by the Gypsy presence and the steps needed to bring about a solution. These varied from enclosures to policing of the commons by keepers, paid by a small rate contributed willingly by the local residents.

The Select Committee eventually reported that it was both unnecessary and undesirable for any part of the Common to be sold or enclosed and as a result the proposals were subsequently withdrawn. A clash of interests and responsibility, over the rights of the commoner and the duty of the Lord to curb a menace taking place on his land, thus resulted in inactivity and a continuation of the Gypsy 'problem'.

By the late nineteenth and early twentieth centuries the county of Surrey had developed into a main centre for British Gypsies. Pushed out of London by the combined actions of the Metropolitan Police, land agents, sanitary authorities and building developments, the nearby open spaces of Surrey provided a suitable and convenient alternative. Furthermore, in Surrey, the Gypsies had the possibility of employment at Ascot races and on the local fruit, vegetable and hop farms. During the winter of 1896 their numbers were so great that it was estimated that 10,000 were encamped in the county. Although it was undoubtedly a wild exaggeration, the census revealed that there were 1,242 dwellers in barns, sheds, tents, caravans and the open air in Surrey in 1891.

After a life of travel and living in tents, barns and vans, Robert Pateman ended his days at Farnborough, Kent, where his sons had adopted the habit of winter lodging in houses. Vernon Morwood, writing in the mid 1880's, noted this tendency: 'some of the Gypsies during the winter months take up their tents and live in houses. But when they do so, they make the place of their abode in the lowest parts of the metropolis and they rent accommodation in the most wretched houses in the low localities of our large towns.'

From being a temporary winter habit, the balance swung increasingly in favour of reduced traveling and permanency, a tendency that dated around the latter third of the century. At first it seemed that only a few individuals were taking up permanent residences for the whole year, though still relying on itinerant callings as their source of income, but from the late nineteenth century the existence of large numbers of house dwelling Gypsies came to be noticed by a variety of writers. By this time the slow drift into a more expansive slide into sedentarisation, and, eventually, colonies of Gypsies were identified:

'The Gypsy element is found in many if not most villages in the south of England. I know one large scattered village where it appears predominant – as dirty and disorderly looking a place as can be imagined, the ground round every cottage resembling a Gypsy camp, but worse owing to its great litter of old rags and rubbish strewn about. But the people, like all Gypsies, are not so poor as they look, and most of the cottages keep a trap and pony with which they scour the country for many miles around in quest of bones, rags, bottles, and anything else they can buy for a few pence, also anything they can pick up for nothing.'

Robert Pateman lived in a cottage in Willow Lane, Farnborough, with his son James. The cottage was on the edge of Tugmutton Common where James had lived since 1881. Whereas Robert had traveled long distances and for long periods, his children adopted a more restricted itinerant life style. By the latter decades of the nineteenth century the majority of Gypsies traveled shorter distances for fewer months, with the inevitable result that larger and more permanent sites grew up on the edges of the towns and cities, in places like Farnborough. With the increased geographical concentration of the population there was no longer the same economic need to travel in small groups over wide areas.

Periods

The first appearance of the surname Pateman in parish registers occurred in 1574 at Ickleton in Cambridgeshire. Interestingly, this is a short distance from where Robert Pateman was born at Luffenhall in Hertfordshire (according to the 1871 Census; the 1881 Census says he was born in Hoo, Kent). The earliest Patemans seem to have lived in the parish of Ickleton up to about 1615 and then began to spread out into other parts of Cambidgeshire. The first appearance of Patemans was in London in 1596.

These dates are also significant because they correlate with the first records of Gypsies appearing in the UK. We know that Gypsies were first mentioned in the Scottish records of 1505 and that Gypsies danced for James V at Holyrood House in 1530 – the year that the first Act was passed to control the 'Gypsy menace'. We also know that the first mention of Gypsies in England was in 1514 at Lambeth and some Gypsies were entertained by the Earl of Surrey at Tendring Hall in Suffolk in 1520. Gypsies were also recorded in Thornbury (1521), Cornwall (1522) and Huntingdonshire (1544) where a large band of Gypsies were arrested and deported to Calais. Also in 1544, another group of Gypsies were arrested in Lincolnshire and deported from Boston to Norway. Fourteen further deportations of Gypsies occurred between 1530-54. Where did the Patemans who first arrived in Ickleton, Canmbridgeshire in 1574 come from – perhaps they had traveled south from Lincolnshire? There is some evidence of Patemans thriving in Lincolnshire particularly at Long Bennington and Heckington in the late 16th century. Long Bennington is to the west of Sleaford and Heckington is to the east of Sleaford, where I moved to in 2004. It seems that my move from Kent to Lincolnshire was the reverse of a trend which started in the 16th century when the first Patemans moved south from Lincolnshire, Cambridgeshire and Hertfordshire, via Middlesex and Surrey, to Kent.

Another John Pateman (of Herne Bay, Kent) is carrying out a one name study of Pateman. His great grandfather, James Pateman, was born at Bassingbourne near Royston in 1831. Bassingbourne is very close to Ickleton and Luffenhall. James married a shoemaker's daughter from Branston (which is very near to Sleaford, Long Bennington and Heckington) in 1859. James Pateman was a carpenter by trade and after his marriage he moved initially to Richmond in Surrey and then to South Norwood where he died on 1 January 1916. It is assumed that he moved from Bassingbourne to London to jump on the building bandwagon between 1860-90. His journey south mirrored that of Robert Pateman. Robert and James were born close to each other; they both traveled south via Surrey and Kent; and they are buried within a few miles of each other. Could they be connected – or is this just one of those many coincidences that crop up in family history and which, without corroborating evidence, must remain conjecture rather than conclusion?

I have used historical events to set the scene and paint the wider picture of the period in question. I use background, historical and contextual information taken from contemporary accounts, novels and secondary sources. The life and times of Robert Pateman and his family is also the history of the nineteenth century. The world into which Robert Pateman was born in 1821 was very different to that in which he died in 1890. Robert lived through both the agrarian and the industrial revolutions. In the process society was transformed. Every aspect of life was changed. Progress bought many improvements to ordinary people but in the rush for change much was lost as well. The population grew and the bond between people and the land was damaged or broken. There was a shift from the countryside to the towns. Traditional ways of life – including that of the English Gypsy – were threatened or destroyed. Land was enclosed, living a nomadic lifestyle became increasingly difficult. During Robert's life time some major legislation relating to Gypsies was enacted:

- 1822 Vagrancy Act - simplified previous laws regarding vagrants, rogues and vagabonds, etc., and consolidated them into one Act
- 1822 Turnpike Roads Act - any Gypsy encamping on the side of a turnpike road was liable to a fine of 40s.
- 1824 Vagrancy Act - any one pretending to tell fortunes by palmistry, or otherwise to deceive; any one wandering abroad and lodging under any tent or cart, not having any visible means of subsistence, and not giving a good account of himself, was liable to a penalty of three months' imprisonment.
- 1835 Highway Act - penalised Gypsies who camped on the highway to a fine of 40s.
- 1871 Pedlars Act – an extension of the 1810 Hawkers and Pedlars Act, which required the purchase of a licence for hawkers and pedlars.
- 1875 Public Health Act – made provisions concerning the accommodation for hop pickers
- 1876 Commons Act – empowered local authorities to make bye-laws effectively closing commons to Gypsies.
- 1881 Pedlars Act – extension of the 1871 Pedlars Act
- 1883 Public Health (Fruit Pickers Lodgings) Act - extended Public Health Act regarding accommodation for pickers of fruit and vegetables
- 1885 Housing of the Working Classes Act – applied provisions of the Public Health Act to nuisances in tents, vans, etc. District Councils were empowered to make bye-laws in this respect.
- 1888 Hawkers Act – extended previous Acts regarding hawkers
- 1889 Infectious Diseases (Notification) Act – provisions of the Act applied to moveable dwellings just as it applied to houses
- 1889 Local Government Act – allowed County Councils to make bye-laws for the prevention of vagrancy.

This legislation coexisted with other external factors which threatened and encroached upon the traveling way of life. The most notable of these were the attempts by missionaries and philanthropic humanitarians to force settlement on the travelers; persecution and harassment by law officers and state officials; the challenge posed by technological developments and industrial advance to traditional crafts and employments; the enclosure movement and building and development schemes which took away many of the regular and customary camping grounds.

The enclosure movement gathered momentum throughout the century, taking away increasingly large areas of common land. The impact on the nomadic population was felt early on with accounts of Gypsies complaining of the difficulties occasioned by enclosure dating from the opening decades of the century. Much land was enclosed under Private Acts between 1834 and 1849, under the Commons Act of 1876 and by an Act of 1851 passed for the disafforesting and enclosure of Hainault Forest. Epping Forest, the other great resort of the Gypsies, also suffered a series of enclosures throughout the first part of the nineteenth century. Furthermore, a considerable quantity of land had been partitioned by agreement and also under the sanction of the Statute of Merton. In the two years from 1871 to 1873 the area of commons had been reduced from 8,000,000 to 2,633,000 acres. The effect of this on the Gypsies was dramatic:

'Their old haunts are no longer their homes. The wide stretching table land around their present temporary retreat, once their own, as if by right of purchase, is now cultivated and enclosed; ploughed fields are interspersed among the smooth, turfy, breezy downs, and utility has replaced the picturesque. The Gypsy tent rises no more from the green sward…so it is in the woodlands. Trees are felled, and houses built, and the wanderers…seek their leafy abodes in vain.'

Similarly, the roadside verge was no longer a convenient or practical alternative in quite the same way as it had been in years past. The wide 'slang' by the roadside of mid century England, where the horses could pasture free of charge, were now guarded and reduced, and the pressure to move on from the rural police and local authority officials was consistent and tiring in its effect. A Gypsy named Lovell stated unhesitatingly that these developments had 'finished the old style Gypsy'.

The situation for the Gypsies was scarcely any better in the towns. For example, in London the regular haunts of the Gypsies at Crystal Palace, the 'Potteries' district of Latimer Road (where Robert stayed in 1861), and elsewhere, were subject to housing and building programmes. By the 1880s Notting Dale, Willesden, Wormwood Scrubs and Kensal Green were all closed to the travelers. Reclamation of waste land, building projects and railway extensions were, for the Gypsy travelers, the urban equivalents of rural enclosures.

The effects of these combined developments were various. Enclosure and the rural police tended to force Gypsies off the country roads and into the towns. Here they congregated in large encampments, located generally on land rented either from sedentary landlords though also occasionally from the more wealthy Gypsies, or else in rented accommodation in low tenements of the slum areas. Homes were found in the damp cellars and garrets of the towns and cities. The drift towards permanent settlement was taking place in town and country alike, affecting the Gypsies of Yetholm, London, Dorset, Kent and all the counties between.

Hoo

It is the combination of people, places and periods which give this family history such a rich context and texture, as they weave geography, history and biography into the lives of an ordinary Gypsy family. In particular, three main threads run through this story – the three alliterative words in our title – Hoo, Hops and Hods.

The Hundred of Hoo is a well-preserved and well-kept secret. The Rev. F.J. Hammond, who was born and bred in Kent and who was Vicar of Allhallows for twenty-seven years, relates that, as a boy, driving with his father over Bluebell Hill – the ridge separating Maidstone from Rochester – he asked what the country was that they could see stretching out north beyond the Medway. His father told him that he believed it to be the Hundred of Hoo. 'Believed' is the operative word.

As Mr. Hammond himself puts it in his book, *The Story of an Outpost Parish*, 'It was understood to be an out-of-the-way, wild sort of place in which, unless obliged to do so, people did not live.' Holinshed, the chronicler, who died in 1580, after recording that Hoo was nearly an island, repeated a current rhyme: 'He that rides into the Hundred of Hoo, Besides pilfering seamen, will find dirt enow.'

Lambarde, author of *A Perambulation of Kent*, does not bother to mention the district at all. This is strange, as he certainly must have been there. Hasted, the most famous of the Kentish historians, writing at the end of the eighteenth century, is extremely gloomy about it: 'Formerly it used to be noted for the wealth of the yeomen who inhabited it, but there are now few but bailiffs and lookers who live in it, the farmers and occupiers of land dwelling in Rochester and Strood, and elsewhere; nor is there a gentleman's house, or a clergyman residing in it, owing to the depth of the soil, the dirtiness of the roads, and the unwholesome air from the neighbouring marshes.'

Hoo is integral to our story – it was here that Robert Pateman was born in 1821, if we are to believe the 1881 census. And it was here, or very near here, that five of his children were born: John (1844, Cliffe), James (1846, Cooling), Henry (1856, Frindsbury), William (1857, Rochester), Anne (1858, St Mary Hoo). Whenever Robert went off on his travels to Surrey and Middlesex he always returned to the Hoo Peninsula, which he might have regarded as 'home', or the nearest equivalent to it that a nomadic Gypsy may have. And one of the reasons which may have bought him back to this part of Kent might have been the agriculture – fruit picking, vegetable picking and, of course, hop picking.

Hops

Romani families – Gypsies, as they were usually described – were among the best organized of those working in the hop fields, though it must be remembered that, for all the 'snide comments' made in respect of these people, they often worked on farms and must have had some qualities useful for farmers, in order to retain their employment. The anonymous author of the mid-1880's story, *Esther Ray The Hop Picker* (Religious Tract Society) appears to have known the environment at first hand, even though the narrative in general follows the moral flavour of Victorian tracts:

'The Gypsies are the ones for picking. I have heard tell of a Gypsy man, with three children, who picked 61 bushels a day, and carried off 15 pounds (£15) at the end of the three weeks' hop picking. But 'tisn't always such a tally could be made up. The hops must grow thick to do it, and don't you see, these Gypsy families are so sharp witted, there's no being up to them. Sometimes, they always manage to plant themselves in the best parts of the ground, and they've got a way, when the hops are measured, of letting them lie loosely, and so making the most of them.'

The Gypsies usually set up their own encampment, i.e. as a group distinct from the melee from the metropolis. So many tents were set up, in Romani fashion, that some areas were known as 'Canvas Town' and from a distance looked like one of those Army tented sites seen so often during the Boer War period. Better off members of the clan came in their covered caravans, 'painted so gay in yellow and red, it makes weak eyes smart to look at them'. The writer also notes the culinary qualities of the cooking: 'Why, the very smell from their pots, when they're on the fire boiling, is most enough for a meal'.

In passing, this may point to the energy that the Romani folk were able to devote to their work. It is well known that the Boer War brought out the relative physical unfitness of British working class youth, many being turned down for Army service as a result. Gypsies were no strangers to poverty but had survival qualities, possibly accounting for some of the widespread popular prejudice reflected in the words of the widow (of a now deceased hop picker) in *Esther Ray*, i.e. that Gypsies 'are a good for nothing lazy set, and that is just why hop picking suits them…'tis light, pays well, and doesn't interfere with their outdoor life.' This seems to beg the question; since piecework was employed and Gypsies were said to do well at it, some ability and effort must surely have been involved.

Diligent literacy workers, welfare volunteers and clergymen visited the hop picking camps, often with the blessing of the landowners and growers, who knew well enough the trouble caused by drunkenness. Any distraction – even a religious one – might be worth trying! Probably the most unlikely attraction was the magic lantern show, put on in the barn or even in the open air, the screen hung on hop poles, and the hop plants acting as a sort of backdrop. It was important that a good story was featured, and also some comedy for the young, and even when the presenter – the local minister, perhaps – got into a muddle with his script, the audience was remarkably patient. 'The hop pickers are happily not critical,' remarked a visitor to one of these shows, 'and do not pounce upon mistakes.' But he added that hazards were always close at hand: 'I have known the pocket of the lady who played the harmonium to be picked during the singing of a hymn, and the slides to be stolen after they had been used in the magic lantern.'

John Pateman lived in Bredgar and possibly worked on Pett Farm which had 150 acres of good orchard, hop, arable, pasture and woodland including three and three quarter acres of hops. Elizabeth Pateman was born in Burham where the chief crops were wheat, beans, barley and hops. Elizabeth lived for many years in St Mary Cray, which was surrounded by orchards; apple, cherry, pear and plum and there were also hopping and strawberry fields. Henry Pye grew hops at Turkey Hall and Cliffe, where James Pateman was born, had 80 acres of hops.

On 26 October 1853 thirty hop pickers, including 16 from one family, were drowned when the wagon in which they were returning from a day's work in the hop gardens toppled over the side of a bridge into the River Medway at Hartlake near Tudeley. They were swept into the murky torrent, running exceptionally fast at the time because of heavy rains. Henry Pateman was born in Frindsbury which had 56 acres of hop gardens in 1840, increasing to 125 acres in 1847. Walter Pateman was born at Stockbury where the chief crops were corn and hops. But the occupation, above all others, which consistently emerges in this narrative is that of brickmaking, hence the 'Hods' in our tiltle.

Hods

There are many associations between Robert Pateman and his family and bricks but we do not know whether they took part in the brickmaking process, or whether they just lived on or near brickfields. The Gypsies pitched their tents and halted their vans in areas of transition, on brickfields and on waste ground, on sites of intended buildings and where buildings had been pulled down.

George Borrow described the Notting Hill Potteries, where Robert stayed in 1861, as 'a neighbourhood of transition; of brickfields, open spaces, poor streets inhabited by low artisans, isolated houses, sites of intended tenements, or of tenements which have been pulled down.' The same area was described in *The Illustrated London News* (13 December 1879) as a tract of land which was 'half torn up for brick field clay, half consisting of fields laid waste in expectation of the house builder, which lies just outside of Shepherd's Bush and Notting Hill.'

Harriet Pateman married Thomas Henry Wood, who was a brickfield labourer, and so were their sons – but did this mean they dug the clay, or moulded it? Were they hackers, feeders or a dryers?

The clay was dug in the autumn and piled in heaps to weather and break down, not least by frosts during the winter. In the spring it was tempered, that is turned over with spades and trodden to produce an even plastic consistency. Soft plastic clays would have some sand added, but glacial clays would need sifting of stones. Later developments involved crushing the clay with rollers. Where blending of clays or admixture of a paste of chalk was required, a horse operated pugmill was used.

The tempered clay was taken from the pile by a feeder to the moulding table. Early bricks were literally hand moulded pat a cake style, but wooden moulds enabled uniformity of size. The clot moulder sprinkled sand on the table and kneaded the clay into the rough shape of a brick. The moulder then dashed it into the mould previously sanded, making sure it penetrated into the corners, and then trimmed off the surplus with a strike (a well wetted stick) or a cutting wire on a bow. The unwanted clay was returned to the clot moulder.

The moulder then turned out the raw brick onto a pallet board, knocking it to release the brick. A take off boy took them to the hackers who wheeled them away in hacking barrows and stacked them in rows, up to eight or ten bricks high, and covered them with straw, or under a long open sided wooden shed. Bricks at the bottom of the hack would have straw marks on one side. When half dry they were scintled – placed in a herring bone fashion – to allow air circulation.

The full drying process could take three to six weeks. A team of feeder, clot moulder, moulder, take off boy and two hackers could produce 3,500 to 5,000 bricks in a twelve hour day. Drying and firing was a summer activity. With the advent of kilns in the nineteenth century, coal fires were prepared in the firing sheds alongside and shovelled into the flue holes. When all were drawing they needed replenishing with coal every two hours. The kiln burned for about five days, when it was sealed and began to cool down.

Robert Pateman was born at Hoo St Werburgh which was well known for brick building. There were three brick making factories in Hoo in the nineteenth century and the bricks were sent to London via the Medway. In his essay on 'Tramps' Dickens refers to bricklayers who 'often tramp, in twos and threes, lying by night at their "lodges" which are scattered all over the country. Bricklaying is another of the occupations that can by no means be transacted in rural parts, without the assistance of spectators. Sometimes the "navvy," on tramp, with an extra pair of half boots over his shoulder, a bag, a bottle, and a can, will take a similar part in a job of excavation, and will look at it, without engaging in it, until all his money is gone'.

James Pateman was described as a bricklayer's labourer. Elizabeth Pateman was born at Burham, close to the Aylesford brick, tile and pottery works. Henry Pateman was born at Frindsbury which had six brickfields in 1847. In 1861 the residents of Hollow Bottom, where Noah Pateman was born, included a general dealer, a dealer, three bricklayers and William Cooper, a basket maker.

In 1881 Robert was living at Mitcham, which also had a brick works: 'I do not know where they found a market, or whether the soil of Cannon Hill was specially suited to the manufacture of bricks, but it is quite certain that the grunts and groans of the primitive machinery used in their making, and the rancid pungency emitted by the smoking kiln were never ending fascinations. Boys who penetrated to the forbidden "Brickie" in the broad light of day were looked upon as bold adventurers by their sisters and the smaller fry; but those who ran the gauntlet of the Gypsy peril when the white mists of evening were stealing through the camp and giving a ghostly quality to the flitting forms were counted thrice valiant heroes.'

Gypsies in the 19th century

In the 1871 Census Robert Pateman was described as a Gypsy. There is at least one piece of anecdotal evidence that Gypsies were in England in the late 1400s - it revolves around some society hostess who gave a soiree, dressed as an 'Egyptian' and telling fortunes. Samuel Ridd in the mid 1500's also inferred that Gypsies were around in the 1400s and had first arrived in the South of England.

'Gypsy, gypsy, live in a tent, can't afford to pay your rent.' Taunts like this school yard chant have followed the Gypsies for hundreds of years. On arrival in Britain they immediately aroused fear and suspicion. Until 1783, simply being a Gypsy made an individual subject to the death penalty, and as early as 1653 a recorded secondary usage for the word was 'cunning rogue.' JPs were urged to enforce the laws in order to root out these rascals and idle beggars, 'symptoms of Popery and blynde superstition', as the Bishop of Lincoln wrote in 1622.

The authorities had very little success, and Gypsies continued to roam the countryside in their tents and wagons, stopping at night in pitches for which no maps had ever been drawn but which were as well known to the travellers as the fingers on their hand. All these places had the same characteristics. There was water nearby, and a large area of grass where the horse could graze. The ground needed to be firm and level. Mud was a great nuisance for the Gypsies, who slept on the ground; moreover if their cartwheels sank too deeply into the grass overnight the wagons would be very difficult to move in the morning. It was usual for them to spend the Winter on a familiar strip of land outside town and doing their travelling from Spring to Winter.

Until the middle of the nineteenth century, all Gypsies slept in tents made of bent sapling wood, probably ash or hazel, with a covering of felt or canvas or blankets. The tents came apart easily, and by day the rods were tied in bundles on either side of a horse or donkey's saddle while the covering was rolled up and carried on its back, or in the cart. Even after carts, vans or vardos came into use, families still had tents; the parents, perhaps with the youngest child, would sleep in the van while the other children stayed in tents pitched by the fire. Large families were considered desirable, so they could never have all crammed into the vardo together.

Family duties were clearly defined. The women cooked, cleaned, did the washing and went out to find the food, while the men looked after the donkeys, horses, and the camp. In the morning, after a meal, the women set off to beg or read palms in the villages, or to sell whatever they had made in the way of mats, pegs or wickerwork. They would previously have agreed a new meeting-place for that evening. It was necessary for the men to remain behind. They could pack up and disappear in a flash if the authorities and later the police came, as was frequently the case, to harass the travellers.

Horses held a tremendous significance for the Gypsies. Only the men worked with them. Gypsies had special rules of hygiene, which divided the world into clean and unclean objects. All babies were born in tents on the edge of the site, because the act of birth was a potential source of pollution. Mother and child stayed on their own, eating from special plates for some weeks, and then the tent, bedding and utensils were destroyed. Women, except when past child-bearing age, were considered to be possible threats of pollution, and were expected to follow strict rules of dress and movement, never to walk in front of their men while they sat, or to step over plates of food; and to stay away from the horses.

Death took place outside the caravan as well. Gypsies had a great fear of ghosts and went to enormous lengths to make sure that the ghost or mulo of the dead person did not return to haunt them. The death tent was guarded, while the rest of the family or tribe sat round the fire, hoping that its light would ward off the ghost. The corpse was often dressed in inside-out clothing and placed on the shafts of his vardo, with the feet facing out, on the way to the graveyard. Favourite possessions and money were placed in the grave, so that the dead man would have no reason to leave his burial place. Relatives kept watch over the grave for fear of robbers, because removal of part or all of the body meant that the mulo could not rest.

Their strange customs and constant mobility made the Gypsies objects of suspicion. Some writers of the nineteenth century wrote romantically about the freedom of life away from towns and factories and timetables. However, George Borrow wrote *The Bible in Spain*, *Lavengro* and *Romany Rye* after spending a good deal of time wandering about, meeting Gypsies and tinkers and living on the road himself. His books first made popular the idea that Gypsies originated in Rajasthan in north west India. Scholars became riveted by their language and customs, and eventually a Gypsy Lore Society was formed. It published a journal which examined minutely the connections between the Romany language and Sanskrit, and the marriage rituals, tribal taboos and habits of the Gypsies, whom the journal-writer believed to be pure-blooded descendants of the early nomads of India. The language of the tinkers was Shelta. The popular conception of Gypsies as idle vagabonds changed in response to literature. They were seen instead by some as 'natural' people who had found a way to live, with dignity, outside the constraints of civilised society.

Tinkers, Gypsies, showmen, circus and menagerie-owners all lived on the road, travelled in wagons and pitched tents at night in places well know to them as safe for centuries past. In *The Uncommerical Traveller* Charles Dickens described one of these wayside halts. `All the tramps – the Gypsy tramps, the cheapjack, the show-tramp - find it impossible to resist the temptations of the place, and all turn the horse loose when they come to it, and boil the pot. Bless the place, I love the ashes of the vagabond fires that have scored the grass.' The pot would probably have contained boiled meat and potatoes, whether it was breakfast or supper time, and quite possibly the meat would be a rabbit, caught by one of the family's lurchers. A good dog was priceless, because it could catch you a rabbit and bring it home and you would not have committed trespass in order to get your meal.

Judith Okely has placed Gypsy employments under four headings: the sale of goods not made by the travelers (horses, fruit, vegetables, pots, pans, needless, pins, jewellery); the offer of services such as tinkering, knife and scissor grinding, umbrella repairing, chair bottoming and entertaining; seasonal labour (agricultural work, fruit and hop picking); the provision of goods and services largely the monopoly of the Gypsies (pegs, baskets, beehives, fortune telling), incorporating traditional rural crafts and long established skills. Robert Pateman worked across the whole spectrum of these employments.

In terms of peddling goods and fortunes, Robert Pateman was a licenced hawker (1866) and greengrocer (1890). The items offered for sale changed with the seasons, depending on the availability of raw materials for the manufacture of craft goods and the vagaries of seasonal demand for different wares. The variety of goods is impressive both for its range and adaptability: flowers, artificial flowers, holly, mistletoe, herbs, fruit, vegetables, gravel, wood, coal, brushes, brooms, pots, pans, tinware, wooden spoons, trenchers, bowls, shoe horns, cups, crockery, dusters, hardware, jugs, brooches and watch keys.

The importance of the hawker, pedlar and street seller in the rural and urban environment should not be under estimated. They filled a gap created by an irregular demand and supply situation, whether caused by temporal or financial factors. The pedlar or hawker was the purveyor in general to the poor, the class of traveling tradesmen were important, not only as forming a large portion of the poor themselves, but as being the persons through whom the working people obtained a considerable part of their provisions and raiment.

With regard to the sale of services, Robert Pateman was a chair mender (1844). The trades of chair bottoming and umbrella mending appear to have been especially popular with the travelers living in or near cities. These street menders were a common sight about London, carrying from house to house their bundles of canes and rushes and performing the necessary repairs on the doorsteps or in the gardens. The usual charge was from 8d. to 1s. per chair, according to the quality of the cane, the size of the seat and the estimated wealth of the customer. The cost of the raw materials, the split and dressed cane, varied from 2s. 6d. to 4s. per pound weight, which covered from six to eight chairs. The work was precarious, though, and the profits were rarely sufficient to maintain a minimum standard of living on their own and needed to be supplemented by other work.

In the category of craft skills, Robert Pateman was a basket maker (1846), a traveling peg maker (1861) and a skewer maker (1881). Basket making was common among Gypsies and, although by the 1880s they were able to buy cheap, ready made baskets imported from France, some travelers preferred to continue the craft tradition. The demand for baskets of all descriptions meant that the Gypsies had to turn their skills to the manufacture of receptacles for fruit, coal, wood, lobsters, beer and a range of other commodities. By this flexibility borne out of necessity they managed to retain control of this limited but steady market.

Perhaps the two most traditional of all Gypsy crafts were those of skewer making and clothes peg making. In order to make the pegs the Gypsy needed a ready supply of willow, which was taken from the roadside, and a supply of tin, obtained from shops and rubbish tips. The only tools required were a pair of pincers, hammer, stake, knife and nails. The Gypsy would sit in front of the stake, about two inches in diameter and a foot high, and the stages that are followed were described by W. Raymond who visited a Gypsy camp in 1905: 'That's to cut off the clothes peg on,' said he. He sat down on a bag…drew a sheath knife, took a willow wand already peeled, and measured the length by means of a piece of hazel cut half through at the right distance and split down to the cut. Then he hammered the knife through the willow, using the stake as a block. He chucked the little five inch piece upon a heap of hundreds of others which he had cut during the day.'

The wood was then dried before being finished by nailing around it a ring of biscuit tin, which was to prevent the split from going too far down. Occasionally, the manufacture was carried out by all the family, with each member specializing in one operation and so providing a fine example of the family division of labour. Around the turn of the century a day's work at this would bring in, at most, the grand total of three shillings.

Skewer cutting was a common employment among the poorer Gypsies and, like peg making, a great amount of labour would result only in modest returns. Although 2,000 skewers could be cut in one day, this was likely to take from seven in the morning until late at night, for which they would receive about 1s. for every 14 pounds' weight. One Gypsy analysed the work involved: 'It takes a deal o' work to earn a penny at skewer making. A dozen cuts to a skewer, and a dozen skewers for a penny, that's a hundred and forty cuts a penny.' Such industry was based in traditional rural craftsmanship and involved imagination, skill and long hours of labour.

Under the heading of seasonal employments, Robert Pateman was a labourer (1846), agricultural labourer (1856), and general labourer (1861). The months from March to November formed the height of the traveling season. Fairs and race-meetings formed a major feature of the itinerant's calendar. They gave some structure to the timing and route of itinerancy, vesting it with purpose and direction. Such occasions served the economic function of providing a convenient location for large numbers of people to engage in the serious business of horse dealing and the less serious pleasures of games and amusements. Also, they acted as a social forum drawing travelers from around the country and becoming the meeting place for families and friends.

Apart from the fairs, seasonal work was provided by the changing demands of the farming calendar which for a period of a few months required large numbers of temporary, migrant workers to be employed. Agricultural employments were to be found chiefly in the Southern and Eastern Counties, where it was possible to follow the stages of the agricultural cycle through the months by crossing from farm to farm and county to county in pursuit of the ripening crops. From April to June work could be found in the market gardens of the London suburbs and in haymaking, followed by turnip hoeing, pea picking (or 'peas hacking'), wheat fagging, strawberry picking and assisting with the corn harvest. In September the round of employments was completed by fruit and vegetable picking and hopping, principally in the counties of Kent, Sussex, Surrey, Hampshire, Herefordshire and Worcestershire.

Pea picking was carried on chiefly in the market gardens of Essex, Lincoln, Suffolk and Kent, and to a lesser degree in Norfolk, Worcester and Yorkshire. It has been estimated that between a quarter and a third of the persons employed in this occupation were van dwelling Gypsies. They were said to be especially favoured as they provided their own accommodation; and, because they were accustomed to temporary abodes and an outdoor life, they were thought to have a standard of living and level of health far above that of the ordinary seasonal labourer. Women and girls were often employed in preference to males, their nimble fingers being considered particularly advantageous. Payment was at a flat rate of 8d. a day. Although the season may have lasted up to eight weeks the duration of the harvest on any one farm was short, perhaps a few days. On at least one occasion the pickers stayed in a single village throughout the summer, but this was made possible only by their turning to other work, notably vegetable harvesting. It was the common practice for the Gypsies to move on.

Following the harvesting months of July and August the Gypsies arrived at the fruit and hop farms in early September. Fruit picking was again largely reserved for females, working a sixteen hour day. This sexual division of labour was not apparent in the hop fields, a seasonal employment for men, women and children of the poorer classes from near and far. Those counties with a high acreage under crop were the most dependent on the mass importation of 'foreign' labour and it was estimated that 80% of those employed in mid and east Kent were strangers. In general, the hoppers were drawn from the Irish poor, the families from the slum areas of London, the unemployed, and 'nearly all the Gypsies in England'.

Gypsies in Kent

Having considered Kent and the Hoo Peninsula, and Gypsy travellers during the nineteenth century, let us bring the two together and look at Gypsies and travellers in Kent. Gypsies tended to travel in large groups: the Act of 1530 against 'Egyptians' complained that they moved around 'in great company.' Typically a group would consist of several inter-related families.

Gypsies had favourite camping spots. In the parish of Chilham Old Wives Lees, Godmersham Hill and White Hill had encampments between 1825 and 1838 and at Seasalter between October and December 1835 the constable removed four tents of Gypsies on 27 October, three tents from Foxes Cross Lane on 30 November and three carts full on 21 December.

Gypsies seem to have preferred more remote country areas to stop in rather than the outskirts of villages. William Ellis, who farmed in Little Gaddesden, Hertfordshire, for 50 years in the early to mid eighteenth century, recalled that Gypsies lay in fields 'almost half a mile distant from our village, by which the men can stroll about in the day time unperceived, and make themselves their own spies against the following night.' He said they were known to steal clothes hanging out to dry, chickens and even sheep, begged at houses and told fortunes. Per Kalm, on his tour of England in

1748, encountered 'at several places large troops of wandering Gypsies, with a number of their wives and children.'

The legal status of Gypsies was uncertain in eighteenth century England but research suggests that they were generally tolerated in east and mid Kent, even those travelling in large groups, until they stepped over the boundaries of what would be tolerated, then the authorities intervened. In the 1760s Gypsies were particularly worrying to the authorities in mid and east Kent. In March 1761 some of a 'large gang' of Gypsies were in Maidstone gaol for felony, one for burglary, and one was in the House of Correction at Dartford.

In 1766 an outbreak of horse stealing saw Justices at Wingham Petty Sessions expressing worries that 'many idle and disorderly persons, commonly called Gypsies, have lately been guilty of stealing horses, and other felonies in or near the county of Kent, several of whom have been apprehended and committed to gaol, and many others are now lurking about, and secreting themselves in the eastern parts of the said county. The family of Mary Ann Coulter, wife of William Pateman, came from Wingham and Staple in Kent.

In the autumn of 1766 three men were dealt with at Canterbury Quarter Sessions for horse stealing. Horse stealing was regarded as the most serious of property crimes next to burglary and remained a capital offence throughout the eighteenth century. Two of the horse stealers, including a Gypsy, were executed at Maidstone on 7 August 1766.

Surveys made by Hoyland in 1816 and compared by Okely in 1970-72 showed that the majority of Gypsies travelled within a region consisting of several counties and that the area travelled may not have altered much in the interval. It is evident from east Kent Gypsies that this was also the case in the seventeenth and eighteenth centuries. Gypsies had a relatively small area of movement and the same families were found in east Kent from the seventeenth century up to the present day. The largest east Kent ones were Lovell, Lee and Scamp but there were also Boswells, Smiths, Coopers and Ingrams.

Taking Lovells as an example, 14 were apprehended as vagrants in Kent between 1739 and 1780, one was born at Romford and a few came from east Sussex but the rest were born in Kent. Robert Lovell, apprehended in 1775, was baptised at Milton near Sittingbourne in 1743, where his parents, who were not married, were working at the hop harvest. Two Lovell familes travelling together had their children baptised at Murston in 1728. On the 1841 census William Pateman and his family were living in Milton and Mary Ann Pateman, was living in Murston.

Gypsy families intermarried with each other – Scamp married Lee on at least two occasions – or did not get legally married. They often had their children baptised late or not at all. Despite this, it is possible in some cases to prove that the same family stayed in a small area for years or even several generations. John Pateman and his sons, John and Theophilus, spent most of their lives in Bobbing, Borden and Bredgar.

Not all Gypsies were described as vagrants, but did harvest work and were tinkers and knife grinders. John Scamp, apprehended in 1740 travelling with his wife, mother and two children, had last worked as a yearly servant in Staffordshire four years before but now travelled the country selling knives and scissors and his wife and mother told fortunes. John Pateman (1731-1803) worked for John Doe for one year as a labourer. John Pateman (1772-1849) hired himself for a year to William Murton.

Nine Gypsies taken up in Tonbridge on 7 September 1799 were sleeping in a tent in the open air. Some came from Chatham and Faversham in Kent while others had travelled from London, Berkshire and Hertfordshire. They had all met up to 'come into the country to hop picking and harvesting.' It is not known where the group formed but the fact that they are all found camped together suggests either some form of advance communication or travelling a certain route and collecting others on the way. It is certain that they linked up only with other Gypsies.

Travellers were a familiar sight on the roads. Their way of life and life histories can be reconstructed from their Settlement Examinations, either when they were taken up as vagrants or simply when being examined to their settlements, and from what was written about them by officials and settled parishioners. Many Examinations suggest that a travelling way of life was inherited from parents and that the person had led a travelling life since childhood. For many vagrants the area within which they travelled was quite small. As a result of Settlement Examinations: John Pateman was moved from Bobbing to Borden in 1772; John Pateman was moved from Bobbing to Bredgar in 1802; Theophilus Pateman was moved from Bobbing to Borden in 1802; John Pateman was moved from Hoo to Bredgar in 1817.

Settlement Examinations throw light on the Gypsies way of life. Lysons, writing about Norwood, Surrey, in 1786 said of Gypsies that 'in the winter they either procure lodgings in London or take up their abode in some of the more distant counties' and there is certainly evidence in their Examinations that the Gypsies found in Kent stayed in one place during the winter months. Stephen Lee 'occasionally lives in the Mint in the Borough of Southwark and works in different parts of the town by driving a barrow with a tinning pot, and works as a tinker.' William Pateman was a tanner both in Milton, Kent, and also in Bermondsey, in the Borough of Southwark.

Some vagrants did move over a wide area. Several generations of some Gypsy families can be traced through a series of their Examinations as vagrants in different places. Others begged because they had left their service, they had run away from masters to whom they were apprenticed or their master had died. Vagrants often met up with others and travelled with them. Those travellers who were born into the life knew very well how to survive, where to look for lodgings and who to approach for money. Many travellers had travelling occupations. These included pedlars and petty chapmen, chimney sweeps, chair bottomers, hair buyers, braziers and broom and mat makers and sellers. Others worked as harvesters and hop pickers during the season and begged when no work was available. Chimney sweeps and itinerant musicians had apprentices who could also get into a travelling way of life. Others sometimes pilfered and stole, or set out to defraud, travelling with false passes and briefs for losses by fire and sea and asking charity on the strength of them.

Robert Pateman's story is also that of many nineteenth century Gypsies. His travels around Kent, Surrey and Middlesex, and his associations with *Hoo, Hops and Hods*, are an important reminder and re-affirmation of Gypsy history and culture.

2. Gypsies or Gorjers?

- John Pateman (1742-1803)
- John Pateman (1772-1849)
- Theophilus Pateman (1778-1864)

If one generation suffered more than any other, it was probably those who were young between 1720 and 1750, but throughout this age sections of the people suffered cruelly from preventable causes. It must also be said that the amount of sheer abuse in eighteenth century England, especially in London and the big towns, was high. The records of the time are full of cruelty, of apprentices beaten and murdered, children taught to rob, or sold, and of mobs whose favourite festival was a hanging-day at Tyburn.

Before the 1834 Poor Law Act, there was no national benefit system in place. Caring for the poor was up to the citizens of each individual parish, who would be required to pay the 'poor rate'. A parish overseer would use the money to provide food, clothing and coal to those in need. Obviously some parishes were much better than others, but as the magistrates practically let the parish overseers do as they pleased, they, often unpaid, sometimes degenerated into corruption. Their ruling passion was to economise on the rates, and often farmed out their poor to a contractor, who could use them as he liked.

The Elizabethan Poor Law of 1601, like all previous statutes showed no sympathy towards vagrants and the poor. Technically it was no crime to be destitute but any paupers found outside the parish that was responsible for them could be in serious trouble. Newcomers thought likely to become chargeable to a parish could be removed by two justices of the peace. If paupers were found to be destitute and claiming poor relief elsewhere, they would be returned to their place of 'last legal settlement.'

By an act of 1598 there were three possible places they could be returned to – the parish where they were born, a parish where they had lived for one year, or a parish 'through which they had last passed without punishment'. These options left plenty of scope for disputes between parishes over who was responsible.

The 1662 Act of Settlement tightened the law and redefined the meaning of settlement. In practice someone could be considered as legally settled in a parish if they had rented a tenement worth £10 a year or more, or if no complaint had been made against them for 40 days. An act of 1685 decreed that the 40 days was to run from the day that written notice was given to overseers. This would perhaps have only served to warn the overseers of the need to take prompt action.

From 1692 legal settlement could be earned by paying local rates, by being bound apprentice, or by being hired as a servant and working for a full year. One could argue that the idea of 'settlement' was actually of benefit to the poor, as the law recognised that they had settlement somewhere, and whichever parish it was could be compelled to support them. Wives, widows, dependent children and other family members would be considered to have the same legal settlement as the head of the family. Settlement however, could change – people constantly moved to find work, children could be born in one parish then move with their parents to another, and being apprenticed in a parish conferred right of settlement there. Complications and ambiguities still led parish officers to go to court to attempt to rid themselves of unwanted financial burdens.

The reason why it mattered so much was that, from Elizabethan times it had been the responsibility of the parish to levy a poor rate on its inhabitants, in order to provide money to relieve the poor of the parish. Strenuous efforts were made to keep the rate down and ensure that payments were only made to those who were eligible. It is apparent from the records that churchwardens and overseers were keen to remove paupers back to their parish of origin, or at least get someone else to pay for their upkeep.

A huge amount of paper work was generated in the courts as a result of all their efforts and these papers are of great interest to family historians. They not only contain lists of names, but some documents provide a great deal of useful information about the lives of the people involved and their families. They can give the names and relationships of the people involved, provide clues to where people have come from, and give details of their profession and recent 'life history'.

These records were kept locally, but they often relate to people who migrated surprisingly long distances, fell on hard times and were returned to where the court decided they came from. Many of the cases heard by the Middlesex Sessions, for example, relate to people from outside London and included Irish and Scots and people from Strasbourg, Jamaica, Parma, Guinea and Gothenburg.

There are various 'vagrancy records', each created for different purposes. There were warrants for the arrest of vagrants. Or petitions from the contractors who undertook to remove the vagrants asking the court to compel the overseers of the parish to reimburse them for their costs. The money would normally be for feeding and transporting the vagrants, but sometimes they appealed for extra to pay for burying those unfortunate enough to die on the way. There were also some lists of vagrants, with the name and place of settlement given, that were submitted as part of contractors' accounts. There are even documents from people tendering for vagrancy removal contracts. Other records relating to vagrants and the Poor Law can be found in the archives of individual parishes, Boards of Guardians and Poor Law Unions. These records include admission and discharge registers for those who were admitted to workhouses, lists of those receiving poor relief, and apprenticeship indentures. There are also the Rate Books that list those residents who were made to pay for all this activity.

Elementary education had not advanced since Stuart times, being almost restricted to charity schools inspired by religious societies, or to that provided in large parishes by the workhouse. Yet the age was one of growing philanthropy, even if slow. Thomas Coram set up the Foundling Hospital in 1745 to help a few women who for whatever reason did not want to keep their baby.

In the first half of the eighteenth century before George III's accession the national advance was slow and uneven. The population of England and Wales in 1760 was estimated at nearly seven million and nearly one million of these lived in London. Exports roughly doubled in value between 1700 and 1770, but a minute revenue of some £15 millions showed the petty scale of the British State. This limited progress was due to the fact that the whole mechanism of life was antiquated. Internal trade was crippled by primitive communications. For, though on main thoroughfares the turnpike roads were rapidly growing, taking tolls which trustees applied to their upkeep, others were left to the Tudor laws which made parishes maintain highways by compulsory labour; with the result that scores of roads were simply mud tracks, in winter becoming torrents or bogs in which carts were stranded and coaches broke their axles.

Mile posts on the main thoroughfares marked the distances from London. Along the London Road in Kent, for example, Borden and Bobbing were just before the 39th mile post and Sittingbourne was off the 40th. The first stage coaches were introduced during the seventeenth century and in 1734 for the first time relays of horses were provided for the stage coach. This enabled the journey time of the Newcastle to London Flying Coach to be reduced from twelve days to nine.

In 1760 Britain was still a grain-exporting country, and not much food was imported from abroad. Grain of various kinds formed the most important item of food - barley, oats, and rye as well as wheat. Fruit and vegetables of many kinds were grown and hops for making beer. There were stock animals for food - cattle, pigs, sheep and poultry. In addition to food crops, there were forests, whose trees were used for building and for ships, and flax for linen weaving was grown in several parts of the country.

The thing which would strike you at once about the English countryside at this time would be the un-hedged fields. We are used now to farms which have a farmhouse and farm buildings, surrounded by fields, fenced or hedged. In some of the fields we expect to see crops growing, in others animals feeding, but in the 18th century most of the good farming country was being farmed quite differently, on what was known as the open field system.

The cottagers were usually poor people who had built small houses, or some kind of dwelling, on or near the common and had come to have certain common rights. They might keep a couple of geese, or a pig, on the common, even though they had no share in the open fields. They perhaps gathered firewood, berries, nuts and mushrooms, and managed to make some sort of livelihood by working at harvest time, by begging if times were hard, and poaching when they got the chance.

Between the parson and the cottagers were a number of people like the parish clerk, who owned a few strips of land, and in return looked after matters like the keeping of records, seeing to the election of the Parish constable and the Parish overseer of the poor. In some places the schoolmaster was also paid by the gift of some strips of land which he farmed in his spare time. Then there were always some craftsmen - the miller, the cobbler, the harness maker, the blacksmith and others, who did work which had to be done in the village, and were paid by the farmers. Even the smallest farmer would get a certain amount of money by taking some of his produce to market. With this he would buy the things which he did not grow himself.

Eighteenth century towns were small by our standards. Many more people lived in the country than in the towns. But this did not mean that they all lived in agricultural villages. A great deal of the country's industry was carried on in villages and small settlements. There were mining villages - not only around coal mines, but tin, lead, iron, alum and silver in different parts of the country. There were iron works where the iron was smelted; weaving villages in the cloth areas of East Anglia, the West Country, Lancashire and Yorkshire, centres around Sheffield where knives and other tools were made, and areas in which knitting, by hand and machine, lace-making, rope-making, nail-making, quarrying, pottery, and very many more trades were carried on, all outside the large towns. Even in the mainly agricultural districts, the wives and children of farm workers, and sometimes the farm workers themselves, might do some work at home, preparing wool or cotton for spinning, spinning it at a hand wheel, knitting, or some other craft connected with manufacturing industry.

In country districts of England in which there was no textile industry, there was not as much chance of wives and children of labourers getting work to do in their own homes. For the girls especially the best chance of earning a living was to work as a domestic servant. The number of people, men and women, who worked as servants of various types was very high, and during the next hundred years the number increased considerably.

The main occupations, then, of the ordinary people of England when George III came to the throne were as servants, out-workers - skilled or unskilled - labourers, artisans (skilled workmen who had served an apprenticeship), farm workers, soldiers (there were quite a few camps around Medway) and sailors. In the cities and especially in London, there were also many people who lived very precariously by begging, stealing or a mixture of both.

There were a surprisingly large number of innkeepers, for in those days of slow travel, before the coming of the railways, people of all classes were often in need of meals and a room. Inns ranged from large comfortable places with plenty of servants and splendid meals, to cottages where the poorest sort of people, including beggars and thieves, slept several to a room. Inns or beer-shops proved then, as now, a centre for social activity in towns and villages.

Shopkeepers varied from the pedlar, with his pack of ribbons, lace and pins, who travelled through the country districts selling to farmers' wives and maidservants in districts which were out of reach of town shops, to the city merchant. More substantial pedlars, selling pots and pans, and other household goods, travelled by cart, making regular tours of country fairs and markets, and apothecaries or herbalists filled the role of doctor in many districts.

Agricultural labourers would be employed by farmers who rented their farms from local landowners. They would live in cottages owned by the landowner and the rent would be deducted from their weekly wage. Owing to a shortage of these cottages before the industrial revolution in the nineteenth century, it meant it was difficult to get a place of your own when you married. Consequently, couples either did not get married at all or married later. Many women were pregnant before they were married and because of the high mortality rate had small families.

John Pateman (c.1742-1803)

John Pateman (c.1742-1803) = Catherine Becon (1732-1807)
- John Pateman (1772-1849)
- Theophilus Pateman (1778-1864)

John Pateman was born circa 1742. There is no record of his baptism so we do not know exactly when and where he was born, but we assume it was in the Medway region of Kent, close to the Hoo Peninsular. We know nothing about John's family, but a Thomas and Anne Petman were living nearby in Chatham, where their sons were baptised: Thomas (16 October 1743), Richard (21 April 1745) and John (22 March 1746). This could be John Pateman.

Catherine Bourn was baptised on 12 March 1732, at Hothfield, Kent. Catherine's father was Robert Bourn and her mother was Katherine Tamset. They were married on 31 December 1729 at Hothfield. Catherine had three brothers: Robert (1734), Thomas

(1737), and Francis (1740). Catherine married Thomas Becon (born 1715, Lenham, Kent) on 11 October 1751 at St Mary Bredin, Canterbury.

Catherine and Thomas moved to Borden in 1751/2 and had three children in quick succession: Robert (baptised 12 January 1752), Elizabeth (baptised 21 July 1754) and Thomas (baptised 30 May 1756)

Borden

According to Edward Hasted's *History of Kent* (1798) the name Borden seems to be derived from the Saxon words Burg and Dena, signifying a mansion or town among the woods: 'This parish lies nearly midway between Newington and Sittingbourne, and contains about 1,550 acres of land, of which 200 are wood. The high London road runs along the north side of it, whence the ground rises southward for about a mile, (leaving the house of Cryals at about half that distance) to the village of Borden, through which there is but little thoroughfare.

It is plainly seen from the high road, encircled by orchards of fruit trees, with the church and Borden Hall standing within it, a little to the eastward is the vicarage, a neat pretty dwelling. The land about the village, and northward of it is very fertile, being mostly a hazely mould, the plantations of fruit here, though many are not so numerous as formerly, for being worn out, no new ones have been planted, and several of them have been converted into hop-grounds.

This part of the parish though it may certainly be deemed pleasant, yet from the water from the wells not being good, is not accounted healthy. Southward of the village the ground still rising, it grows very hilly, and the land poor and much covered with flint stones, and the soil chalky, which renders the water wholesome, and this part much more healthy. About half a mile southward from the village is the house of Sutton Barne, and a small distance eastward Wrens, now called Rains Farm, and a small hamlet called Heart's Delight. On the opposite side from Sutton Barne is the hamlet of Wood, formerly called Hode Street, situated on high ground; at a small distance eastward from which is a long tract of woodland, in which there is a great plenty of chestnut stubs, whence they are usually known by the name of chestnut woods. These woods reach down the side of the hill to the Detling road, and the western boundary of this parish.'

The church of St Peter and St Paul at Borden is reckoned to be about 800 years old and was possibly built on the site of a Roman temple by monks of Leeds Abbey. The Norman tower is the oldest part of the present church and its most eye catching feature is the fairly elaborate carving around the west door.

The parish, though, was founded in 1160 when the first vicar was appointed and today Borden is an undisturbed little village about a mile south west of Sittingbourne from which it has managed to remain very positively separate. The approach from Sittingbourne takes the visitor past several modern homes but where the road bends past the church, old farm buildings and some picturesque timbered cottages give a glimpse of the old village.

In August 1802, William Wise, churchwarden, paid John Greensted 14/- for carrying the bells to Milton Quay in his cart. The following March Greensted went to fetch the new ones. The Leeds (near Maidstone) ringers came and played the opening rounds or changes a week later. This indicates that Borden was in a fortunate position of being able to cart its bells to the nearest port and then have them transported, possibly by barge, to the Whitechapel foundry in London. So other villages on or within the proximity of the Thames and Medway presumably were able to do the same, thus avoiding the task of hauling them along some of the county's poor roads, even in August, when they were likely to be dry and hard.

In the seventeenth century, however, Henry and John Wilnar, possibly an Ightam family, cast bells at Borden for some twenty years. John Wilnar died in 1640 and his brother Henry in 1644; both were buried in Borden churchyard. Examples of their bells survive at Bredgar, Ivychurch, Cowden, Addington, Eastry, Challock, and other places.

The Wilnars cast their bells at Oad Street where in 1959 what is believed to be their casting pit was discovered by Eddie Barton. He was ploughing Boundary Field, which is on Woodgate Farm, to the west of Munsgore and north of Woodgate Farmhouse. He came to a slight hollow which made him think of the story he had been told as a boy by a very old man. The story went that the devil in a fit of anger had thrown a bell from the church tower and it had fallen to the earth in Boundary Field, making a hole. As Mr Barton ploughed he found that the soil in the hollow was of a different colour from that of the rest of the field. He found pieces of iron conglomerate which he took to Maidstone Museum. They now have no record of this but the site was recorded at the time by Ordnance Survey. There was a well nearby which Mr Barton covered or capped, and a bank of pure sand. In the Wilnars' time there would also have been plenty of timber.

We do not know why Catherine and Thomas came to Borden in 1751/2. Perhaps it was to work on 'the plantations of fruit' and the 'hop grounds'. Catherine was six or seven months pregnant when she married Thomas. It was very common for girls to be pregnant before they married during the eighteenth century and illegitimacy was at an all time high especially in the towns.

There is a gap of 12 years between the baptism of Thomas junior (the last of the three children) and the death of Thomas senior in 1769, when they could have had more children. It does not say what he died of in the Borden register or give his age. There is nothing for Thomas and Catherine on the IGI (International Genealogical Index) for Becon and its derivatives in Kent, Surrey, Sussex and Essex. They do not appear in the registers for Borden, Bobbing and Bredgar.

After the death of Thomas on 5 December 1769 at Borden, it would have been a very challenging period for Catherine, as for any widow with children at this time. Her eldest three children would have been 16, 14, and 12, and all capable of working, but if she had more younger children it would not have been so easy. If she did not have any immediate family to help her, or some kind of means of supporting herself, it would fall to the parish to assist her and the children.

Bobbing

The big mystery is where was John Pateman born and when did he come to Bobbing, Kent? Edward Hasted says in 1798: 'The parish of Bobbing lies almost the whole of it on the northern side of the high London road, nearly at the 39th mile stone. It is not an unpleasant situation, though at the same time it has not the character of being very healthy. It contains about 780 acres of land, of which 40 are wood, the soil is generally poor, much of it on the high ground is either gravel sand, or a mixture of clay, but in the lower parts especially in the northern towards Milton, there is some good fertile level land.

The high road runs along the southern boundaries of it, excepting at Key Street, where it extends some way up the Detling road; hence the hill rises to high ground, on which, about half a mile from the road, is the church, and close to the church-yard the ruins of Bobbing Court, with the few houses that compose the village on the other side of it. At a small distance from these ruins southward, on the brow of the hill, at the end of the toll of elms leading from the high road, Arthur Gore, Esq. of the kingdom of Ireland, built on Col. Tyndale's land a few years ago, a small shooting seat, which has since been further improved. The house commands the view of the London road, and a fine one southward beyond it; below the descent of the hill, norward from the church, is Bobbing-place, a low situation near the boundaries of this parish next to Milton.

At the south-west corner of the parish, on the London road, is a small hamlet of houses called Key-street, with the ale-house in it. Here is a large house lately erected by Mr William Boykett, who resides in it. There is an ancient allowed fair here, held formerly on St. Bartholomew's day, now by alteration of the stile on September 4th yearly, the profits of which belong to the Lord of Milton Manor.' Maybe it was St Batholomew's fair which bought John Pateman to Bobbing?

The Settlement Act was designed to control and regulate the movement of the entire population of the UK – but particularly of the poor. Naturally, as Gypsies live to travel, they were at great risk of being caught contravening the Act. What happened was, when travellers or strangers arrived in a parish and looked likely to claim help or support from the parish (or, in the case of a woman, a place to give birth), they were subject to an Examination by Justices of the Peace to find out where their 'legal place of settlement' was. This could be their place of: birth, apprenticeship, marriage to a settled parishioner, employment for over a year, residence in a property with an annual rental value of more than £10, or service as a parish officer (such as Overseer of the Poor or Churchwarden).

The earlier Settlement Examinations (1740-1770) contain the most information about the vagrants and people connected in some way to them. Later statements record only the bare minimum of information about why and where people are being moved, or about apprenticeships or service. This is particularly noticeable for Irish and Scottish vagrants and those born at sea. This may reflect a social trend - were there fewer people in service? Or do brief notes reflect a change in the law – courts perhaps needing less information to make a decision? Perhaps it simply reflects an increase in the number of vagrants – the magistrate or court clerks may not have had the time to keep detailed records.

The Examination of John Pateman (Settlement Certificate No.50) in 1772, for example, does little more than confirm that he was to be moved from Bobbing to Borden. Once the place of settlement had been established, the poor traveller (and any accompanying dependents) would be escorted back there by the Parish Constable. There are obviously very few of these conditions that Gypsies could fulfil apart from the place of birth – which no doubt helps to explain why they were traditionally so keen on having their children formally baptised and recorded in a church close to where they were born.

There were no Patemans in Borden, Bobbing, or Bredgar and the surrounding area before 1772. The earliest records of any Patemans in the nineteenth century in a twenty mile radius were at Speldhurst, Kent and Hartfield, just over the border in East Sussex. Of course John Pateman could have come over the river from Essex or beyond. He could also have arrived in Kent by sea and landed at Chatham, the Isle of Sheppey or any other small ports along the Thames estuary. Other possibilities are John was illegitimate, he was never registered, or he could have changed his Christian name, something Gypsies did quite frequently.

Whatever his background, John Pateman somehow came to know Catherine Becon. According to a Marriage Licence signed by John Pateman himself on the day before his marriage to Catherine on 11th April 1772, he 'appeared personally and made Oath that he is of the Parish of Borden, and was a bachelor of the age of 30 years and upwards and intended to marry with Catharine Becon of the Parish of Borden aforesaid a widow and that he knoweth of any lawful Lett or Impediment by Reason of any Reconstruct entered into before the 25th day of March 1754, Consanguinity, Affinity, or any other legal Cause whatsoever, to hinder the said intended Marriage; and that he prays a Licence, to solemnise the said Marriage, in the Parish Church of Borden aforesaid; in which said Parish he further maketh Oath that he had hath his usual Place of Abode for the Space of four weeks last past.'

The marriage certificate (dated 12 April 1772) contains the signature of John Pateman and 'the mark of Catharine Becon'. On another marriage document (also signed by John Pateman) dated the 12th April 1772, which is difficult to read and understand, it states that John Pateman had been working for John Doe for one year as a labourer. The document mentions a sum of two hundred pounds being paid, but it is not clear by whom or for what. This was a considerable amount of money for this time. His age is given as 30, which makes him about 10 years younger than Catherine. Whether he knew her true age is open to speculation. However, even if it was a match made in heaven, or not, she was pregnant, and if he had no family or fixed abode it would have been very timely for him to marry a widow who had a home and ready made family.

For Catherine it meant she was no longer reliant on the parish, or any family, for support. Within four months of getting married John and Catherine had their first child, John Pateman (baptised 2 August 1772, Borden). There was then a gap of six years before the birth of their second child, Theophilus Pateman (baptised 14 October 1778, Bobbing). Catherine was 46 when Theophilus was born and there was a 26 year gap between the birth of her first child (Robert Becon, 1752) and her last child (Theophilus Pateman, 1778).

Even though John was a lot younger than Catherine he still died first at the age of 61 and was buried in Borden on 18 August 1803. Catherine died three and a half years later on 10 January 1807 at Bobbing at the ripe old age of 75. She was buried in Borden on 18 January 1807.

John Pateman (1772-1849)

John Pateman (1772-1849) = Sarah Cook (m. 1799) = Charlotte Mirtle (m.1821)
- George Pateman (1807-1840)
- Jessie Pateman (1816)
- Robert Pateman (c. 1821-1890)
- John Pateman (1821-?)

John Pateman was baptised on 2 August 1772 in Borden. In 1798 he hired himself for a year to Mr William Murton of the parish of Bredgar. Soon after the expiration of his year's service, John married Sarah Cook on 11 October 1799 in Bredgar. John and Sarah signed the marriage certificate with a cross, indicating that they could not read or write. The witnesses were Richard Shirley and Mary Agar.

Bredgar

According to Edward Hasted (1798): 'Bredgar or Bradgar, as it was sometimes spelt, is the next parish southwards from Tunstall. Although the road from Sittingborne to Hollingborne-hill, and thence to Maidstone passes through it and the village of Bredgar, it is rather an unfrequented place lying obscurely among the hills, and bounding eastward to the woods. It contains near 1,300 acres of land, of which 100 are wood-grounds. The village, which stands on high ground, nearly in the centre of the parish, having the church and college, or chantry in it, is a healthy and not unpleasant situation, being surrounded mostly by pasture grounds, but the remaining part of the parish is very hilly, the soil poor and chalky, and much covered with flints, being rather a dreary country'.

He makes an addition at a later date saying: 'The road through this parish to Sittingborne and Milton, which passes through this village, has a tolerable thoroughfare, and a considerable traffic is carried on through it by carriages of various descriptions, from below the hill to the keys of Milton and Sittingborne, loaded with corn, hops, wood, etc for London and other parts; and coals, ashes, coke and other materials are conveyed back again in them to the different villages below Hollingborne-hill. The land of this parish is very much improved of late, by being laid down with the flocks of sheep and fed on them.'

Bredgar is one of those hideaway Downland villages, 350 feet up on the north slopes of the North Downs. The M2 has cut away the north end of the village, which is roughly bisected by the B2163 Sittingbourne-Hollingbourne road, with a nucleus formed by the pond and the church.

The typically Downland flint church of St John the Baptist at Bredgar has drawn the village around it for something like 800 years and looks set to do so for many more years yet. There has been a church here certainly since the eleventh century although the present one is mainly late fourteenth century, probably on the site of an earlier wooden one. Its tower doorway is one of those that are distinguished by surviving Norman stone decoration, probably preserved from an older building.

Buildings around the church and pond include several prominent old timbered houses and behind trees near the pond lies the College which was founded by Robert de Bradegar in 1393.

Mr Cary, a shoemaker of Leeds, near Hollingbourne, was returning from a Bredgar feast when he was stopped by footpads and robbed of eight guineas, 15 shillings and sixpence. The story concluded: 'It is thought they dogged him from Bredgar'.

According to a Settlement Examination dated 4 February 1802, John and Theophilus were living in Bobbing and were settled in Bredgar and Borden respectively. Settlement Examinations were documents drawn up after the pauper had been questioned with the intention of discovering where they had come from. They are, in a sense, the evidence that that one parish presents to prove its case that the vagrant should be somewhere else.

John and Sarah's first son, George Pateman, was born in 1807 at Bredgar. They subsequently moved to St Werburgh Hoo, where their second son, Jessee Pateman was baptised on 15 December 1816. He only lived a week and was buried on 22 December 1816.

Settlement Examinations can be quite short, or go into a great deal of interesting detail about the vagrant, his or her family, their occupations and where they lived. They often clearly establish the family relationships of those being moved. An example is that of John and Sarah Pateman who were returned to Bredgar on 5 February 1817, following another Settlement Examination:

'John Pateman, wife Sarah and child George aged 10 years. Settlement Examination - at Hoo, settled Bredgar. John Pateman now resident in and chargeable to the parish of Hoo in the said county of Kent on his oath saith that about sixteen years ago he hired himself for a year to Mr William Murton of the parish of Bredgar in the said county and under such hiring served him for one whole year in the said parish and received twelve guineas as the years wages; that to the best of his knowledge and belief he hath done no act to gain a settlement since; and that very soon after the expiration of his said service he was married, at the parish church of Bredgar aforesaid, to Sarah his now wife by whom he hath one child named George aged ten years who is now with him.'

As in this case, Settlement Examinations often give the names, occupations and addresses of masters of apprentices and employers of yearly hired servants. John Pateman hired himself for a year to Mr William Murton of Bredgar. Consequently, John and Sarah were removed from Hoo and returned to Bredgar.

In theory Settlement and Removal made it very difficult for the large section of the population who were not property owners to move from one place to another. In practice there was a considerable amount of mobility. These records – which date from 1662-1834 – provide vital clues to family historians. But these records also give insights into social and economic conditions. It is possible to find out where the majority of vagrants come from, for example.

Many families were returned by other parishes to Bredgar during the eighteenth century. There are 75 surviving certificates relating to people, most of whom were only returning from neighbouring parishes such as Turnstall, Stockbury, Bicknor, Wormshill and Misted. But of course movement was in both directions and the parish churchwardens and overseers also removed those without legal settlement who became a charge on the parish. These again were in the main local people but the whole system must have caused considerable misery.

Apart from those who tried to settle in Bredgar there were also the travellers, some of them Gypsies, and naturally there were always more at harvest time. Poor 'Yorkshire Jenny' caused Bredgar people expense when she died there in 1735, described as a stranger. Sometimes there was not even a Christian name as when the following year 'a woman stranger in childbed' was buried.

Emergencies occurred now and then which the vestry had to deal with. One such came in 1778. George Sellen, a carpenter, had died in February leaving his wife Ann and eight children whose ages ranged from fourteen to one. Mrs Sellen herself died in December and all the children became the charge and care of the vestry. A special meeting was called where they met with Richard and Susanna Wood. Susanna was Mrs Sellen's sister. It was agreed that the Woods should have all the household effects, and in exchange they would take the eldest child Mary, off the parish's hands. William aged thirteen would be taken on by Mr Wood as a seven year apprentice.

Gypsies had always visited Bredgar regularly and helped with the farm work, and one time a large country house, Downsells, had become very run down and was actually lived in by Gypsies. It had been divided into four cottages and in one of these lived old Mrs Clubb. Children nearby used to visit the old lady, and during her last illness and at her death they took her flowers. One little girl will never forget her last visit when she was taken in to see the corpse. To her amazement the coffin stood upright. This funeral was at Tunstall, and Gypsies came from miles around to pay their last respects; the procession reached from Tunstall to Bredgar. There was no sleep that night for the neighbours, for the Gypsies spent it trotting their ponies up and down Swanton Street, showing off their paces and driving bargains with their relatives. The morning after the funeral the wagon and possessions of the old lady were burnt in the corner of the garden with full Gypsy rites.

Gypsies may have been attracted to Bredgar by the hops, fruit and vegetables which were grown there. Pett Farm, for example, had 150 acres of good orchard, hop, arable, pasture and woodland, including three and three quarter acres of hops. The cherry orchards were said to be particularly profitable. Other local farms included Manns Place and Stiff Street farm. Stiff Street was in good repair and like Manns was farmed by Thomas Cornwell. It was described as 'having a brick, plaster and tiled roomy farmhouse – now occupied as two dwellings and having five downstairs rooms and six bedrooms with large walled garden. Rain water tank and deep well, a set of capital farm buildings flint built and tiled. Stabling for eight horses with large chaff house recently built timber and iron roofed. Roomy cattle lodge, brick and iron barn with curved roof cement floor and partly matchboard lined. Implement lodge adjoining.'

Charlotte Mirtle

We do not know when Sarah Cook died, but John Pateman (widower) married Charlotte Mirtle (widow) on 18 February 1821 in Chatham. Both of them signed their marriage certificate with a mark rather than a name, so presumably they could not read or write. We do not know anything about Charlotte's parents or siblings. Her first husband was Benjamin Fowler, who she married on 1 July 1815 at Kintbury, Berkshire. We do not know if they had any children.

Charlotte was the mother of John Pateman's last two sons: Robert and John. No baptisms have been found for these boys in Kent, and it is possible that they may have been born outside the County, possibly in Bedfordshire and/or Hertfordshire. This may be connected to Charlotte's association with Berkshire. It suggests that John and Mirtle may have travelled a great deal and that the seasonal pattern of work – or family connections – may have encouraged them to follow the route from Kent to Beds / Herts.

It is interesting to note that a triple christening took place on 22 October 1826 at Toddington, Bedford. The parents were John Pateman and Sarah. The baptised were John Pateman, Robert Pateman and Mary Pateman. Is it possible that these were the children of John Pateman and Sarah Cook and that John decided to have them baptised in 1826? Although he was no longer married to Sarah at this time, if she was the mother, then her name would be given for the baptism record.

In 1833 Charlotte was a witness at the marriage of her brother-in-law Theophilus Pateman and Mary Payn in Milton, near Sittingbourne.

On the 12th February 1840 John's son George Pateman died at the age of 33 years with consumption in Stoke, Hoo, Kent.

Censuses have been held every ten years since 1801. However, detailed enumerator's returns were not kept until 1841 and a condition was made that none of the census returns could be consulted until they were 100 years old. The 1841 Census names each person in the household, gives ages (exact for children under fifteen, but often rounded down to the nearest five for the adults), occupations and whether or not born in the same county.

In 1841 and 1851, census enumerators were only required to record the names of persons living in houses. Those not living in houses were to be grouped into categories: those in barges or boats, those in barns or sheds, and those in tents or in the open air. The number of persons in each category was to be entered in a printed table in the enumerator's book; there was no requirement to record their names. The rules were not followed precisely, and some Gypsy families do appear in the 1841 and 1851 census returns.

On 6 June 1841 John Pateman (60, labourer) and Charlotte (55) were living back in Bredgar. Frances Pateman, (28, Agricultural labourer, Pond Place, Kent), the wife of George Pateman, and her son William (3, Pond Place) were living at Newington.

John Pateman died on 28 December 1849 aged 76 at Bredgar. On his death certificate he was described as a labourer who died of old age. There is 'the mark of Mary Ann Thomas present at the death Bredgar'. John was buried on 3 January 1850 in Bredgar.

On the 1851 Census Charlotte was living at Silner Street, Bredgar, with Sarah Clinch a widow aged 80 years. A Hannah Clinch lived next door, also a widow, aged 76. Charlotte died on 18 March 1852 aged 67 years from a diseased heart in the infirmary at Maidstone. On her death certificate she was described as a 'single woman' and there was 'the mark of Ann Mannoring present at the death.' Charlotte was buried in Bredgar on 23 March.

Theophilus Pateman (1778-1864)

Theophilus Pateman (1778-1864) = Mary Agar (m. 1800) = Mary Pain (m. 1833)
- William Bass Pateman (1801-1885)

Theophilus Pateman was born on 3 May 1778 and baptised on 14 October 1778 in Bobbing, Kent. Mary Bass was baptised in 1760, but we do not know where and we do not know anything about her family. She married Edward Agar on the 8 January 1780 at Boughton under Blean, Kent which is between Faversham and Canterbury. At some stage they moved to Bobbing, Kent where they had at least four daughters: Sarah (1784), Elizabeth (1786), Martha (178?) and Frances (178?). Martha and Frances were baptised on the same day, but baptising children together did happen, so we are not sure if they were twins or not.

Theophilus may have met Mary Agar at the wedding of his brother John in Bredgar in October 1799. Mary Agar was a witness at their wedding. Mary was a 40 year old widow and 18 years older than Theophilus. They were married on 7 September 1800 at Bobbing. Theophilus signed the marriage certificate with a cross, indicating that he could not read or write. At the time of the wedding Mary was pregnant with their only child (William). At 22 years of age Theophilus inherited four step-daughters. The eldest step-daughter, Elizabeth, was only 6 years younger than Theophilus. This is certainly history repeating itself as his father married a widow who was ten years older than himself and who was pregnant when they married, and inherited a ready made family.

William Bass Pateman was baptised on 12 April 1801 in Bobbing. In 1802 Theophilus and Mary obtained a Settlement Certificate to return to Borden on the 4 February. This may have been to be near his elderly parents, or they may have gone for the work.

Martha Agar married Edward Pepper in 1815 and Frances Agar married William Rochester (from the parish of Minster in Sheppey) in 1816, at Bobbing. Elizabeth Agar married Edward Yerlett at Minster in Sheppey in 1820.

In 1823 Mary, who by this time was 63 years of age, died in Borden and was buried on 7 October. They had been married 23 years and Theophilus was 45 years old. Theophilus remained in Bredgar after Mary's death, but his name does not appear in the Rent Books in 1830, 1832 or 1833, which suggests that he may have been travelling.

Mary Cossingham Pain

Mary Cossingham was baptised in 1786 in Ware, Hertfordshire. Her parents and siblings are unknown. We do not know why she moved to Kent. Mary married John Pain in Borden on 26 November 1809. John Pain, the son of John and Elizabeth Pain, was baptised in 1779. John and Mary Pain had five sons: Charles (1806), James, David (1818), William (1819) and Richard. There were Pain's living in Borden going back to 1722 and in Kent back to Frittenden in 1510. Borden was a small village and the Pateman and Pain families would have known each other. We do not know when John Pain died.

Theophilus Pateman married Mary Pain on 18 April 1833 in Milton, Kent. The fact that they were widow and widower is not mentioned in their marriage entry in the parish records, but David Pain was living with them in 1841, and in 1851 Charles and William Pain and their families were living in Borden.

Theophilus and Mary returned to Borden in 1834. Theophilus was an agricultural labourer. These 'ag labs' were employed by farmers who rented their farms from local landowners. They would live in cottages owned by the landowner and the rent would be deducted from their weekly wage. Theophilus Pateman appears in the rent books for Borden in 1820-29, 1831, and 1834-1840.

These cottages rented by Theophilus Pateman would have been small with the main downstairs room being a kitchen, and one or two rooms for sleeping downstairs, or upstairs if two storey. There was no running water, and not even a sink, in the house. All the water had to be collected from a well or a stream nearby and stored in earthenware pans. All the walls would have been uneven and the ceilings low. The small windows admitted little light, but a great deal of air, particularly in the winter, because the leaden frames did not fit securely into the wooden window-frames. The downstairs floors were paved with brick, and as there was no damp course, the walls and the floors were usually wet in winter. The little furniture they did have in the kitchen would have consisted of a rough wooden table with either benches, stools, or if lucky chairs with wicker seats, and maybe a settle (the name for these straight backed seats) by the fireplace. Above the fireplace a wooden shelf would have held a candlestick or two which could also be used to hold a rush light.

There was so little to eat and the daily variation in their diet was so small that cooking occupied little of women's time. Some were lucky enough to have a bread oven, many didn't. As the family grew, washing, patching and mending the clothes took up several hours a day. Maybe once or twice a week she boiled some of the clothes in a big iron cauldron. She did the rest of the washing just outside the back door, unless it was raining or bitterly cold when she did it in the kitchen, or if she was lucky in a small back kitchen. The cottage would have been swept with a birch broom. Villagers usually bought their brooms - which were made of birch twigs bound to a rough wooden handle by thin strips of hazel - from a broom-maker. The brick floor of the kitchen was often covered with a fine layer of sand, which was renewed every week after the floor was scrubbed on hands and knees.

The average working day for the agricultural labourers would be 14 hours or more, and they might have to walk some distance to get to their work. In bad weather there would be no opportunity for drying clothes, and working all day in wet clothing resulted in rheumatism, which was a common complaint among the agricultural poor. They would wear smock-frocks, the women having long dresses with aprons, shawls and mob-caps. A hat was an important part of a woman's everyday attire, and kept their hair tidy. When clothes wore out it was a struggle to replace them.

The biggest job, and the most profitable because of the extra pay, for the whole year was the harvest. Every available man, woman and child in the village was employed on the harvest. Even so, sometimes there was still too much work for them to do alone, and many farmers employed people who travelled around the country helping with the harvest. They were paid per day, plus free beer, and at night they slept in the barns or sometimes under the hedges.

They all started work in the field as soon as the dew had evaporated from the corn, cutting it close to the ground with a heavy, short-handled hook. A couple of women, or a woman and child, worked with each reaper, tying the corn with three or four stalks into a small bundle called a sheaf. Eight or ten of these sheaves were then rested against each other so that they stood upright and could dry out in the wind and the sun. The sheaves had to be turned every day or so to make sure that all the corn dried thoroughly. When it was all completely dried out, it was loaded with a two-pronged pitchfork on to a farm wagon and carted off to the farmyard where it was stored, or built into a haystack.

During the harvest, work continued until late at night and it was thirsty work. The farmer provided the workers, at various intervals during the day, with weak beer made in the brewery at the farm. The men carried it out into the fields in wooden harvest bottles - small oak barrels with handles made of rope or plaited horse hair. Some of them held a gallon of beer. Others used stoneware bottles with a curved handle on the neck.

When the last wagonload of corn had been brought in from the fields, the most exciting event of the whole harvest, if not of the whole year, took place. All the men, women and children who had taken part in the harvest, plus one or two of the village craftsmen, like the blacksmith, the thatcher, and the wheelwright, sat down together at a long table often in one of the barns or the dairy. Usually the farmer sat at one end with his wife at the other end. The farm workers had their best meal of the year with as much home-brewed beer to drink as anyone wished - roast beef, a side of mutton, and vegetables, followed by plum pudding. After the meal clay pipes and tobacco were placed upon the table and a very merry time was had by all.

The harvest supper was one of the highlights of the year, but there was no respite in their round of toil, which continued the following day as usual. Many of the men did not go home that night, but lay down in the dairy or a barn, so that they would be ready for work again at six o'clock the following morning. Sundays and Christmas Days were their only holidays, though many did attend the church service on Good Friday morning.

Other highlights of the year besides the harvest and Christmas Day, were the annual fairs in the market towns. The morning was devoted to the serious business of selling horses, cattle and sheep, and the afternoon and evening to entertainment. Whole families walked in from miles around and saved for weeks so that they could visit the stalls and buy gingerbread and nuts for their children and themselves; or try their luck on the side shows including the shooting range; and send their children on the roundabout pulled by a horse.

About a month later was the hiring fair. There was the same blowing of horns and beating of drums outside the gaily decorated stalls in the streets, but it was attended by fewer children. Its main purpose was for farmers to hire for the coming year cowmen, shepherds, ploughmen and the young lads to help them, who lived at the farm and were paid once a week. The men all wore some sign of their calling in their hats. The ploughman had a twist of whipcord; the cowman a wisp of cow hair; the shepherd a piece of wool. When the farmer had hired a man, he would seal the bargain with a coin. Most of the men went off to the nearest inn, where they spent the afternoon and evening drinking and chatting to the local girls and domestic servants who always seemed to be present on these occasions.

No other period of the year brought such great activity and so much excitement as the summer, with fruit and hops to be picked, and the harvest. In autumn the potatoes had to be lifted; beans, clover and wheat to be sown; and weeding had to be done. Winter, with its rain, snow and ice, was the bleakest season of the year, when the cold, damp cottages were cheerless in the short evenings. The main jobs on the farm were making manure heaps, building stables, and threshing the corn to separate the grains from the stalks which at this time was done by hand.

If the agricultural workers fell ill or if there were bad harvests, they and their families would be totally dependent upon charity. This was administered by the local squire or parson or by the guardians of the poor. Unemployment pay was non-existent. Sickness benefit was not introduced until 1911.

The basic expenditure of the labourers around this time was rent, bread which was their main source of food, potatoes, vegetables, tea, sugar, soap, laundry blue, thread, candles, salt, fuel, butter and cheese. For many the provision of meat, fish, fruit, milk, clothing, footwear, entertainment, reading matter, medicine, schooling or insurance, all of which are now taken for granted, was very hard to come by. It is also worth remembering that the Adulteration of Food, Drink and Drugs Act was not in force until later in the nineteenth century. In the absence of inspection of food, the labourers of this time could be victimised by dishonest practices such as watered beer, bread adulterated with chalk, and tea with used tea leaves.

Theophilus might have been lucky enough to keep a pig or poultry. A pig was often relied upon to supplement the family income and its loss from swine-fever would be little short of a disaster. No doubt the odd carrot, turnip, apple or pear surreptitiously lifted from the fields and orchards would find its way to their table. But if a game bird or a rabbit was poached, this ran the risk of incurring severe penalties.

A respite from the daily grind would come on Sunday, when husbands, wives and children would attend the parish church. There they would listen to sermons in which the clergy attempted to reconcile the poor to their lot by preaching the doctrine of contentment in that station of life to which God had been pleased to call them. The congregation would approach the communion rail in strict descending order of precedence - farmers first, followed by agricultural labourers, and, last of all, domestic and farm servants. The days when Jack was to think himself as good as his master were still a long way in the future.

Chestnut Street

On 6 June 1841, Theophilus Pateman (60, agricultural labourer, Kent), Mary Pateman (50, Kent) and David Pain (20, agricultural labourer, Kent) were living in Chestnut Street, Borden. The ages on the 1841 census for Borden have been rounded off: Theophilus would have been 63, Mary 55, and David 23.

By 1841 Theophilus' son William and his wife Mary had moved to Milton, but nevertheless they did live in Borden with their first seven children until then, which meant life would not have been dull. In 1850 William and Mary Pateman and all of their children, except Harriet and her family, moved to Bermondsey, Surrey.

From the 1851 census, exact ages, status, relationship to the head of the household and county and parish of birth are given. As most people were illiterate the enumerator spelt the names how he thought they should be. This also applied to the clerk entering details in the parish registers.

On 30 March 1851 Theophilus Pateman (74, agricultural labourer, not known), Mary Pateman (65, Ware, Hertfordshire) and Sarah Goodhew (13, lodger, Hartlip, Kent) were living at 58 Chestnut Pound, Wood Cottages, Borden.

In the 1861 census, for the first time persons not living in houses were to be recorded by name and entered on a separate page at the end of each enumeration district. On 7 April 1861 Theophilus Pateman (85, agricultural labourer, Bobbing, Kent) and Mary Pateman (75, Ware, Hertfordshire) were living at Chestnut Street, Borden. Living with them were George Woodeson (39, lodger, agricultural labourer, Iyhurst, Berks), Susan Woodeson (wife, 32, Storrington, Sussex), George Woodeson (son, 6, Brighton, Sussex) and John Boughton (unmarried, 64, agricultural labourer, Stillin Minis, Kent).

Theophilus Pateman's occupation was given as agricultural labour which you really cannot believe considering he was 85 years old. There was no retirement and a pension at the age of 65. He and Mary probably took in lodgers to supplement their income and if Mary was suffering from chronic bronchitis maybe Susan Woodeson, being young, could help in the house with some of the more challenging jobs, like fetching water from the well. Whatever their circumstances it would have been a very challenging time for both of them.

Even though Theophilus was older than Mary it was she who eventually succumbed to a stroke and died on 21 June 1863 aged 77. The informant was Amelia Payne. Theophilus Pateman died on 11 February 1864 in Borden aged 89. He was a farm labourer and the cause of death was 'natural decay, certified.' The informant was 'the mark of Maria Payne, present at the death, Borden'.

Gypsies or Gorjers?

At this point we need to consider the question: were John Pateman and his sons, John and Theophilus, Gypsies or Gorjers (a term used by Gypsies to describe non Gypsies). Not everyone described as a traveller or a vagrant was a Gypsy. By gathering evidence or documentary references to an individual or a family, it may be possible to identify a Gypsy connection using a combination of typical occupations, forenames, surnames and other data. Reference to travel or movement may give a clue to Gypsy origins. Most Gypsies lived in tents, though travelling vans were adopted by some from the mid nineteenth century. Travelling people were described variously as: Gypsies, Egyptians (until the eighteenth century), travellers, vagrants, strollers, tramps; of no fixed abode, living in tents, van dwellers.

It is not clear how John and his sons travelled between Bobbing, Borden, Bredgar and other places. It is also possible that they travelled longer distances, beyond Kent, and possibly as far as Hertfordshire and Bedfordshire. They could have been Gypsies who became 'Gorjified'. Robert Dawson gives the example of a Boswell family which 'looks to me as if it has become gorjified…They are clearly Gypsies who have settled, with the possible exception of William, who continued to travel'.

On the other hand, as Dawson has also pointed out 'we have to abandon the belief that Gypsy = nomadism. Of course, many Gypsies did move around, but the overall records prove that some settled, and then set off again, or stayed for long periods in one place.' They may have been settled for part of the year (winter) and travelled the rest of the year. Some of the places where they lived – and possibly settled – such as Bredgar and Hoo, were associated with Gypsies.

Gypsies provided goods and services to local communities in the course of their travels. The terms dealer and general dealer were frequently used by Gypsies from the late nineteenth century, but these terms were also used to describe other trades and shopkeepers. A marine store dealer was a dealer in scrap materials. Gypsy occupations included: hawker, licenced hawker, pedlar; basket maker, mat maker, beehive maker, brush maker, chair bottomer; tinker, tin man, razor grinder, knife grinder; dealer, general dealer, marine store dealer, wardrobe dealer; peg maker, umbrella mender, chimney sweep, horse dealer

John senior worked for John Doe for one year as a labourer. John junior hired himself for a year to Mr William Murton of the parish of Bredgar. Theophilus was an agricultural labourer. These all suggest a settled pattern of work with a regular employee, rather than a life on the road, but they could have done both.

Gypsies often used standard forenames – such as Samuel, William, Mary, John – but were also fond of unusual names. Examples of male names: Elijah, Goliath, Hezekiah, Hehemiah, Noah, Sampson, Shadrack, Theophilus, Amberline, Belcher, Dangerfield, Gilderoy, Liberty, Major, Nelson, Neptune, Silvanus, Vandlo

Examples of female names: Anselina, Athalia, Britannia, Cinderella, Clementina, Dotia, Gentilla, Tryphena, Urania , Fairnette, Freedom, Mizelli, Ocean, Reservoir, Sinfai, Unity, Vancy.

Most surnames used by Gypsies are also common in the Gorjer population. The best known and most widespread Gypsy families include: Boswell, Buckland, Faa, Hearn, Heron, Lee, Lovell, Smith, Wood, Young. The following families all travelled in southern England: Brazil, Cooper, Doe, Hughes, James, Keet, Loveridge, Mills, Pateman, Penfold, Stanley, Wells

This list is by no means exhaustive, but the use of surnames to identify a separate race of Romany Gypsies is highly flawed. It fails to distinguish between the different groups of travellers with any degree of certainty, uniting as 'pure' Gypsies all travelling families with 'pure' surnames and the 'vagabonds' and 'hawkers' of the parish registers.

John Pateman and his sons were all married in church which was not a Gypsy custom. The marriage rite that has been most widely practiced among English Gypsies is the simplest imaginable – the mere joining of hands in the presence of witnesses.

Most Gypsies did not read or write. If they had to sign official documents they used their 'mark' – often a simple cross. But John senior signed his marriage certificate, which indicates that he could read and write; John junior and Theophilus did not sign their marriage certificates.

If they were not born Gypsies, it is possible that they married into Gypsy families. Thomas Acton has suggested that from the time of their first appearance in this country Gypsies would have been mixing 'culturally, linguistically and genetically with the local population'. Available evidence would seem to back up this claim.

From the eighteenth century records of marriages with Gorjers have been preserved, indicating that such relationships were neither rare nor exceptional. Between 1701-1750 only 12% of Gypsy marriages were with Gorjers, but between 1751-1800 this increased to 34%. Proof of intermarriage between travellers and non travellers is even more plentiful for the nineteenth century: the figure remained high during 1801-1850 (30%) and 1851 – 1900 (35%). As Dawson has said, 'note that about a third of all unions were with Gorjers, emphatically giving the lie to the 'pure blood' nonsense'.

Dawson gives examples of male Gorjers marrying female Gypsies and starting new Gypsy families: Elizabeth Boswell married James James in 1729, 'perhaps thereby the start of the Romani James family which remained a Gypsy family in Hampshire until late in the nineteenth century when they began to spread further afield'. When Anne Boswell married John Heaps in 1777, 'this union almost certainly created the small but interesting nineteenth century Romani family of Heaps.'

Vernon Morwood points out that 'When Gypsy women marry our men they of course take their names, which may account to some extent for many English surnames being used by men considered to be Gypsies. The children of such parents, however, in the majority of cases, marry those members of the Gypsy tribes who are of purer Gypsy blood than themselves, so that in a generation or two their offspring present all those physical features by which genuine Gypsies are so distinguishable.'

Morwood gives the example of Isaac Jowles, who was known in Somersetshire as 'king of the Gypsies'. Jowles was a native of a village in Wiltshire, and followed the occupation of a stone mason; but he was not Gypsy born. Having had, when a young man, an unpleasant dispute with his family about some property, he left home, and was not heard of for many years. He married a Gypsy woman, by whom he had two daughters. When these girls were young their features were very beautiful; their Gypsy characteristics were, however, decidedly predominant. In due time they married Gypsy men, and had children by them, 'between whom and the purest offspring of the Gypsy race it would have been difficult to detect any physiological difference.'

Another example given by Morwood is that of a man named Stephens, a native of Gloucestershire, who married a daughter of Myrick Locke, the reputed 'king of the Gypsies'. Stephens lived to be an old man, and left behind him several sons and grandsons, 'so that it is not unlikely his name became very common among the Gypsy tribes of this country. These sons, having married Gypsy women, their offspring present the same physical, mental, and moral characteristics as those do who have descended from old Isaac Jowles'.

Morwood also cites the Carew family: 'Amongst English Gypsies are several members named Carew, who are the descendents of the notorious Bamfylde Moore-Carew, who, although the son of a clergyman, left his home and joined the Gypsies, with whom he remained some years. The Carews referred to, having so much intermingled with genuine Gypsies, present in a very marked manner the same singular features as other Gypsy nomads do. It appears, so far, tolerably certain that these intermarriages and others will in a measure account for some of our surnames being common among the Gypsies.'

Francis Groome offered three Romany pedigrees showing various degrees of intermarriage with Gorjers and in one of these, of Abraham Wood, marriages with Gorjers outnumbered those with Gypsies. Groome himself recognised that, despite his desire to prove the opposite, not only was the trend towards intermarriage more pronounced by the latter decades of the century but also that it was extremely difficult to draw a clear line between Gypsies and non Gypsies.

The evidence given above is far from conclusive. There are indications that John Pateman and his sons were relatively settled, with Gorjer occupations, but they could have travelled as well. Their forenames could be Gypsy or Gorjer, but Pateman is recognised as a Gypsy surname, at least in the southern counties. Given the large amount of intermarriage between Gypsies and settled people in the nineteenth century it is highly possible that the Patemans could have married into travelling families.

Not all vagrants were born into the life. Some came from settled parents but took up a travelling life. Matthew Marsh, who was taken as a vagrant at Woodham Ferrers, Essex, in 1786 was 23 years old and said he had lived with his father in Bobbing until two years previously when he left home and travelled about the country and got his living by selling ballads and chapbooks.

The parallels here with the Pateman family are interesting. John Pateman and his sons spent much of their life in Bobbing, and in the nearby settlements of Borden and Bredgar. While they did not stray very far from this relatively small area of Kent, their children travelled far and wide. We do not know when or how Pateman became a Gypsy family. What we do know is that the next generation of Patemans were Gypsies, and lead a travelling life for most of the nineteenth century.

3. Tanners and Bermondsey

- William Bass Pateman (1801-1885)

In the open field village, you had the houses standing together along the main street of the village, with the fields and commons spread out around them, and everyone in the village knew his place in the life and work that went on. Some of the customs were written down, like the list of the vicar's tithes. Some of them were never written - like the right of some poor cottagers to put their geese on the common. But since everyone in the village knew of these customary rights, there was not usually any argument about them. The open field system went on for centuries. Why, then, did the changes come?

The chief reason for change was that the number of people living in England was beginning to get very much greater. In the hundred years between 1750 and 1851, the population of England and Wales nearly trebled to just over eighteen million. People did not realise exactly what was happening until after 1801, when the first census - a Government count of all the people in the country - was held. After that, there was a census every ten years, and although the early ones were not very accurate they soon showed clearly that the population was steadily increasing. No one knows exactly why this happened at this time. It was happening especially in the countryside. People in the towns were living in such over-crowded and unsanitary conditions at the end of the eighteenth century and beginning of the nineteenth century, that more children died and the death rates generally went up, but in the country as a whole more people were being born, and they were living longer.

The increase in the number of people to be fed put strains on the old ways of growing food. Also Britain was at war with France from 1793 until 1814 when Napoleon finally abdicated, and with the war came inflation. A system which had jogged along, just about managing to feed a fixed or only slowly growing population, was not able suddenly to start producing more. More people to be fed meant that more money could be made from good farming. So naturally landlords wanted to get more out of their estates. The people of the country needed the food, and the landlords wanted to try and give it to them.

The old open field system was undoubtedly slow and wasteful and so parishes gradually started to become enclosed. What this meant was that an Act was presented to Parliament, asking for permission to enclose the common fields. Parliament agreed, and appointed three lawyers to go into the whole question. It was the job of these Commissioners, as they were called, to find out, first of all, whether the owners of three-quarters of the land (not three-quarters of all the landowners) wanted to enclose. Then they had to find out who owned all the various strips of land, and what claims each person had to common and grazing rights. Then they had to draw a new map, dividing up the fields and commons between all those who had land or claims on the old open fields. They had to allow for roads on the new plan, often they made these roads with wide grass verges which could be let for grazing or haymaking, the money from the rent going to help with the cost of keeping the road in good repair. When they had sorted out these and many other questions, they held meetings of all landowners, and listened to any appeals against their findings.

If there were no appeals, or if the appeals did not succeed, they finally signed the papers and plans. These papers, known as the Enclosure Award, were kept as the record of the land ownership for that particular area. Each landowner should now have a piece or pieces of land equal in value to his old strips. He had the job of fencing and draining his land, and he could then go ahead and farm it as he pleased. However, in 1836, a General Enclosure Act enabled enclosure to proceed without the cumbersome preliminary of a private Act of Parliament, provided it had the consent of the majority of the people concerned; and a further Act of 1845 set up a board of Enclosure Commissioners, in London, to supervise all enclosures.

We also have to remember that before the above Acts, part of the wealth that agricultural labourers helped to create would go to the Church in the form of tithes paid by the landowners and tenant farmers. In the eighteenth century these had been paid in kind, for example in farm produce. But by the beginning of the nineteenth century this system was becoming inconvenient to payer and receiver alike. In some places the Church made a private arrangement for the tithes to be paid in cash and we can see why parsons were very comfortably off at this time. But by the Tithe Commutation Act of 1836 the position was regularised; the tithes everywhere had to be paid in cash and payment in kind was finally abolished. This really was the start of the industrial revolution.

From the point of view of growing more and better food, there is no doubt that the move was an excellent one. But how did it affect the villages? For the big farmers this was the chance to use new methods, and so draw ahead of the old slow ways of their village. For a great many of the small landowners the legal expenses of the enclosure act, the draining and fencing of land where the new roads were to be built, fencing in other odds and ends which did not belong to any one owner, was not easy. You can imagine that a man who had managed to jog along and make a poor living from a couple of strips in the open field would not be likely to have the ready cash for all this. So a great many of the small landowners sold their allotments straight away. Money does not last as long as land. Even if the small man did not yield to the temptation to spend all his money at once in the nearest town, it would still only last him and his family a short time. Then he would be a labourer, and depend on what he could earn by working for someone else, either in the village, or if there was no work there, he would have to move on to the nearest town and look for work.

The cottager without any land would probably be worse off still. If he could bring proof that his right went back for many years, he might get a small allotment when the common was enclosed, but many hundreds of cottagers and squatters would have no rights at all, even to the land their cottages stood on. Their scruffy donkeys and half-starved geese would have to go, and with them their chance of a livelihood in the village. There are many versions of a rhyme about the cottagers, who were often accused by the landlords of being thieves and Gypsies:

They clap in gaol the man or woman
Who steal the goose from off the common,
But let the greater thief go loose
Who steals the common from the goose

So the small landowner and the cottager were either forced to leave the village, or had to stay on as labourers, depending on someone else to give them work. And when we remember that the population was increasing, we can see that it must have seemed as though the enclosure movement was driving people off the land into the unhealthy and overcrowded towns. It may well have been that in some areas the enclosed farms provided more work for labourers than the old strips, but there were many more looking for work. The feeling of injustice, the belief that they had been robbed by the rich enclosing landlords, remained very strong amongst the poor people of England, and their children.

On 17 October 1801 Lydd's heroic sailor Lieutenant Tom Edgar, who sailed around the world with Captain James Cook, died aged 56. In 1776 he joined Captain Cook on his last voyage in the exploration ship *Resolution*. Cook on an earlier epic journey had reached Tahiti and charted the coasts of New Zealand and eastern Australia. On 1 March 1859 William Bass Pateman's son, James Edward Pateman, followed in Captain Cook's footsteps and sailed to New Zealand in the *Cameo* with his family and 218 passengers, seeking a new life in the New World. Fifteen years later he was joined by his younger brother, James Coulter Pateman, who set sail for New Zealand on 17 April 1874 on board the *Hereford*.

It was in 1788 that Captain Arthur Phillip established a penal colony near Botany Bay which he described as 'the finest harbour in the world'. He called the colony Sydney and in that year commanded six transports carrying 736 convicts. Refusing to carry slaves, Phillips said Sydney was a fit place for these tough human beings to make a fresh start in life.

Many Gypsies were also transported, to New Zealand, Australia, the Caribbean and the Americas. As Robert Dawson has pointed out in his study *British Gypsy Slavery* (2001), Gypsies were transported for a number of reasons including: criminality, vagrancy, poaching and for taking part in political agitation such as the Gordon Riots and the Chartist Movement.

Victoria became queen on 20 June 1837 at the age of 18, succeeding her uncle William IV. On the 1 July 1837 civil registration began for all births, deaths and marriages. The returns were sent to the General Registry Office by district Registrars and, in the case of marriages in Church, by the incumbent of the parish. This has assisted the researching of this family history.

William Bass Pateman (1801-1885)

William Pateman (1801-1885) = Mary Ann Coulter (1807-1872)
- Harriett Pateman (1825-1894)
- Mary Ann Pateman (1827-1899)
- William Pateman (1829)
- James Edward Pateman (1831-1905)
- Ellen Ann Maria Pateman (1833-1837)
- Sarah Ann Pateman (1835-1897)
- George Henry Pateman (1838)
- Elizabeth Ann Pateman (1840)
- John Henry Pateman (1842-1886)
- James Henry Pateman (1844-1893)
- Esther Mole Pateman (1846-1849)
- James Coulter Pateman (1849-1879)

William Bass Pateman was baptised on 12 April 1801 at Bobbing, Kent. William's baptism looks like William Bath and not Bass. However, on his son James Henry Pateman's birth certificate in 1844 it says father William Bass Pateman. Earlier certificates just said William Pateman. Although William was the only child of Theophilus and Mary he did have at least four step-sisters.

William and his parents moved from Bobbing in 1802 after they obtained a Settlement Certificate for Borden where his grandparents John and Catherine lived. His grandfather died a year later and his grandmother when he was six years old. As there was no schooling he would have been a farm boy from about the age of eight years.

Mary Ann Coulter was born in 1807 and baptised on 5 March 1809 at Staple, Kent. Her father was Edward Coulter (baptised 1776) and her mother was Mary Medgett (baptised 1775 at Wingham). Her siblings were Sarah, William, Henry, Charlotte, James, Jemima, Edward, and George Coulter.

Wingham and Staple

This is what Edward Hasted said about Wingham and Staple around 1798: 'Wingham is situated in a healthy pleasant country, the greatest part of it is open unenclosed arable lands, the soil of which, though chalky, is far from being unfertile. The village, or town of Wingham, is nearly in the middle of the parish, having the church and college at the south-west part of it; behind the latter is a field, still called the vineyard. The village contains about fifty houses, one of which is the court lodge, and is built on the road leading from Canterbury to Sandwich, at the west end of it runs the stream, called the Wingham river, which having turned a corn-mill here, goes on and joins the Lesser Stour, about two miles below; on each side of the stream is a moist tract of meadow land. Near the south boundary of the parish is the mansion of Dene, situated in the bottom, a dry, though dull and gloomy habitation; and at the opposite side, next to Staple, the ruinated mansion of Brook, in a far more open and pleasant situation. There are two fairs held yearly here, on May 12, and November 12, for cattle and pedlary.

The parish of Staple lies north-eastward from Adisham, from which and the rest of the hundred of Downhamford, it is separated entirely by the hundred and parish of Wingham intervening. The parish, which is but small, lies in a pleasant healthy country, mostly on high ground. The soil near the village, and towards the stream, is very good corn land, but towards the southern part it is rather poor, and much of it chalky. The village, called Staple-Street, consists of about ten houses, having the seat of Groves, (a mansion in the parish) and the church near adjoining. Beyond which the parish extends into the vale eastward, as far as Durlock bridge, on the stream which rises at a small distance from it, and runs from hence to Danne-bridge into the Wingham stream. On the high ground on the opposite side of the valley, is the hamlet of Shatterling, built on the high road leading from Canterbury through Wingham, towards Ash and Sandwich, where the soil becomes very poor and a deep sand, up to which road the park grounds of Grove extend. On the opposite side of the parish is Crixall house, once a gentleman's seat, but now diminished to the common size of a farm-house. Near it is a piece of healthy ground, called Crixall Rough, with a noted toll of trees on it, a conspicuous object to the surrounding country. There is no woodland in the parish. A fair is held here on the 25th July, for toys and pedlary.'

The very attractive east Kent village of Wingham is built around the T-junction formed where the B2046 north south road meets the A257 Canterbury Sandwich road. It is a relatively large village, with a handsome, tree lined High Street. It has a prosperous look about it and, indeed, it has enjoyed a measure of prosperity since Saxon times when it was one of the richest manors in Kent. In the thirteenth century a college for six secular canons was founded here and Canon Row, opposite the thirteenth century church of St Mary the Virgin, remains as a reminder that the college was, in fact, one of the most notable medieval colleges in Kent. It was dissolved in 1547 by Edward VI and the buildings were sold.

The village has had a front seat in much of the history of this part of Kent. Archbishop Thomas Becket passed through Wingham on his way back to Canterbury from exile on the continent, unaware that he would be slain in his own Cathedral less than four weeks later. Richard I (the Lionheart) stopped here on his way to London when he returned from captivity in Austria in 1194, and King John stayed here in 1213. In 1255, the King of France gave an elephant to Henry II as a gift and the animal must have caused quite a stir as it walked through Wingham on its way to Canterbury. Edwards I, II and III all visited Wingham during the thirteenth and fourteenth centuries and Elizabeth I followed in their footsteps in 1573.

After about 1540, when the church had been allowed to get into such a state that one day it just fell down, a Canterbury brewer called George Foggard sought and was given permission to collect money for rebuilding it. He was evidently a persuasive collector for it seems he raised £224, quite a considerable sum for that time – so considerable, indeed, that Master Foggard could not bring himself to part with it when the time came and the money never did find its way into the fabric of the rebuilt church. One consequence of that was that the church was rebuilt with a nave arcade of octagonal chestnut pillars instead of stone ones, to keep down the cost.

The church boasts a number of impressive monuments, none of which eclipses the seventeenth century Oxenden monument in the south transept. In black and white marble, it is an ornately carved obelisk on a square base with ox-head corner supporters for the four putti at the corners. A fourteenth century window of the Earl of Kent, who retired to a convent, broke her vows and secretly married at Wingham a French Wars veteran called Sir Eustace de Aubrichecourt. The marriage caused quite a scandal at court and outraged the Church which imposed penances upon the pair, requiring them to eat nothing but bread and drink nothing but water for a whole day once a week, and recite the psalms every day. In addition, the bride had to walk barefoot to Becket's shrine at Canterbury. The couple seem to have accepted the penances stoically and to have fulfilled them for more than 50 years, during which time they had one son.

In 1795, William Miller was born in Wingham, grew up to join the Army and travelled to South America where he fought with Simon Bolivar, the Spaniard who freed part of Peru from Spanish dominance and gave his name to the new state of Bolivia. Miller so impressed the Spaniard that he was given command of his whole army in South America, but the call of Kent proved too strong after a year or two and he returned to be made a freeman of Canterbury. He did not stay long, though. He was a rover at heart and died at sea in 1861.

There are numerous inns named White Horse, Black Horse, Black Bull, Red Cow, Red Lion, etc, but the only example in Kent called The Black Pig is the inn of 1588 in Barnsole Road, Staple. It is puzzling to know why it is the sole one as Kent originally had its own breed, the Kent Black Pig, also called the Black Kent. It has been compared with the Old English Large Black that was descended from the 'Old English Hog' of the sixteenth century, in turn descended and bred from the wild boars of the Weald, but the Kent Black Pig had smaller, drooping ears, far less hair and it was much finer textured and stood higher off the ground.

The Kent Black was possibly a similar breed to the Dorset Black, one of a number of several black breeds confined to southern and eastern counties in the nineteenth century. A number of these breeds were formed in that period by pig breeders to meet their own and customers' requirements. Most were short lived, but some survived for a time and were locally popular. There was also a Kent White Pig, rather long-legged, narrow backed and similar to the early Suffolk White Pig, with medium length ears, thickly hairy and said to have a thick rind or skin.

According to a Kent saying a 'Kent Hog' was a Kentish born man who would give anything away – as long as it was of no further use to him! There are also many Kent dialect words and other expressions associated with the hog or pig. Apart from its curly tail and straight back the Staple inn sign pig has a fair likeness to a Kent Black Pig, which had an almost straight tail and a back tending to slope from its hind quarters down to its shoulders and head.

Staple and Wingham were visited by Gypsies, looking for work, as described by William Howitt in 1838: 'In July and August they move into Kent for harvest work, where they continue. Through September, great numbers of them find employment in the hop districts of the county. They constantly encamp on the commons. In the park of Greenwich, the Gypsy women are to be found exercising their vocation of fortune tellers. On this account many of them encamp about Blackheath, Woolwich Heath, Lordship Lane, near Deptford, and Plum Street, near Woolwich, the Archbishop's Wall, near Canterbury, Staple and Wingham Well, near the same city, and Buckland, near Dover.'

There were two groups of Coulters/Culters in Kent. In 1559 there was a marriage of Tho Culter and Joane Briggs at Nonington, a village not very far from Staple, and probably the ancestors of Edward Coulter. Then in 1541 there was a marriage of Tho Culter and Margaret Medgate at Offham near Maidstone. There were many Coulters living in Bearsted from 1611 and Aylesford, near Maidstone, starting in 1734. There were burials for Edmund Coulter at Newington in 1817 aged five months and Charles Coulter in 1820 aged one day.

Mary Medgett's parents were William and Mary Medgett nee Elgar. There are not that many Medgetts/Madgetts' in Kent, but they do go back to Folkestone in 1610. They could have been a French family. Edward Coulter and Mary Medgett were married in 1795 at Wingham; Edward Coulter signed his name, Mary used a cross. The witnesses were John and Elizabeth Coulter and they also signed their names.

We don't know why the Coulters moved up from Wingham to the Medway area. It was probably the need for work. By 1823 after the boom years which followed the end of the Napoleonic Wars a general depression settled across the county and poverty was growing everywhere - nowhere worse than in the towns of Deal and Sandwich with Wingham and Staple not very far away. The dispersal of the fleet in the Downs and the suppression of smuggling, which many men coming back from the wars in the area turned to, brought a total suspension of trade. In Deal more than 500 pauper children were fed daily alongside the 450 inmates of its two poorhouses.

The linen thread making of Maidstone, the cloth making of the Weald villages and the silk weaving of Canterbury had virtually ceased. The coastal communities of Folkestone, Ramsgate, Whitstable and Faversham suffered from the seasonal maritime hazards caused by a succession of bitter winters. Unemployment was rife in Chatham while the towns of Gravesend and Milton were experiencing vast hardship.

The Rev G.R. Gleig, vicar of Ash, near Staple and Wingham, at the time described the French wars as a `golden age' for East Kent. The demand for labour was great, working men received half a crown a day, wheat sold for ninety or a hundred shillings a quarter, working people throve and were contented. There was full employment during the wars. For Kent farmers every shilling expended brought back two shillings. That was followed by galloping inflation which had a devastating effect on real incomes.

William married Mary Ann Coulter on 19 July 1824 in Gillingham, which is a few miles away from Newington and Borden. Mary was only 17 years old and under the age of consent and he was 23 years old. Mary's sister Jemima Coulter was a witness at the wedding, along with George Carey, so there was at least one member of her family there. None of them signed their names, they all used a cross.

Harriet Pateman (1825-1894)

William and Mary's first child, Harriet Pateman, was born in Borden on 24 July 1825. She married Thomas Wood, a labourer, at Milton parish church on the 13 April 1845. Thomas' father's name and occupation were left blank. Neither of them could sign their names in the register. They had at least six children: George William Wood (baptised 20 May 1846, Sittingbourne), Mary Ann Wood (baptised 6 May 1848, Sittingbourne), Edward James Wood (baptised 24 July 1854, Sittingbourne), John Henry Wood (baptised 21 August 1856, Murston), Thomas Henry Wood (born 27 November 1862, Church Road, Murston, father - brickfield labourer), Henry E Coulter Wood (baptised 9 July 1865).

In 1881 Harriet Wood was living with her husband, Thomas (who was still working on the Kent brickfields) and their two sons, Thomas and Henry, at 3 Dean Street, Milton, Kent. Harriett Sarah Wood died on 27 January 1894, a widow, at 51 Frederick Street, Sittingbourne aged 68 years from Influenza and Exhaustion (16 days). William George Wood her son of 20 Quay Street, Milton was the informant and signed with a cross.

On 9 December 1826 a Removal Order stated that 'William Pateman, wife Mary and child Harriett aged 2, years removed from Borden to Bobbing'. Removal orders were the next stage in the legal process after a settlement examination. A removal order was a court document giving authority for the removal of vagrants. They stated which parish wished to remove them, the name of the vagrant and sometimes that of the magistrate. They also said which parish it was intended to return the vagrant to. In addition they sometimes gave details of the route - which parishes the vagrants was to go through to get there. Some parishes were used as 'transfer of authority points', regular stops on the route, or embarkation points.

From 1820 onwards, annotations appeared on many of the removal orders, confirming the arrival of vagrants at their place of settlement. Payment of expenses was also recorded in some cases. The removal order normally restated the reason why someone was to be moved to a particular place. William Pateman and his family were removed because they 'lately intruded and came into your said parish of Borden not having gained a legal settlement there, nor produced any certificate owning them to be settled elsewhere, and are actually chargeable to the same: We, the said justices, upon examination of the premises upon oath, and other circumstances, do adjudge the same to be true, and also adjudge the place of their last legal settlement to be in the said parish of Bobbing and that no sufficient security has been given to discharge the said parish of Borden.'

Sometimes parishes disagreed about the settlement of a vagrant. As the parish and its inhabitants had to pay for the upkeep of any paupers within their area, they did their best to discourage vagrants from settling within their bounds. There are many cases where the overseers and parish officials appeared in court or compelled the officials of another parish to attend to explain why named individuals should not be placed with them. This may have been the case for William and Mary, who subsequently obtained a Settlement Certificate to live in Borden

Mary Ann Pateman (1827-1899)

William and Mary Ann's second child, Mary Ann Pateman, was baptised in Borden on 3 June 1827. She married Thomas John Pearce, a tanner, on 23 July 1846 in the parish church at Frinstead. They both signed their names. Thomas lived at Frinstead, a village about four miles south-east of Milton. His father, also Thomas, was a publican. His brother, Edwin, was a farrier. Mary Ann and Thomas had at least six children and moved to Bermondsey.

Mary Ann Pearce died on 1 May 1899 from mitral regurgitation at 2 Wearside Road, Lewisham, aged 72 years. Her daughter Ann Harding was present at the death and the informant. On the certificate it stated she was widow of James Thomas Pearce - Farrier (Master), so Thomas stopped being a tanner and became a farrier like his brother Edwin. When Bermondsey's trade and industry was at its height road transport was horse drawn. At 217 Long Lane there was an old stable block on three floors that was once a 'multi-storey horse park'.

On the same day as Mary Ann Pateman's baptism at Borden there was a baptism for Elizabeth Paine daughter of James and Charlotte Paine of Sheerness, Minster, Isle of Sheppey. On 22 May 1825 there had been a baptism of James William Paine son of James and Charlotte Paine living in Minister. This must be a brother of John Paine, Mary Pateman's first husband. This created a double connection with Minster, Isle of Sheppey where Elizabeth Agar married Edward Yerlett in 1820. James and Charlotte probably came back to be with the rest of the family for the baptism.

William Pateman appeared in the rent books for Borden in 1826-40. In 1827 William rented a cottage from Mrs Norris.

William Pateman (1829)

William and Mary Ann's third child, William Pateman, was baptised at Borden on 19 July 1829. He moved with his family to Bermondsey and on all the census returns until 1881 he was described as single. On the 1881 census it said his wife was Martha ? (1831, Southwark, Surrey) and he lived at 9 St Martins Road, Lambeth with his wife and Elizabeth Hill (daughter of his sister, Sarah Ann).

On William's baptism record, William Bass Pateman said he was a tanner and not a labourer. The Enclosure Act started to force people into the towns for work and this could have been a reason for William Pateman to look for another source of income besides being an agricultural labourer. In 1835 a Report said: 'Crime in many towns, especially Maidstone and Chatham, has reached an unprecedented level. Small armies of pickpockets, burglars and prostitutes are living wholly or partly by crime. The vicar of Staplehurst said recently that 'predatory bands…. Are causing manifest danger to life and property…. We have no civil force (in Kent) to put them down.'

There were many tanners trading in Kent in the nineteenth century. According to *Kelly's Directory* for 1859 (the earliest date that a trades directory was published) there were four in Canterbury, two each in Milton-next-Sittingbourne, Tonbridge and Tenterden, and one in Ashford, Bexleyheath, Cranbrook, Dartford, Deal, Dover,

Edenbridge, Gravesend, Hollingbourne, Maidstone, Ramsgate, Sandwich, Southborough, Tunbridge Wells, West Malling and Wingham. One has only to think of the numbers of sets of harness in use and the quantities of labourers' boots to realise how much leather was needed in an age before synthetic rubber and plastic.

It is very likely that William would have served an apprenticeship; in fact the stages of a man's career were Apprentice, Journeyman, and Master. The apprentice learned the trade from a master craftsman who also had other employees, termed journeymen. The word comes from old French jornee (modern journee - day) and means one who works for day wages.

James Edward Pateman (1831-1905)

William and Mary Ann's fourth child, James Edward Pateman was baptised on 9 October 1831 at Borden. This was the first of three of their son's to be baptised James. He was later called Edward James Pateman. He married Mary Bray in the Parish Church of St Marylebone, Middlesex, on 19 November 1857. On his marriage certificate it stated he was a miner. He may have worked in the Kent coalfields or for the railways building the hundreds of tunnels necessary for the lines to come into London. They lived at 73 Hamilton Terrace, Marylebone and both signed their names, but Edward said his father's name was William George Pateman.

Edward and Mary's first child, Eliza Sophia Pateman, was born on 19 January 1859. Six weeks later they sailed from Britain on the *Cameo* on the 1 March 1859. There were two hundred and eighteen passengers on board. They arrived at Lyttleton, New Zealand on 11 July 1859 nearly four months later. Edward worked on the West Coast gold fields when he first arrived and later he became a Police Officer in the force at the gold field. While they were living at Lyttleton his daughter Eliza Sophia died and was buried on 9 June 1860 at Lyttleton Holy Trinity Church aged 16 months.

Edward and Mary's second child, Edward Claude Pateman, was born in Christchurch on 18 May 1861 and was baptised at St. Lukes Church, Manchester Street, Christchurch, on 27 October 1861.

Mary Pateman died on 18 September 1862 with disease of the heart aged 34 years. Seven months after Mary died, Edward James Pateman married his second wife, Charlotte Smith (spinster, 38) on 15 March 1863 in Christchurch. She was described as a dressmaker. They moved to Christchurch in 1864.

Edward and Charlotte's first child, James Coulter Pateman, was born in 1866. He died on 29 January 1887. Edward James always blamed Edward Claude for the death of James Coulter. One day the two boys were getting firewood from the swamp. On the way home they had to open a gate. Edward Claude was on the wagon loaded with wood and James Coulter was on his horse. James got off his horse and opened the gate. The horse on the wagon took fright and bolted, knocking James over and killing him on the spot. He was only 20 years old. He was buried at Woodend Methodist Church, Rangiora, north of Christchurch.

Edward and Charlotte's second child, Ellen Mole Pateman (Nellie), was born around 1869 and as a girl became mentally ill. She remained like this all her life. She died on 28 April 1917 aged 47. She was buried at Woodend Methodist Church, Rangiora.

Charlotte Pateman died on 2 September 1897 aged 64. She was buried at Woodend Methodist Church, Rangiora. By this time Edward James Pateman owned 50 acres of land at Little River and described himself as a farmer. Around about 1900 Edward James went back to England, to see his family again, despite the fact nearly all his brothers and sisters were dead.

Edward James married Eliza Witte in 1901. He was 70 years old, and Eliza was 40. She had been born in England and her parents were Bernard Henrich Witte and Mary Bowden Tongman.

They had been married four years when Edward James was thrown from his horse and cart after the horse stumbled, and he died 17 days later on the 27 May 1905 as a result of nervous shock and heart failure. Eliza Pateman died on 3 March 1940 at 41 Mays Road, Christchurch aged 80.

Although William Pateman and his family probably did not have an easy life, it is likely that they were better off living in a village than those who lived in large towns. In 1832 there was a cholera epidemic in Kent. A report in September of that year said:

'According to military medical officers it is "uncommonly rife" about the Medway warships, prison hulks and in soldiers barracks. Scores of people are dying from a disease whose cause and cure are unknown and a strict quarantine has been imposed on all continental vessels in the Kent ports. This week between 250-300 sail ships are under quarantine restrictions in the Medway station at Stangate Creek. Quarantine is also imposed at Dover, Faversham, Whitstable, Milton and Ramsgate.

With so many open sewers and filthy streets Chatham has one of the highest mortality rates in the country and it is here the disease was first reported in Kent. Cholera enters the body by way of the mouth and is contracted by consumption of food and water that has been contaminated by excreta of a cholera victim. It is also spread by flies that have fed on diseased excreta.

The first victims were those on the prison ship *Cumberland*. Within a few days cholera had claimed more than 80 convicts including the surgeon who was treating them. It then spread into the town killing many…… The deaths increased with the arrival of the warmer weather…. Two young children from Milton died along with the woman who had been employed to clean the filthy hovel where they lived. At Mile Town, Sheerness, 12 died within a few days - all persons of low circumstances. Minster has fared even worse with 47 deaths from 107 cases.

Last week the *Maidstone Journal* reported; 'We are happy to learn that this frightful disease has somewhat abated in the last two days. That is not the case in London where the disease has spread. It is believed that more than 5,000 have died and cholera is now spreading through the country at an alarming rate.'

Ellen Ann Marie Pateman (1833-1837)

William's father, Theophilus Pateman, married Mary Pain on 18 April 1833 at Milton. William and Mary Ann's fifth child, Ellen Ann Marie Pateman, was baptised at Borden on 22 September 1833. Ellen died on 2 September 1837 aged four years at Chalkwell, Milton. Her father was a tanner and the cause of death was measles. The informant was Susannah Trigg, Chalkwell. Ellen was buried on 10 September 1837 at Newington.

Sarah Ann Pateman (1835-1897)

William and Mary Ann's sixth child, Sarah Ann Pateman, was baptised at Borden on 11 October 1835. Sarah married Edward Liniker Hill (of 53 St Ann's Road, Stepney) on 23 November 1859 in the parish church of Stepney, Middlesex. His father was James Hill, a mariner. Edward was also a mariner, but he later called himself a merchant seaman.

They had five children: Edward James Hill (born 20 August 1862 Wrights Buildings, Bermondsey), Elizabeth Hill (1866, Bermondsey), Minnie Hill (1868, Middlesex), James John Hill (born 14 October 1869, Wrights Buildings, Bermondsey), Rebecca Annie Hill (baptised 11 November 1872, St. James, Bermondsey).

At the time of the 1881 census Sarah was a widow charwoman living in Bermondsey with her father and her daughters, Minnie and Rebecca. Sarah Ann Hill died on the 13 September 1897 at 57 Princes Road, Lambeth at the age of 62 years from Pneumonia and fatty degeneration of the heart and other organs. It must have been sudden because an Inquest was held on the 16 September.

George Henry Pateman (1838)

William and Mary Ann's seventh child, George Henry Pateman, was baptised at Borden on 2 May 1838. We believe he married someone called Alice, but a marriage certificate has not been found so far. To other members of the family they were more 'well to do' than the rest and never had any children.

Elizabeth Ann Pateman (1840)

William and Mary Ann's eighth child, Elizabeth Ann Pateman, was born at Milton on 3 February 1840. Her father was a tanner and her mother was Mary Ann Pateman, formerly Coulter. Elizabeth was baptised at Milton in 1840. We do not know who/if she married, but she had one child, Matilda Elizabeth, born on 13 October 1858 at the Union Workhouse, Milton. The name of the father is not shown. Matilda died on the 7 April 1859 at the Union Workhouse, Milton aged 6 months from Marasmus, a severe wasting in infants, when the body weight is below 75% of that expected for age. The condition may be due to malabsorption, wrong feeding, metabolic disorder, repeated vomiting, diarrheoa, or disease. She was buried on 11 April at Bobbing. Her grandfather and grandmother were still alive, but very old, and living in Borden. Elizabeth said she was a domestic servant. We do not know what happened to her after this. She did not appear on any of the Bermondsey Census Returns with the family.

Milton

On 6 June 1841 the census address given for William, Mary Ann and their children was Crown Lane, Chalkwell, Milton, Kent and their ages were rounded up: William Pateman (40, journeyman tanner, Kent), Mary Pateman (30, Kent), Harriet Pateman (15, Kent), William Pateman (12, Kent), Edward Pateman (10, Kent), Sarah Pateman (5, Kent), George Pateman (3, Kent), Elizabeth Pateman (1, Kent).

Their daughter, Mary Ann was missing but we found a Mary Pateman living at Murston on the 1841 Census at the house of a surgeon. This could be Mary Ann whose age was given as 15 years but she was probably only 14 years old. It does not give her occupation but we assume she was a domestic help.

This is what Edward Hasted had to say about Milton around 1800 : 'In the southern or upper part of the parish, next to the London road, is a small hamlet, called from the soil, Chalkwell , in which there are two modern-built houses of the better sort, the lower most of which has a large tan-yard belonging to it; near it there rises some springs, which fill several large ponds, the reservoirs for a corn mill below them, after which they run along the east skirts of the town, which are continued swamp of watery bogs, into the creek below...... The town of Milton has considerably increased, as well in the number of its houses and inhabitants, as in its wealth and trade.... The trade of it chiefly consists in the traffic carrying on weekly at the four wharfs in it, where the corn and commodities of the neighbouring country are shipped for London, and goods of every sort brought back again in return; and in the fishery for oysters......they are esteemed the finest and richest flavoured of any in Europe.

The Market, which is a very plentiful one for all sorts of butcher's meats, poultry, is held on a Saturday weekly, at the shambles, in the centre of the town. Adjoining to them is the market-house, having a clock, and a bell which is rung not only for the purpose of the market, but for the calling of parishioners to church, for funerals, and for occasional parish meetings....... At a small distance northward from the shambles is a kind of court-house, being a very low old-timbered tenement, where the courts of the manor are kept, and other meetings held; at other times it is made use of as the school house, underneath it is the town prison.

There is a fair, which used to be held on the feast of St. Margaret, July 13, now, by the alteration of the stile, on the 24th of that month, and the two following days. In the north-west part of this parish, among the marshes, there is a decoy for wild fowl, the only one that I know of, in this part of the county. The fowl caught in it, are much esteemed for their size and flavour. Great numbers of them are weekly taken and sent up to London.'

Like a number of other villages elsewhere in Kent, Milton has been virtually absorbed into the apparently endless inflation of an overwhelming neighbour, in this case Sittingbourne. So much so, that the two are spoken of in the same breath. But Milton (properly Milton Regis) was a royal manor long before Sittingbourne mattered at all and in Saxon times the Isle of Sheppey was just part of the manor of Milton, where stood the mother church for chapels in villages for several miles around. Milton was Alfred the Great's town of Middleton and its creek side location would have made it a significant little port. Holy Trinity Church claims to be the second oldest in Kent still in use. There was certainly a church on the site in AD 680, although most of the present flint and stone building is fourteenth century.

It was that same creek side location that brought the nineteenth century paper mill that completely overwhelmed the little eighteenth century fishing village. The mill's need for water drained the creek and the creek side area became lost among industrial development. The tide still flows into one branch of the creek and Holy Trinity Church, with its exceptionally massive tower, keeps watch over the Milton and Kemsley marshes.

A headstone in the churchyard of Holy Trinity Church tells us that Simon Gilker 'was killed by means of a rocket November 5th, 1696, aged 48.' Gilker was the local Administrator of the Poor Law among other duties. Not a job likely to bring you many friends in the community in those days. The event that caused his death is unknown but the rocket was probably a ship's signal rocket set off from a navy ship at Sheerness or nearer in the Swale or perhaps even at Milton Regis, a royalist port. Because of the significance of the date of death he may have been witnessing some form of ship board commemoration from the shore, or attending a local celebration, when the rocket went off course. It is improbable, even in his official capacity, he would have been liberating rockets for the occasion. Maybe he was just an unlucky bystander. Whatever the circumstances, it seems that in 1696 Simon Gilker became the first firework casualty in England.

Tanning

The tan-yard at Milton was surrounded by springs, large ponds, reservoirs, watery bogs and a creek, all essential for the process of tanning. The area also had many chestnut woods which would have provided the bark for the tanning process. In his book *Tanning Hides and Skins* (1801) the author Mr Desmond describes the process of tanning as follows:

'The hides from the cattle, cow and ox, were brought to the tannery either fresh or slightly salted for processing. They would then be washed in running water, well cleaned, and fleshed in the usual way. In order to remove the hair they immersed the hides for two or three days in a vat filled with gallic lixivium, and a mixture of sulphuric or vitriolic acid, or oil. Once the hair was quite loose it was then scraped off with a round knife, on a horse, or beam. Calf and goat skins were soaked in lime water.

The preparation of the hides and skins consisted of impregnating and saturating them with a principle obtained from tan, this gave strength and firmness, preserved a sufficient flexibility, and allowed the skins to be indissoluble and incorruptible in water either hot or cold. …… When the hides are completely saturated, that is fully tanned, which is known by cutting off a bit of the edge, remove the leather, and let is dry slowly in a shady place.

Five or six days are generally sufficient for the immersion of the hides in the same vats, as by that time they come to an equilibrium in point of saturation with the liquor; that is to say, they acquire all the strength the liquor can give them. They are then to be shifted into a stronger infusion, where they may remain the same number of days. In mild weather, if the liquor is of a proper strength, three or four immersions, of five or six days each, will be sufficient to tan the hides, which in the old mode required eighteen or twenty months to be completely tanned……… It is not the length of time during which the same water stands on the bark, but the number of waterings, that will completely separate the tanning principle from it. As the heaviest and best part of the liquor always falls to the bottom of the vats, it should be stirred up from time to time.

In tan-yards where there is not a sufficient body of running water for soaking and washing the skins, in order to extract the lime from them, the present mode of extracting it in 'grainers', by means of hen or pigeon dung, or other alkaline substances, may be continued, but the skins should never be put into the same liquor in which hides unhaired with the gallic and vitriolic acids have been tanned.'

In another book on tanning by Henry Procter in 1885 he says: 'The primitive way of drying leather was to hang it on poles in the open air, but this in our uncertain climate has become quite obsolete. The oldest plan now actually in use is to hang on poles in a shed generally raised some height above the ground, so as to catch the wind, and provided on all sides with louver boards arranged so as to open and shut as required. In windy and wet weather at all times, the louvers must be kept nearly or quite closed, and on the sunny side of the shed the same precaution is generally necessary. Again, in very damp weather the leather does not dry at all, and in frosty seasons it is apt to freeze, by which sole leather is made soft and spongy, and dressing leather though whitened, is said to be less capable of carrying grease. To prevent freezing, and to enable leather to be dried in damp or cold weather, it became customary to provide sheds with ranges of steam-pipes on the floor; this though decidedly a valuable addition, has not proved by any means an entirely satisfactory solution of the problem of leather drying.'

Leather manufacture was divided into different stages, tanning, in which the raw hide was converted in to the more or less flexible material known as leather, currying, in which this leather is further manipulated, and treated with fatty matters, to soften and render it more waterproof, and to improve its appearance. Finishing and dressing was the process necessary in tanning the more flexible leathers used for boot-uppers, hose-pipes, belts for machinery and saddlery equipment, as well as gloves and chamois leather. Because it was specialised work William would have been paid more than an agricultural labourer. Evidence of this is the fact that besides maintaining a very large family, many of the children were educated enough to write. This cost money because there was no free education until 1870.

Mary's father Edward Coulter died at Newington in March 1840 a month after Elizabeth Ann was born.

John Henry Pateman (1842-1886)

William and Mary Ann's ninth child, John Henry Pateman, was born on 24 January 1842 at Sitingbourne. His father was a tanner and his mother was Mary Ann Pateman formerly Coulter. John Henry was baptised at Milton in 1842.

On 11 April 1869 John Henry Pateman (full age, bachelor, dryer, 74 Grange Walk, father – William Bass Pateman, dryer) married Elizabeth Jane Bennett (full age, spinster, Twickenham, father – Richard Bennett, gardener) at Holy Trinity Church, Twickenham, Middlesex. They both signed their names and the witnesses were Richard Bennett and Julia Harriett Bennett.

They had two children: Rose Lillian Maud (born in 1870 in St. Olave, Bermondsey), and Harry Ernest Coulter (born 30 June 1872 at Bridge Street, Leatherhead.)

On 3 April 1881 John Henry Pateman (39, tanner, Sittingbourne, Kent) was living at 10 Little George Street, Bermondsey with his wife Elizabeth (38, Twickenham, Middlesex) and their daughters Rose (11, scholar, Bermondsey, Surrey) and Henry (8, Leatherhead, Surrey).

On 30 June 1886 John Henry Pateman died, aged 44, at St. Bartholemews Hospital in the City of London. He was a leather finisher of 71 Grange Road, Bermondsey. The cause of death was stomach cancer. The informant was the Superintendent at St Bartholemews Hospital.

Henry Ernest Coulter Pateman married Matilda Pattison on 17 January 1894 at St Mary Magdalen parish church and Henry's occupation was a grocer. His address was Grange Road. His sister, Rose Pateman, was a witness.

Henry George Pateman (1844-1893)

William and Mary Ann's tenth child, James Henry Pateman, was born at Milton on 26 July 1844. He was later called Henry George. As a 20 year old tanner he married Elizabeth Louisa Fagg, on 10 July 1865 at St. James's Church, Bermondsey. The bells of St. James' were cast from cannon captured at Waterloo. They gave their address as Spa Road and Henry signed his name, but Elizabeth signed with a cross. Elizabeth was baptised in 1844 in Bermondsey. Her father was Michael Fagg a Leather Dresser.

Henry George and Louisa had seven children: William Henry (1866, Bermondsey), Ann Elizabeth (1868), Rose Louisa (1870), Grace Alice (1873), Henry James (1875-1922), Edward George (1877) and Louisa Maud (1880-1881).

Henry George died on 11 December 1893 at Edmonton Workhouse. Elizabeth Louisa died in 1930 in Worcestershire.

Esther Mole Pateman (1846-1849)

William and Mary Ann's eleventh child, Esther Mole Pateman, was born on 23 October 1846 at Sittingbourne. Her father was a tanner. Esther died on 11 October 1849 at Sittingbourne aged 2 years 11 months. She was the daughter of William Pateman, tanner, and the cause of death was 'scarlatina, no medical attendant'. The informant was 'the mark of Mary Ann Pateman, present at the death, Sittingbourne'. Esther was buried at Newington on 14 October 1849.

James Coulter Pateman (1849-1879)

William and Mary Ann's twelfth and last child, James Coulter Pateman, was born on 26 January 1849 at Milton. He kept the name of James and married Mary Ann Price. On the 1871 census he described himself as a tanner. On 17 April 1874 James Coulter Pateman and his wife Mary went to New Zealand with their daughters Emily and Elizabeth on the *Hereford*. It was an assisted passage costing £43.10.0 and James' occupation was given as a carpenter. When he arrived in New Zealand he met his older brother James Edward (later Edward James) who said that, if he worked hard, for every £100 he made he would give him another £100.

James and Mary Ann had three more children, all born in Christchurch, New Zealand: Ellen (born 6 December 1874), Henry (born 24 January 1877) and Maud Sarah (born 8 January 1879). James Coulter Pateman died on 18 August 1879 with typhoid Pneumonia (8 days) at Christchurch hospital. His occupation was given as a labourer. He was buried on 20 August 1879 at Barbadoes Street Cemetery, Christchurch - Plot 689B. His older brother Edward paid for the children to be educated. For how long we do not know. It would have taken quite a while for the news of James death to get back to England.

Mary Ann Pateman, aged 33, re-married a Job Cartwright (bachelor, aged 44, Bushman) on the 11 June 1884 at his house in Waikerikeikeri, which is near Canterbury, New Zealand. Job was born in Staley Bridge, Lancashire, England and was the son of Allan Cartwright, grocer, and Hannah nee Dawson. We do not know if they had any children.

Bermondsey

On the Census dated 30 March 1851 William and his family were living at 12 Wrights Buildings, Bermondsey in the Borough of Southwark: William Pateman (head, 50, tanner, Bobbing, Kent), Mary (wife, 44, Bearstead, Kent), William (son, 22, tanner, Borden, Kent), George (son, 12, Borden, Kent), Elizabeth (daughter, 10, Milton, Kent), John (son, 7, Milton, Kent), Henry (son, 6, Sittingbourne, Kent) and James (son, 3, Sittingbourne, Kent).

They also had a visitor and another family living with them: Ralph ? (visitor, 22, tanner, Milton, Kent), Thomas Pearce (head, 26, tanner, Borden, Kent), Mary Ann Pearce (wife, 24, Borden, Kent), Ann Pearce (daughter, 4, Sittingbourne, Kent), Thomas Pearce (son, 2, Maidstone, Kent).

Thirteen people living in one house. It must have been very cramped and crowded. William Bass Pateman and his son, William, were both tanners, as were his visitor, Ralph, and his son-in-law Thomas Pearce. We do not know why William moved up from Kent to Bermondsey, but we assume it was to get work in the tanning industry. There were numerous tan-yards in the vicinity as well as an area called Leather Market. The move may also have been part of a more general migration from the countryside to the towns and cities.

The young and the single – or the village craftsmen – ventured to the towns, followed the canals (later the railways) or emigrated. When, after 1834, the Poor Law Commissioners sought to stimulate such migration, preference was given to 'widows with large families of children, or handicraftsmen…with large families'. William Pateman would have fallen into this latter category. The 1851 census (which recorded birth places) showed that 'in almost all the great towns the migrants from elsewhere outnumbered the people born in the town.' A very large proportion of nineteenth century Londoners were immigrants from the village.

Some were lured from the countryside by the glitter and promise of wages of the industrial town; but the old village economy was crumbling at their backs. They moved less by their own will than at the dictate of external compulsions which they could not question: the enclosures, the Wars, the Poor Laws, the decline of rural industries, the counter-revolutionary stance of their rulers.

Ever since the Middle Ages the chief place in England for the manufacture of leather was Bermondsey, which could get a good supply of animal skins to make into leather from the butchers of London. In 1392, a proclamation ordered that the butchers should have a place in Southwark for dumping such `garbage'. Leather-making was actually just one of the unpleasant, smelly, smoky or dangerous trades which the citizens were glad not to have within the city walls but across the river in Southwark and Bermondsey.

Bermondsey, like Milton, had a good supply of water in its many streams and ditches which rose and fell every twelve hours with the tide in the river Thames. Tanners' yards are marked on Rocque's map all along Long Lane and by the Grange. In early times there were woods in Bermondsey where oaks may have grown, but at this time there were woods, as their names suggest, not far away at Forest Hill and Honor Oak. The Bermondsey workers could be sure of a good market for their leather to the citizens of London, just across Old London Bridge. Until 1894, when Tower Bridge was built, there was no bridge lower down river than London Bridge.

There are reminders of the leather industry in the street names. Leading off Bermondsey Street are Tanner Street and Morocco Street, which is named after a kind of leather made from goatskins. Leathermarket Street led to the Leathermarket, a fine building erected in 1879. Even public houses have names from the leather trade, for example, Simon the Tanner. Nos. 146-148 Long Lane built in 1730, were once the home of well-to-do leather merchants. One of the oldest and most important tanning firms was Bevington's which only moved out about 1981. Their impressive building is still standing in Abbey Street. Three brothers, Samuel, Henry and Timothy Bevington started leather manufacturing at the Neckinger Mills in 1801. They made good use of the Neckinger stream which flowed through their works. Whether the Patemans' worked for them we do not know.

Bermondsey would have been a great contrast to Milton. William, Mary Ann and the family lived in 12 Wrights Buildings, off Spa Road, a street with terraced houses either side having the front door straight onto the pavement. There was a small window downstairs, and one upstairs with shutters either side. There were two rooms downstairs and two up, and, because the roof sloped down at the back there was probably not much room upstairs, especially in the back bedroom. There was a scullery or wash-house with a door into the back yard and a toilet behind it.

In *Collins' Illustrated Atlas of London* first published in 1854, at the end of Wrights Buildings the street had fields and meadows, but later a glue and size works was built there. However, compared to many in Bermondsey the Pateman's were not too badly off. Their street later changed its name to Vauban Street and 75 years after the Patemans' first moved in, it was declared part of an unhealthy area by the Public Health Committee on 4 May 1926. The Neckinger Estate was subsequently built on this site. Vauban Street today is a very run-down, depressing and sad picture. It is likely that in a few years the flats in this street and surrounding area will once again be declared unfit for habitation.

Bermondsey Spa

By way of complete contrast, in the eighteenth century well-to-do ladies and gentlemen believed it was good for their health to drink the water from a 'spa' or spring containing some mineral salts. Bermondsey Spa was discovered in 1770 by Thomas Keyse in the grounds of his tea gardens in what is now Spa Road. He provided many kinds of entertainment for visitors. In addition to 'taking the waters' they could visit the picture gallery, of which he was very proud, as he was himself an artist, and the great Sir Joshua Reynolds had visited the gallery. In the evenings there were musical concerts and grand firework displays. By 1881 the population had risen to 86,652 from 17,169 in 1801. The population of London and the whole of England increased enormously during this period. In Bermondsey, where trade and industry flourished, people came from other parts to seek work in the tan-yards, the breweries, the docks, railways and factories.

Where, and how, did they all live? For those in regular jobs or a little better off there were pleasant Victorian houses of a type which people appreciate today. But for the thousands of very poor people in Bermondsey, row upon row of narrow streets and alleys were hastily put up, completely covering what had once been open fields. Families shared crowded little houses, built back to back, as close as possible. Sometimes as many as nine people lived in one room. Often there was no water supply, only a tap in the street to serve up to twenty-five houses, and there was no proper sanitation.

Charles Dickens, the first, or at least the most successful chronicler of London slum life, converted to the page much of what he witnessed in the lives of the labouring classes of Southward and Bermondsey, and particularly the criminal element: 'to show them as they really were, forever skulking uneasily through the dirtiest paths of life, with the great, black ghastly gallows closing up their prospect.' His stories as 'Boz' appeared from 1833, often in the *Morning Chronicle*. At the end of the 1830's he was becoming the most popular author in England. He believed that the English working class were 'as hardworked as any person upon whom the sun shines. Be content if in their wretched intervals of leisure they read for amusement and do no worse. They are born at the oar, and they live and die at it'.

For the poorest of all, the old, the orphans, the unemployed, there was the workhouse in Tanner Street. If you have read *Oliver Twist* you will have some idea of what life was like in a workhouse. In the same novel, written in 1838, Charles Dickens also described Bermondsey's worst area, `Jacob's Island', the place where according to the story, Bill Sikes finally met his end. It was between Jacob Street and the river and at high tide was actually an island, cut off by the `Mill Stream' or `Folly ditch'. Old tumbledown houses overlooked the ditch from which the unfortunate inhabitants had to draw up all the water they needed in buckets, and the same ditch served as a sewer. No wonder terrible diseases, such as cholera, broke out in such a neighbourhood.

In the summer of 1849 a cholera epidemic took 13,000 lives in London. On the southern shore of the Thames it was particularly devastating in Bermondsey: 'The land of death in which it dealt was Newington, hemmed in by Lambeth, Southwark, Bermondsey, and other gloomy parishes through which the pestilence stalked like a destroying angel'. In September, Henry Mayhew, co-founder of *Punch*, visited Bermondsey to report on the epidemic for the *Morning Chronicle*. Of one street he noted:

'Along the reeking banks of the sewer the sun shone upon a narrow slip of the water. In the bright light it appeared the colour of strong green tea, and positively looked as solid as black marble in the shadow - indeed it was more like watery mud than muddy water; and yet we were assured this was the only water the wretched inhabitants had to drink.'

About 1860, these horrible ditches were filled in and the old houses demolished around the time of the `big stink'. In 1859 the smell from the River Thames was so obnoxious that it forced the `Powers that Be' to start work on building a new sewer system in London. Today although the inlet, which was once Jacob's Island, is still there it is a very different picture. Warehouses that once stored all the produce brought into the London docks have been converted into luxury apartments. The inlet is now spanned by a bridge made of polished steel and wood. This forms part of a walk-way along the embankment where many of the warehouses have been converted into luxury apartments, restaurants and offices overlooking the Thames.

Wrights Buildings

On 7 April 1861 William and his family were living at 12 Wrights Buildings, Bermondsey : William (head, 61, tanner, Borden, Kent), Mary (wife, 53, Staplehurst, Kent), Henry (son, 16, tanner, Sittingbourne, Kent), James (son, 12, errand boy, Sittingbourne, Kent), Mary (wid., 44, shirt maker, Folkestone, Kent).

In what must have been extremely cramped conditions, another whole family were sharing the same address: Edward Sullivan (head, 21, iron roofer, Cork, Ireland), Catherine Sullivan (wife, 27, Woolwich, Surrey), John Sullivan (son, 4, scholar,

Bermondsey, Surrey), Richard Sullivan (son, 3, scholar, Bermondsey, Surrey), Edward Sullivan (son, 1, Bermondsey, Surrey), Ellen Sullivan (sister, 13, scholar, Bermondsey, Surrey).

Only Henry and James were still at home with their parents in 1861. William may have been sub-letting his house to the Sullivan family to bring in some extra money. On 21 June 1863 William's mother Mary died at Borden. On 11 February 1864 his father Theophilus died, also at Borden. It is likely that William would have returned to Kent for their burials.

William was still living at 12 Wrights Buildings, Bermondsey on 2 April 1871: William (head, 70, tanner, Bobbing, Kent), Mary Ann (wife, 64, Wingham, Kent). Living with them were their oldest son, James Coulter (head, 21, tanner, Sittingbourne, Kent) and his wife, Mary Ann (wife, 22, silk winder, Coventry, Warwicks).

Henry and Elizabeth Pateman were living next door at 13 Wrights Buildings. Thomas and Mary Ann Pearce were living at 3 The Grange, with Mary's brother William Pateman (lodger, 41, tanner, Borden, Kent).

On 17 April 1872 Mary Ann Pateman died with acute bronchitis at 12 Wrights Buildings at the age of 65 years. It must have been very challenging to have 12 children and bring them up in that period. Hannah Pearce was the informant and present at the death. In 1873 Wrights Buildings changed to Vauban Street.

Bermondsey was changing fast and it was no longer the same place they had all moved to in 1850. It was becoming very densely populated with large blocks of flats or 'tenements' being built for some working people. Places like Devon Mansions in Tooley Street were erected in 1875, but many old slums, and the bad unhealthy conditions, remained. People still worked long hours for low pay, or were unemployed, as dock work was very uncertain. Many lacked nourishing food and suffered particularly from tuberculosis, from which many died each year. There must have been times when William wondered what his life would have been like if he had stayed in Kent.

However, it was during these hard times that something special developed in Bermondsey, what might be called 'the Bermondsey spirit'. Bermondsey (excluding Rotherhithe) was a small place, only about one mile from east to west and one mile north to south. People lived close together in their little streets and courtyards and worked together in factories, tan-yards, breweries, wharves and docks near their homes. Families stayed together. They knew their neighbours, who were mostly poor, like themselves. It was a real community. People shared their joys and sorrows and helped each other in time of trouble.

Ambrose Street

On 3 April 1881 William Pateman was living at 56 Ambrose Street, Bermondsey: William (head, widower, 80, tanner, Bobbing, Kent), Sarah Ann Hill (daughter, widow, 46, charwoman, Borden, Kent), Rebecca Hill (grand daughter, 8, scholar, Bermondsey, Surrey), Ellen Gregg (boarder, 8, scholar, Middlesex), Minnie Hill (grand daughter, 13, scholar, Middlesex).

We do not know when William Bass Pateman left 12 Wrights Buildings to live with his widowed daughter, Sarah Ann Hill. Ambrose Street wasn't that far from Wrights

Buildings, just off Blue Anchor Road, which is now Southwark Park Road. The friendly, lively local crowds went 'down the Blue', the market in Blue Anchor Road, to spend their hard earned wages. Before modern traffic took over there were over two hundred stalls lining each side of the road.

William Pateman junior was at 9 St Martins Road, Lambeth in 1881 with his wife Martha (50, Southwark, Surrey) and Elizabeth Hill (unmarried, 15, servant, Bermondsey, Surrey). William was a Tanner on the 1871 Census but in 1881 he was a 'publican out of business'.

John Henry Pateman (39, tanner, Sittingbourne, Kent) was living at 11 Little George Street, Bermondsey with his wife Elizabeth (38, Twickenham, Middlesex) and their daughters Rose (11, scholar, Bermondsey, Surrey) and Henry (8, Leatherhead, Surrey).

William and Mary Ann's family were well scattered by this time and most of them were living separate lives from the rest. When a family gets this large it is difficult to all keep in contact, especially with those on the other side of the world.

Sometime after the 1881 Census William Pateman decided to return to his roots and he lived with his daughter Harriet Wood at 3 Dean Street, Milton, Kent. There were only four people living in the house (Harriett, her husband Thomas and their two sons Thomas and Henry) and it must have been more peaceful than Bermondsey, with all those people.

The 1881 Census makes you realise the difference between working and living in a town and in a village. The most any of Harriet's immediate neighbours in Dean Street had living in their houses were seven. However, these houses, or cottages, were probably much smaller than the larger, sometimes three storey, houses in London. Of course, with long working hours the men did not spend much time in the house. A visit to the pub on the way home probably meant they were really only in them to sleep. It was the women with young children who had a challenging time.

William Bass Pateman died on 22 January 1885 at 3 Dean Street, Milton, aged 83, thirteen years after his wife. The cause of death was 'Natural Decay' and he was formerly a Tanner. The informant was Mary Ann Wood, grand daughter, 20 Bridge Street, Milton.

4. The Hoo Peninsula

- George Pateman (1807-1840)
- Jesse Pateman (1816)
- Robert Pateman (c. 1821-1890)
- John Pateman (c. 1821-?)

This chapter is mostly set on the Hoo Peninsula which is bounded by two great rivers, the Thames to the north and the Medway to the south. Much of the Peninsula is reclaimed marshland and marsh fever - or malaria, as we would call it today - took a heavy toll on the local population. The population of the Peninsula declined sharply between the early 18th and late 19th centuries, and it did not rise again until the early 20th century when positive steps were taken to control the mosquitoes and consequently the incidence of malaria. It is worth mentioning that historically Kent followed a different tradition of farming practices than most other areas of the country. There is no real evidence here of fixed crop rotation, as elsewhere. Nor is there evidence that livestock owners possessed the usual common grazing rights on fields in winter. The Hoo Peninsula, perhaps because of its relative isolation and sparse population, followed a still different pattern. Unlike most other areas of Kent the fields on the Peninsula were large and often unenclosed - the largest being at Cliffe and measuring some 2000 acres even in 1778, long before the modern system of open-field farming was developed.

Open meadowland extended from the Thames marshes to the high ground of the Hoo Peninsula. The villages on the Peninsula tended to be nucleated around a centre, as part of the open-field system, as opposed to the isolated farmsteads more common in enclosed landscapes. The scarcity of timber on the Peninsula also accounts for the large proportion of old houses built of bricks from the start. The effects of this different method of husbandry can still be seen today, giving the area a wide vista and open prospect not common to this part of Kent. The 'Hundred', as the name given to the unequal geographical divisions of the old Shires, may have owed its origin to a rudimentary police organization based on a hundred persons or a hundred households. The Hundred of Hoo encompasses most of the Hoo Peninsula. It comprises the parishes and churches of Hoo St Werburgh, High Halstow, St Mary's Hoo, Allhallows and part of Stoke. The Isle of Grain is in the Hundred of Gillingham, while Cooling and part of Stoke are in the Hundred of Shamel. These boundaries are clearly shown on Halstead's *Map of the Hundreds of Hoo and of Chatham and Gillingham*.

Scenically, the Hundred of Hoo certainly has a character all its own. There are various ways of approaching it, but perhaps the best starting place is Strood, the most westerly of the four Medway towns of Strood, Rochester, Chatham and Gillingham. Turn north at the bottom of Strood Hill and after passing through Frindsbury and Wainscot you reach the Hoo St Werburgh Road. Branch left-handed after Four Elms Hill and you are on the road to Allhallows which cuts a diagonal slap across the Peninsula. You will quickly become aware of a change in the character of the countryside. This is not the Kent that you passed through in order to reach Strood – a familiar countryside of small fields and enclosed orchards, of prosperous farms flanked by oast houses, of stretches of woodland with chestnut under wood which is cut every so often to supply poles for the hop gardens, of chalk ridges with hanging groves of beeches, of heavily timbered parks with glimpses of great houses, of ribbon development at its worst along the shining black racing tracks of the main roads, and of deep-sunk lanes which are like green tunnels to drive through.

By the time you have climbed the first hill you will be fully aware of the change. There is a new feeling of spaciousness. Hedges there are, but they are few and far between and wide unfenced stretches of roots and potatoes roll away on either side of the road. Every inch of the land is cultivated, but it is farmed on a broader, less fussy scale. To the right you look across the narrow Medway to the Isle of Sheppey, a fine, unobstructed, unimpeded view, interesting as all views must be which embrace water and shipping and a distant prospect of what might fancifully be regarded as a 'foreign' country. Away to the left is High Halstow Church, perched on the spine of ground which, running from west to east, forms the backbone of the Peninsula. Ahead is more rolling, open, cultivated country, dotted here and there with 'spiry' elms.

The Hundred is all views and distances, and you seem to be more aware of the sky. Stop just short of Fenn Street. Away to the right the distance to the Medway has increased, and there are intervening stretches of marshland. That way lies Port Victoria and the Isle of Grain and the eastern tip of the Peninsula facing Sheerness. Ahead, hidden by the rising ground, is Allhallows, with the little village of St Mary's Hoo lying just off the road in a cul-de-sac to the left. If you turn off westward along the High Halstow road and take the first turn to the right past Clinch Street – and in this as in other parts of Kent a 'Street' is a hamlet as opposed to a village which boasts a church – you will quickly reach the top of the Peninsula's backbone ridge.

Stop at the point at which the narrow lane begins to drop down the hill. On either side of the road there are steeply tilted grass fields dotted with trees as in a park only, for the most part, they are un-pollarded willows. Walk through the gateway on the left and you will find yourself on a grassy platform which commands another and still finer prospect. This time it is the Thames that you are looking at, with the Essex hills rising blue on its farther side. But whereas in the case of the view over the Medway from the Allhallows road it was the river and the shipping on it that caught and held the eye, this time it is the fore-ground that is all-important. Not the immediate foreground, though that is attractive enough with the circle of willows in the sloping field at your feet and to your left the beginnings of Northward Wood – locally called 'The Norrads'. The real interest starts at the foot of the slope.

First, when the ground levels up, there is a stretch of arable land. Then comes a house, Decoy Farm, with its fine old pink brick front and its steep-pitched lichen-covered roof which shows up a vivid orange-yellow against a dark background of ilex trees. And then – and this is the point – immediately behind the house, with no further break or dividing line, the marshes begin, running back for a good mile and a half to the sea-wall and the river – a flat beige-coloured carpet shading into pale green, dotted with grazing cattle, broken by an occasional gate, mound and raised brick causeway, with a few scattered huts and sheds and with one outlying farm hidden behind a screen of trees. Look to the right and you will see the line of the sea-wall curving round into St Mary's Bay and then jutting out again towards Bell's Hard and Allhallows, always with the flat expanse of the marsh running in to the line of the cultivated land at the foot of the continuing ridge. If your eyes are good you will be able to pick out the double line of thorn trees which, along this stretch of the marsh, constitute the boundary between the desert and the sown.

Look left, where Northward Wood, tumbling in disorder over the slope, joins the marsh at the foot of the hill and you will see the water of Decoy Fleet running in from Egypt Bay, a feature in the level stretch which sweeps on westwards towards Cooling. The sun picks out a building on the distant Essex shoreline, shines on the water in the Fleet – there is a barge with a dark-red sail going down river with the tide – and the eye comes back to a gleam of yellow straw in the Decoy stack yard. Leave Northward Wood and its heronry to the peace and seclusion which it desires and deserves, go back along the lane past Church Street, turn to the right, and you will soon be in High Halstow, a typical little Hundred village clustering round its church. Bear right-handed again and in a minute or two, as you drop down the hill to near marsh level, you will be able to look back at the gorsy, brambly reverse slope of Northward Hill.

Away to the left the backbone continues, running westward, its foot hidden by the up-and-down stretches of cultivated land. To your right there are glimpses of the marsh and river beyond the Buck Hole apple orchards. Then, for a time, all attention has necessarily to be focused on the road itself, which twists and turns in the most extraordinary fashion until suddenly you reach an inn, the *Horse-shoe and Castle*. Then comes an ugly red-brick vicarage by the side of the road and a right-angled turn brings you round the end of Cooling Churchyard. Stop once more just past the church. The field on the right has rushes growing in it, a sure sign that it is near-marsh. To the left, the ridge has receded and is crowned by the Chattenden Woods, while on a bare stretch of the crest the long red-brick mansion house of Lodge Hill is just visible.

On again, and you pass the startling white-stone, drum-towered gatehouse and the moated ruins of Cooling Castle; there are more ferocious bends in the road – Cooling is, as it were, defended and guarded by these twists and turns – turn left through Cooling Street, past Perryhill with its meticulously tidy orchards and neat white-topped railings, past the fuzzy end of Chattenden Wood, so typical of the Hundred in its unkempt state and so untypical of other Kentish woodlands, bear right, and the only reminder that you are still on the edge of the marsh country are the hedges of pollarded willows that screen the orchards. With the spire of Lower Higham Church away on your right you reach Chequers Street and then there is the hill up to Higham Upshire. You are now back where you started. If, this time, instead of branching left after Four Elms Hill, you branch right, this road will take you to Hoo St Werburgh and Stoke. Beyond Stoke you have two choices: left will take you to All Hallows; and right will take you to the Isle of Grain.

George Pateman (1807-1840)

George Pateman (1807-1840) = Frances Clarke (c.1813)
- Charles Pateman (1830-?)
- George Pateman (1831-1840)
- Sarah Ann Pateman (1832 -1834)
- William George Pateman (1835-?)
- William Pateman (1837-1845)
- Thomas Pateman (1839-1840)

George Pateman was the first child of John and Sarah Pateman. George was probably born in Bredgar in 1807. His parents had been returned to Bredgar from Bobbing after a Settlement Examination in 1802. His family subsequently moved to Hoo, where their second son, Jessie Pateman was baptised on 15 December 1816. He only lived a week and was buried on 22 December 1816. John and Sarah Pateman were returned to Bredgar again on 5 February 1817, following another Settlement Examination: 'John Pateman, wife Sarah and child George aged 10 years. Settlement Examination - at Hoo, settled Bredgar.' George Pateman married Frances Clarke on 7 December 1828 at Newington, Kent, not far from Bredgar. Frances was baptised on 10 April 1813 at St Mary Magdalen, Woolwich. Her parents were Samuel Clarke and Ann ? of Newington. Edward Coulter (Mary Coulter's brother) was a witness at the wedding along with Ann Hudson. Newington was a village that had strong connections with William Pateman and his wife Mary Ann nee Coulter.

Newington

There are two Newingtons in Kent: one near Folkestone, which has been practically extinguished by the Channel Tunnel terminus, and this one, near Sittingbourne, which is larger and stretches along the A2, almost linking up with Rainham. Neither has imprinted itself particularly deeply upon the county consciousness, although the A2 Newington has at least won a place in county lore. In 1936 a great stone was moved from the corner of Church Lane to the entrance to St Mary the Virgin's church. It is known as the Devil's Stone, identified by a metal plaque which, however, does not tell the story that belongs with it. According to legend, the Devil was once so disturbed by the ringing of Newington church bells that he went to the belfry one night and gathered the bells up in a sack. Then, with the sack over his shoulder, he jumped down. But as he landed, he tripped over the great stone and fell, leaving his footprint stamped into the stone and spilling the bells out of the sack. They rolled down the hill towards Halstow and into a stream which, the story always ended, flowed clear as a bell ever afterwards. The footprint remains to be seen – with a little imaginative perception – to confirm the truth of the story! George and Frances had six children, all baptised at St Mary Hoo by the Reverend Robert Gascoyne Burt. The baptism register stated that George was a fen labourer.

Robert Gascoyne Burt

Robert Gascoyne Burt was born in 1792, after his father's death, and was brought up by his mother who did not die until 1845. His father had purchased the advowsons of St Mary's and High Halstow and these, on his death, passed to his widow. It is clear that Robert's career was marked out from the first, for elderly clergymen were appointed to the two livings in order that they might become vacant by the time that the young hopeful was of an age to be presented to them. In the event, these stopgaps hung on rather longer than had been anticipated. Mr Burt was inducted to St Mary's in 1816 and became Rector of High Halstow eight years later. He held the living of St Mary's for fifty-nine years and that of High Halstow for fifty one. Throughout the whole of his long life he lived at St Mary's Rectory – a nice little eighteenth century brick house with a weather-boarded addition set in a small park and with a magnificent view northward across the marshes to the Thames.

Although he was never Vicar of Twickenham he spent three months out of every twelve at a house which he owned there. These jaunts apart, he liked the seclusion, the peace and the quiet of the Hundred. It is clear that he organised his life in such a manner that his clerical duties were kept down to a minimum. As incumbent of two neighbouring villages, he was accustomed to hold a Sunday morning service alternately at St Mary's and at High Halstow. During his annual absences in Twickenham services just lapsed. When the church authorities most unfeelingly ruled that matins must be read in each parish church each Sunday he imported and installed a curate at High Halstow and built a house for him there.

Tradition has it that he never composed a sermon in his life and very seldom delivered one. The services at St Mary's must have been extremely odd. The men sat on one side of the church and the women on the other. The schoolchildren were herded into a pew in the chancel and were watched over by one Collins, who was armed with a stout stick with which he maintained order. The clerk, Justice by name, frequently dropped off to sleep, waking up to intone 'Amen' at inappropriate moments. Music was supplied at first by a band which, turn and turn about on Sundays, attended the churches of Stoke, Allhallows, High Halstow and St Mary's, and later by a barrel organ, purchased at second hand from Cliffe Church, which played six hymn tunes. This restricted musical fare was subsequently supplemented by one of the parishioners who played the concertina. He was famous for his solo rendering of 'I will arise', but in due course he uprooted himself in no small way and emigrated to the United States of America.

Church collections were spasmodic. When Mr Burt decided that it was time to have one he stationed himself at the church door with a dinner plate which he had most tactfully primed in advance with a sovereign and a penny. No one could then feel that they were giving too much or too little. The rector's private life was equally un-sensational. He married but had no children. Except when he was taking church services he eschewed clerical dress, appearing always in a dress suit which was his customary and ordinary ware. Each year, on a stated day, a new top-hat was despatched to him from an eminent hatter in St James Street. He kept a carriage and a pair of grey horses in which he used occasionally to drive out on fine afternoons. The carriage was re-varnished once in every three years.

He was a kind-hearted and generous man. When the day came for the Pye children of St Mary's Hall to return to school they always went up to the Rectory to say good bye and Mr Burt would invariably give each of them half a crown. On one dismal occasion, when they paid their call, it was to learn that this fount of wealth was out driving. That evening the half crowns were sent down to St Mary's Hall with the rector's compliments. He subscribed lavishly to parish funds and on his death left each of his villages the sum of five hundred pounds. St Mary's is a small enough and a remote enough village today. What must it have been like in Mr Burt's time, when, in order to get your letters you had to send to Stoke Post Office? How did he employ his time? He did not read very much. He did not shoot or ride or hunt. He did not garden. He did not go for walks. He did not write books. He just existed beautifully from Sunday to Sunday, occasionally marrying, baptising or burying his parishioners and going out in his carriage on fine afternoons.

He fell into that category of clergymen of whom a church historian has written 'they were kind and sociable men, advisers of the poor, counsellors of their flock, maintainers of the character of Christian gentlemen.' And indeed sovereigns at Christmas time, bowls of soup when they were ill, and the appearance of his shiny carriage and pair in their lane may well have benefited the parishioners of St Mary's, including George and Frances Pateman, more directly than any number of conflicts of the soul conducted in the privacy of the Rectory study. Charles Pateman was baptised by the Reverend Robert Gascoyne Burt on 18 April 1830. We do not know what happened to Charles, but there is no record of him later, not even on the 1841 Census, so we assume that he died.

George Pateman was baptised in 1831. George died on 9 May 1840 with pulmonary consumption in Newington, Kent, aged 9 years. Sarah Ann Pateman was baptised on 20 February 1832. Sarah Ann was buried at St. Mary, Hoo aged 2 years 8 months on 6 November 1834. William George Pateman was baptised on 26 February 1835. We do not know what happened to William George, but there is no record of him later, not even on the 1841 Census, so we assume that he died. This is probably why they named their next child William.

William Pateman was baptised on 6 August 1837. William died on the 26 January 1845 in the parish of St Mary Hoo, Kent, aged 8 years. He was the son of George Pateman, deceased, and the cause of death was typhus fever. The informant was Sarah Blake, present at the death, St Mary. Thomas Pateman was born on the 5 September 1839 in the parish of St Mary's, Hoo. His father was an agricultural labourer and his mother was Frances Pateman formerly Clark. Thomas was baptised on 18 October 1839. Thomas died on 9 April 1840 at Newington aged six months and three weeks. He was the son of George Pateman, labourer, deceased (his father had died two months earlier in February 1840). The cause of death was whooping cough. The informant was Elizabeth Gable, Sittingbourne, in attendance.

George Pateman died on 12 February 1840 in the parish of Stoke, Hoo, Kent, aged 33 years. He was an agricultural labourer and the cause of death was consumption. Thomas Pateman was present at the death. 1840 was a very bad year for Frances Pateman: her husband died on 12 February, her infant son Thomas died on 9 April and her nine year old son George died on 9 May. Frances went back to live in Newington. On 6 June 1841 Census Frances (28) was living at Pond Place with her parents Samuel and Ann Clarke, and her son William (3). By 1845 Frances had lost her entire family. What happened to her after this we do not know; we have not found a death certificate. The Hoo Peninsula was a very marshy fenland and not the healthiest place to live. The thirteen little tombs huddled pathetically in Cooling church yard indicate the high level of infant mortality in the Hoo Peninsular in the eighteenth century. Ten of the children who lie here died under two years old, within three years of each other, and come from the same family. Marsh fever, or malaria, is believed to have been the cause of many such deaths.

Jesse Pateman (1816)

Jessie Pateman was baptised at Hoo, St Werburg on 15 December 1816. He only lived a week and was buried on 22 December 1816. Gypsies may have been attracted to the Hoo peninsular because the marsh reeds were excellent for basket-making, chair mending, etc. There was also a thriving brick making industry, which may have been associated with the Pateman's, hence the use of 'Hods' in the title of this book

Hoo St Werburgh

According to *Kelly's Post Office Directory*: 'Hoo St. Werburgh is a parish and ancient village of the time of King Edward the Confessor, head of a union and hundred, in the Mid division of the county, lathe of Aylesford, county court district of Rochester and rural deanery, archdeaconry and diocese of Rochester, near the north bank of the Medway, on which it has salt marshes cut up by creeks and a quay for landing coals; it is four miles north-east by a circuitous route from Rochester. The church of St Werburgh is an ancient structure: it has six bells and a fine spire, which serves as a landmark; it contains several brasses and wood carvings and was restored in 1873. The register dates from the year 1587. The living is a vicarage, yearly vale £395, in the gift of the Dean and Chapter of Rochester and held by the Rev. William Boys Johnston M.A. of Christ Church Oxford. Hoo union comprises seven parishes, viz: Allhallows, Cooling, High Halstow, Hoo St Werburgh, St James (Isle of Grain), Hoo St Mary and Stoke; the workhouse is in this parish. The gross estimated rental of the union is £32,777; rateable value £29,108. Walker's charity, of £5 yearly, is for bread. Here are pottery and tile works. The Earl of Jersey, who is lord of the manor, and the Dean and Chapter of Rochester, are the principal landowners. The soil is various: subsoil, clay. The chief crops are cereals. The area is 4,458 acres of land and 33 of water, rateable value £7,210; the population in 1871 was 1,260, including the inmates of the Union Workhouse. Broad Street is half a mile west; Cookham Wood, half a mile south west; Chattenden, a mile and a half north west; Belluncle, a mile and a half north east.'

There was a post, money order and telegraph office and an insurance agent. Officers of the Hoo Union were a clerk, assistant overseer, collector, relieving officer, vaccination officer, medical officer, superintendent registrar and a registrar of births, deaths and marriages. Staff at the Workhouse included a master, chaplain, surgeon and matron. The rural sanitary authority had a clerk, medical officer and inspector of nuisances. There was also a national school and two carriers to Rochester, one from Stoke (passing through every day, except Tuesday and Thursday, from 10 to 11am), and the other from Grain (passing through on Tuesday, Thursday and Saturday). Occupations included publicans (2 – *Five Bells* and the *Chequers*), beer retailer (4), wheelwright (3), potter, miller, carpenter, grocer (2), farmer (11), shopkeeper (5), butcher (2), blacksmith (2), boot and shoe maker, plumber and glazier, surgeon, builder and brick makers (the Wilson brothers, of whom more later).

Hoo St Werburgh is one of those Hoo Peninsula villages distinguished from its neighbours by the name of its church, which differentiates it from St Mary's Hoo to the north east. In fact, the parish became formally Hoo St Werburgh only as recently as 1968. Before that, although the name was used, most of the local people simply called it Hoo – as, indeed, they still do. Originally Hoo, or Ho, indicated a promontory or peninsular. The church of St Werburgh at Hoo dates mostly from the fourteenth century, though it stands on the site of a Saxon predecessor. There are five yew trees in the churchyard, four of them planted only in 1836, but the fifth is a very ancient specimen indeed with a girth of 25ft, and said to be 1,000 years old. The tower and spire were added in the fifteenth century. The spire is 60 ft high and the only remaining spire on the peninsula. It is a notable landmark in the area and the knoll upon which the church stands affords fine views over the surrounding district.

Of interest inside is a stained glass window to Thomas Aveling (1882) of Aveling and Porter who were first to produce the steam roller. In the churchyard is a tombstone to the memory of William White 'murdered in the bosom of his afflicted family' (1808) and thereby hangs a tale, an unsolved mystery. St Werburgh's dedication commemorates the daughter of Wulfhere, seventh century King of Mercia, who founded a nunnery at Hoo which was destroyed by Viking raiders. Her body was removed from Hoo to Chester. She was venerated locally because once, when the nunnery neighbours appealed to her to help them stop geese flying in and ravaging their crops, she called the geese to her and gave them a good talking to, after which they never touched the villagers' crops again.

The embarrassing Dutch raid on the Medway in 1667 brought soldiers to Hoo, to man Cookham Wood Fort, but the fort was never needed and very little of it remains today. Hoo Fort, like its twin, Darnet Fort, was built in the 1860s as part of the defences against the expected Napoleonic invasion. Both were originally intended to mount 25 guns on two tiers, but while the forts were still being built it was obvious that they were going to sink into the marsh under the weight of that much ordnance. In the end Hoo Fort was armed with only eleven 9 inch rifled muzzle loaders, with stores and accommodation for the gunners. They were never fired in anger but both forts remained operational until before the Great War when they were abandoned by the Army, although Hoo Fort remained Ministry of Defence property.

William Wyllie

From 1887 to 1907 the Victorian marine artist William L. Wyllie (1851-1931) lived at the two-storey brick Victorian Hoo Lodge. It stands on one of the highest sites between Hoo St Werburgh and Lower Upnor. His studio was on the top floor, the reason being that from it he had clear views of the Medway. He spent much time on the lower Thames and Medway painting marine and coastal subjects in oil and water colour, including harbour and dock scenes and views of the British fleet. These include *The Rochester River* (1881); *Heave Away – barges shooting Rochester bridge*, (1884); *The Winding Medway*, (1897); *Chatham Reach*, (1904) and *A Medway Fleet,* (1906). He was also an author on painting and coastal and maritime subjects, one book being *London to the Nore* (1905). Maidstone Museum has examples of his paintings.In the late nineteenth and early twentieth centuries, the village was thrust into that mainstream of life when land that had been wholly agricultural until then began to be valued more as an industrial raw material. Gravel was dug there; bricks were made and so was pottery. The barges that carried away the local products busied the river frontage until the 1930s, after which these industries declined.

Thames barges moored at West Hoo Creek (at this point sometimes known as Buttercrock Wharf). The breakwaters here and further upstream are provided by old concrete barges moored securely together. On the riverside of this anchorage or harbour is a concrete coaster, *Violette*, which was launched at Faversham in 1919. *Violette* hit Southend Pier in 1921 and although declared a total loss served as a refueling tanker moored just above Sun Pier, Chatham, up until World War Two. A number of derelict barge hulls still lie along the sea wall near the old Bawley Boat;

Henry Wood, Metropolis, Partridge, Bessie Hart.. Of the several wharfs at Hoo, Buttercrock was used as a sand wharf and dump during the 1920's and then for discharging ballast. *Bessie Hart* and *Partridge* were the last two to trade to the wharf. Frog's Dock was used commercially till 1918. Then the hull of the barge *Northfleet* lay there and was used as a coal store until she sank on her own berth. The berth was leased out in 1954 and now is occupied by the sailing barge *Henry* still fully rigged and sailing actively though converted and used as a home.

The ballast works nearby receive shingle and sand, all in ballast by barge from Grays, Rowledge, Freshwater, Aylesford and Felixstowe. During the construction of the oil refinery at Grain ballast came from Hoo. The gaunt shingle washer and grader that used to be conspicuous as a feature of the landscape, is now being demolished. Visible across the saltings are stumps, remains of a pier built by the Royal Engineers before the 1914 War. This was to have been the last stage of a railway from Lodge Hill Ordnance Depot to Folly Fort on the Hoo Salt Marsh. A swing bridge was constructed to cross the first arm of the creek but the whole project had to be abandoned when efforts to pile drive into the creek failed. No doubt the oyster catchers, little tern and shellduck who come here to breed are only too glad of the seclusion thus secured.

It was not until after the 1914-18 War that the deep water frontage of the Medway at Kingsnorth, not far distant, attracted the oil refining plant of Berry Wiggins, who built their plant close to the site of the old airship sheds. When Richard Church wrote about Hoo in 1948, he referred to it as cut off from the mainstream of life. Since then the mainstream has broadened out a bit in this part of the county and today Hoo St Weburgh is no longer small and not especially remote although it is by passed by the A228 spine road.

Hoo is still the principal village of the Hundred, surrounded by farming land and a good deal of twentieth century development, including the great Kingsnorth electricity generating station, which dominates the local riverside scene and is a more prominent landmark than the tall shingled spire of St Werburgh's church ever was. Today Hoo is really a small town, well provided with banks, shops, public houses, churches and schools and a very good County Library (where much of this research was carried out). *The Chequers* is still one of the three pubs at or near the centre of Hoo. The *Chequers* and the *Bridge* are in Church Street. The *Bridge* is so called probably because it stands very close to a brook which passes under the road.

The *Chequers* has a Mansard roof which is a common feature of several buildings on the peninsula, and is found on pubs, farms or the larger dwelling houses. It is a typical country pub with a rural atmosphere despite its urbanized surroundings. During World War Two, when many troops were stationed in the area and local amenities were stretched to the limit, the frequently overcrowded *Chequers* became known as the *Altmark*. What is the end of the story? There is no ending to a village and therein lies much of its attraction. There is a shifting of outline and changes in predominant activities. In Hoo there are caravan dwellers living by the sea wall where the Romans buried their dead. In long Meadow a pill-box stands beside the old elm used by bygone athletes for pacing their quarter-mile; the once bare horizon is spiked with flame-tipped chimneys of the oil refinery at Grain where many of the Hoo residents are now employed instead of on the farms around the village. But the church remains as one un-shifting centre of the village, and though families holding land in and around Hoo have changed and changed again, there have always been generous benefactors, and those who have been willing to give service to the community.

Hoo St Werburgh is no 'show village' nor can it boast of any world famous or national figures among its inhabitants past or present. But social history is not composed entirely of purple patches – how overpowering if it were. The people of Hoo are proud of their homespun village which provides a foil for Cobham and Cooling, their more illustrious neighbours in the Hundred of Hoo, and thus enhances the quality of life of one and all.

Robert Pateman (c.1821-1890)

Robert Pateman (c.1821-1890) = Mary Ann Enis (c.1819-?)
- Mary Ann Pateman (1840-1844)
- Alice Pateman (1842-1892)
- John Pateman (1844-1883)
- James Pateman (1846-1926)
- Mary Ann Pateman (1851-1929)
- Elizabeth Pateman (1855-1916)
- Henry Pateman (1856-?)
- William Pateman (1857-1921)
- Anne Pateman (1858-?)
- Walter Pateman (1859-1943)
- Louisa Pateman (1861-?)
- Thomas Pateman (1861)
- Noah Pateman (1866-?)

It is not clear when and where Robert Pateman was born. According to the 1871 Census he was born in Luffner, Hertfordshire in 1816. According to the 1881 Census he was born in HOO, Kent, in 1821. According to the age given on his death certificate he was born in 1813. 'Luffner, Hertfordshire' is possibly a reference to Luffenhall, which is a few miles north of Stevenage in Hertfordshire. A large number of Pateman births in the nineteenth century took place in Hertfordshire and neighbouring Bedfordshire and Buckinghamshire, in places such as Stevenage, Bishop's Stortford, Luton, Hitchin, Ware (where Mary Pain was born), Biggleswade and Royston.

I went to the Hertfordshire County Records Office at Hertford and checked the parish baptism register for LUFFENHALL, which formed part of the parish of CLOTHALL. I checked all entries from 1813-23 but found no entries for Patemans or Gypsies. I decided to find some information about LUFFENHALL and consulted the *Victoria County History of Hertfordshire* (1912, republished 1971). Here is the entry for CLOTHALL: 'Kingswood Bury is a farm in the occupation of Mr White in the south west of the parish. Beyond it the ground slopes downwards to the hamlet of LUFFENHALL, built in a single street, and lying partly in ARDELEY. Around it lie three small open fields known as LUFFENHALL, Newell and Swanstey Commons. Over these the farmers have the right of shackage or grazing after harvest; but the farmers generally come to a mutual agreement about their rights of sheep walk, and the greater part of the LUFFENHALL land is enclosed. The hamlet is well watered by the River Beane and its tributaries.'

Maybe Robert Pateman was born on LUFFENHALL Common? I then looked up all the baptisms which took place in ARDELEY (also known as YARDELEY) between 1813-23. I could not find any Patemans but I did find two 'Travellers', both baptised on 4 January 1818: Aaron, son of Jacob and Ann MILLS; William, son of Moses and Sarah HARRIS. Perhaps the Patemans were travelling through LUFFENHALL with these families when Robert was born? As with so much Gypsy family history, there are more questions than answers!

The Surname Profiler website shows where clusters of families were born in 1881 and 1998. The top area for Patemans in both years was Stevenage and the top postal town was Hitchin. This pattern did not change over a period of 117 years. This was not untypical of many other surnames, but is perhaps a little surprising when it comes to a Traveller surname. Maybe this indicates that some branches of the Pateman family tree were sedentary, while others traveled into areas such as Kent and Hampshire. The surname distribution map indicates this pattern – most Patemans in 1881 were clustered around Hertfordshire and Buckinghamshire. By 1998 the clusters included parts of Kent and Hampshire. The frequency of incidence of the Pateman name in the general population did not change – 42/43 occurrences per million names. The predominant ethnicity was British / English. The social demographics (or mosaic type) were characterized as White Van Culture – a 20th century equivalent of agricultural labourer? There was also a fair sprinkling of Patemans in Australia, New Zealand and Canada.

Interestingly, Gypsies are also associated with a place called Luffenham in Rutland. For example, Elizabeth Boswell was born at North Luffenham in 1798. Dawson notes that 'Rutland provided a very central base for travel to many parts of the country.' I went to the Rutland County Records Office at Oakham, and looked up the baptism registers for NORTH and SOUTH LUFFENHAM. There were no entries for Patemans or Gypsies between 1813-23. I re-checked my Gazeteer for place names beginning with LUFF, and found two more: LUFFTON, in Somerset, near Yeovil; and LUFFINCOTT, in Devon, near Launceston. Although there is no record of my Patemans travelling in Somerset or Devon, the 1871 Census gives 'Bath, Somerset' as the birth place of Robert's wife, Mary Ann Enis.

Some possible Kent births for Robert include: 16 December 1810, Frindsbury, Kent, mother Sarah Trimnel; 4 July 1813, Yalding, Kent, mother Sarah Comber; and October 1813, Cliffe, Kent, mother Elizabeth Willis. But it does not seem likely that Robert was born before 1817, as he would have appeared in the Settlement Examination of 5 February 1817 which moved John and Sarah Pateman and their son, George, from Hoo to Bredgar. It seems more probable that Robert was born in 1821 at Hoo St Werburgh. All the available evidence about his family points us in this direction. Robert's family came from Kent, the garden of England, a major centre for hop picking, and a significant source of employment for the Gypsy community. Robert's grandfather, father, uncle, cousin, and younger brothers were all born, lived or died in Kent. Bobbing, Borden, Bredgar, Milton, and Newington are all within a few miles of each other. They are also very close to the Hoo peninsula.

It is interesting to note that a triple christening took place on 22 October 1826 at Toddington, Bedford. The parents were John Pateman and Sarah. The baptised were John Pateman, Robert Pateman and Mary Pateman. Is it possible that these were the children of John Pateman and Sarah Cook and that John decided to have them baptised in 1826? Although he was no longer married to Sarah at this time, if she was the mother, then her name would be given for the baptism record. If so, then Robert could have had a sister Mary – and Robert, John and Mary could even have been triplets, although it was not unusual for children born at different times to all be baptised together.

Mary Ann Enis

We can find no record of Robert's marriage to Mary Ann Enis. According to the 1871 Census Mary Ann was born in Bath, Somerset, in 1819. Mary Ann's surname was spelled variously as Enis, Enos, Enus, Heinus and even Henious!

We have not found a baptism record for Mary Ann Enis, but we have found some records which could relate to other members of the Enis family.

On 3 December 1820 Mary Ann Anis was baptized at Bexley, Kent. Her birthplace was Bridgen, Bexley Parish and her father was William Anis.

In 1821 Frances Sarah Ennis was baptised at St Dunstan, Stepney. The parents were James and Martha Ennis, labourer. Frances was baptized in 1823.

On 20 April 1840 Catherine Ennis (minor, spinster, servant, 1 Garden Row, Turk's Row, Chelsea; father – James Ennis, umbrella maker) married Thomas Cotton (full age, bachelor, brick maker, 1 Garden Row, Turk's Row, Chelsea; father - Thomas Cotton, labourer) at St Luke's Chelsea.

On 26 June 1840 Mary Ann Ennis (full age, spinster, servant, 1 Mosby's yard, Chelsea; father – James Ennis, umbrella maker) married John Fletcher (full age, bachelor, mariner, 3 Durkham Mews, Chelsea; father – William Fletcher, labourer) at St Luke's Chelsea. One of the witnesses was Thomas Ennis, who could have been a brother to James and Mary Ann Ennis.

In 1841 Frances Enis (55) was living with Eliza (15), Abraham (15) and John (15) Enis at Braintree. Her neighbours were Sarah (15, Mary (20) and Mary (1) Pateman.

In 1851 Daniel Anis (30) was living with his wife Elizabeth (26) and their children Mary Ann (7), Daniel (4) and Noah (2) at West Brommich.

James and Sarah Enis

There are six baptisms for the children of James and Sarah Enis which took place between 1835 and 1851, the same period when Mary Ann and Robert were having their children:

Baptised	Name	Abode	Trade	Parish
19 July 1835	Mesach	Wimbledon	Basket maker	St Mary, Wimbledon
22 October 1837	Alice	A travelling person	Basket maker	St Mary, Wimbledon
28 June 1840 Born 1 June	Robert	11 Jubilee Court	Basket maker	St Luke, Upper Chelsea
16 January 1845 Born 2 January	William	3 Bouldins Gardens	Labourer	Holy Trinity, Upper Chelsea
27 December 1849	James Thomas	1 Lawrence yard	Basket maker	St Luke, Upper Chelsea
26 June 1851 Born 10 June	Mary Anne	1 Jubilee Court	Basket maker	St Jude's

Robert Enis died on 30 January 1850 aged 10 years at Lawrence Yard. He was buried in the parish of St Luke, Chelsea, Middlesex.

Mary Anne Enis died on 8 October 1851 aged 4 months at Jubilee Court. She was buried in the parish of St Luke, Chelsea, Middlesex. Described simply as 'poor' there is no record of the location of her grave, payment for the burial or undertaker's name and residence.

In 1851 James Henious (41, basket maker, Salisbury) was living at Jubilee Court, Turks Row, Chelsea with his wife Sarah (40, hawker, Bucks) and their children Musher (15, Surrey, Molesley), Alice (13, Kent, Riverhead), William (6, Chelsea) and Sarah (4, Chelsea).

In 1861 James Ennis (57, basket maker, Wiltshire) was living at Star Lane, Fulham, with his wife Sarah (50) and their children William (17, Chelsea) and Sarah (15, Chelsea).

In 1871 James Eanus (63, basket maker, Wiltshire) was living at Fulham as a boarder with his daughter Sarah (22, Chelsea) and her husband Jayson Keane (24, caretr, Fulham).

While these are all common names (with the exception of Mesach), they also feature in the family of Robert and Mary Ann Pateman. For example, Alice Pateman was born in 1842 at Wimbledon. Robert Pateman was also a basket maker. James Enis could have been Mary Ann's brother.

On 7 February 1869 James Lucas Enis was baptized at St James Norland. His parents were Mesach (basket maker) and Emma of 2 William Street.

On 24 May 1869 William Enis (24, bachelor, chair caner, Clifton Street; father – James Enis, basket maker) married Selina Lee (20, spinster, Clifton Street; father – Riley Lee, basket maker) at St Clements Church in the district parish of Kensington, Middlesex.

On the same day and in the same church William Enis was a witness at the marriage of Solomon Smith (full age, bachelor, chair caner, Clifton Street; father – Sydney

Smith, chair caner) and Naomi Shoesmith (full age, spinster, Clifton Street; father – James Shoesmith (deceased), brazier).

William and Selina Enis had five children baptised at St James, Norlands, Middlesex:

Baptised	Name	Abode	Trade
6 August 1871	Christopher William	3 Thomas Street	Chair bottomer
11 May 1873	Mary Ann	3 Joliffes Yard, Sherwood Street	Labourer
23 January 1876	William	2 Virginia Place	Labourer
28 April 1878	Rosina	10 St Mary's Place	Labourer
6 February 1881	James Isaac	10 Mary's Place	Labourer

In 1881 William Ennis (36, chair caner), his wife Selina (34) and their children Sarah 15, hawker), William (5), Rose (3) and James (3 months) were living at Bloomfield's Yard, Chelsea.

On 10 March 1885 Mesach Ennis (58, bachelor, hawker, 33 St Katherine's Road; father – James Ennis, basket maker) married Emma Fitzgerald (51, spinster, 33 St Katherines Road; father – James Fitzgerald, stone mason) at St James Norlands.

Thomas and Ann Ennis had two children baptized at St Luke's church, Upper Chelsea:

Baptised	Name	Abode	Trade
16 November 1853 Born 13 April 1853	Ann	6 Mosby's Yard	Labourer
29 June 1857 Born 29 May 1857	Henrietta	6 Mosby's Yard	Labourer

There are also birth certificates for Mary Ann Enis (June 1873, Kensington, 1a 135), Mary Ann Enis (June 1874, Kensington, 1a 60) and Selina Enis (December 1894, Kensington, 1a 98).

James and Ellen Enis baptized their four children on 18 March 1889 at St Jude's, Peckham. James gave his profession as a Ginger Beer Hawker:

Born	Name	Abode
20 March 1882	James	15 Clarkson Place
27 November 1883	Henry	15 Clarkson Place
31 December 1885	Ellen	15 Clarkson Place
20 February 1889	Arthur	15 Clarkson Place

James and Ellen had two more children baptized at St Mary, Newington on 1 August 1894. James gave his profession as a coster monger:

Born	Name	Abode
9 September 1891	Ellen	5 Little Mount Street
7 July 1894	Albert John	5 Little Mount Street

Gypsies did not always bother to marry formally. Often the researcher will only find negative evidence that a couple never married, i.e. despite extensive searching, no marriage entry is found. Some marriages did take place. Eighteenth century examples include two marriages in Berkshire in 1789: Major Eyres to Hannah Matthews at Hampstead Norris, and Onslow Ayres to Ann Cole at Yattendon. Formal marriage became more frequent as the nineteenth century progressed.

Several late marriages have been noted. George Ayres and Rosanna Pike married in 1853 at Eversley Hampshire after traveling together for nearly thirty years and having at least six children. Couples were encouraged to marry by the various Gypsy missions, and it is likely that encouragement played a part in the multiple marriage of six Gypsy couples in 1915 in the Hampshire hopping parish of Holybourne. Prior to 1837, references to Gypsies in marriage entries are uncommon, and most Gypsy marriages can only be identified by the names of the parties and witnesses. From 1837, marriage entries record the occupations of the marriage parties and their fathers, and the familiar occupational descriptions appear. Traveller marriages took place in the parishes which were popular for baptisms, though in some cases they are surprisingly few in number.

Marriage was frequently, though not exclusively, to members of other travelling families, and there are some Ayres marriages, official or other wise, to Gypsy families including Doe, Lee, Stanley and Wells. Other Gypsy families traveling in Hampshire include Buckland, Pateman and Penfold. Just because there is no official record of them getting married in church does not necessarily mean that they did not go through some kind of wedding ceremony. There is no evidence of specific marriage ceremonies amongst Gypsies other than agreement between a couple, with witnesses, that they will be life-long partners. There is historical evidence that the knot was tied by the couple jumping hand in hand over a fire / broomstick / working tools. For whatever reason, church marriage was never popular. This was probably as much to do with preference and custom as with persecution.

Circuits and Settlements

Robert and Mary Ann Pateman travelled around Kent, Surrey and Middlesex, following a regular pattern of agricultural work. This circuit can be plotted on a map, using birth, baptism, burial and census records as reference points. Contrary to popular belief, Gypsies of the past did not generally travel large distances in a haphazard way. The course of their journeys was usually well planned and repeated year after year to take advantage of the different trading opportunities offered by the annual calendar of fairs or markets in a particular region of the country. Depending on which part of the country your ancestors looked on as their 'base', you may find that they did not venture beyond a single county. If, for example, that county offered a large number of centres of population, a year round calendar of fairs to attend and opportunities for different kinds of agricultural employment throughout most of the year, there would be little need for the Gypsies to travel further afield.

Robert looked on Kent as his 'base' and spent most of his time travelling around parts of this county. There were a number of large centres of population, particularly in the Medway area where much of Robert's travels took place. Kent offered a year round calendar of fairs and agricultural work. Yet on three occasions he left the county: in 1840 he was in Chelmsford, Essex; in 1842 he was in Wimbledon, Surrey; and in 1861 he was in Notting Hill, Middlesex. The reasons for these journeys may have been either that he was traveling to visit family in Hertfordshire / Bedfordshire; or he was wintering over in what George Borrow called the great metropolitan Gypsyries. With the help of the 1871 census return showing the birthplaces of his children, combined with *A Calendar of Fairs and Markets held in the Nineteenth Century* (Loveridge), we have plotted the course of Robert's travels: Mary Ann Pateman, was born in 1840 at Chelmsford, Essex. We do not know where Robert was at the time of the 1841 Census. Alice Pateman, was born on Wimbledon Common, Surrey in 1842. Robert was back in Kent when his first child, Mary Ann, died at Stockbury in 1844. John Pateman was born in the same year, at Cliffe on the Hoo peninsula. James Pateman was also born on the peninsula, at Cooling, in 1846. John and James were baptized together in 1846 at Cliffe.

John and James were both born in a tent. Early Gypsies are known to have sheltered in barns and outhouses, but tents were adopted during the eighteenth century. The form of tent, the bender tent, was unlike those used by European Gypsies, and was made by stretching cloth or felt over a semicircular frame consisting of a central wooden ridge supported by hazel rods bent into arcs. Horse drawn wagons came into use from about 1830 onwards, but many families continued to use tents well into the twentieth century. Gilbert White wrote in 1775 of Gypsies visiting Selborne: 'While other beggars lodge in barns, stables and cow houses, these sturdy savages seem to pride themselves in braving the severities of winter, and in living *sub dio* the whole year around. Last September was as wet a month as ever was known; and yet during those deluges did a young Gypsy girl lie in the midst of one of our hop gardens, on the cold ground, with nothing over her but a piece of blanket extended on a few hazel rods bent hoop fashion, and stuck into the earth at each end, in circumstances too trying for a cow in the same condition; yet in this same garden there was a large hop kiln, into the chambers of which she might have retired, had she thought shelter an object worthy her attention.'

Mary Ann Pateman, was born at Westwood, Kent in 1851. We do not know where Robert Pateman was at the time of the 1851 census. There are three Robert Patemans on the 1851 census, but none of these match. Elizabeth Pateman, was born at Burham, Kent in 1852. Henry Pateman, was born at Snatts Lane, Frindsbury, near the Hoo peninsula, in 1856. William Pateman, was born at nearby Rochester, Kent in 1857. Robert returned to the Hoo peninsula for the birth of Anne Pateman, at St Marys Hoo in 1858. Walter Pateman was born at Stockbury, Kent, in 1859. He was baptized at Claygate on 3 July 1859 along with Elvey Pateman, the daughter of John Pateman and Matilda Sherrif. This confirms that John and William were probably brothers. The family then traveled to Surrey where Robert was born at Claygate in 1860. Robert senior then moved to Middlesex, where Louisa and Thomas Pateman (twins) were born at Latimer Road, Hammersmith, in February 1861. Winter encampments grew up on the fringes of the cities at places like Battersea, Wandsworth, and Notting Hill, and some Gypsies moved into towns and cities during the winter months to take rooms in lodging houses. Louisa and Thomas were born in a 'van' which could have been a Gypsy wagon or vardo. We do not know where Robert Pateman was at the time of the 1861 Census. There are eight Robert Patemans on the 1861 Census but none of these fit the bill. Robert Pateman returned to Kent for the birth of his last child, Noah Pateman, at Hollowbottom, Bromley, Kent in 1866. There is a pattern to these travels which took Robert from Kent to Surrey and Middlesex. This might have been part of a larger travel cycle which could have also encompassed Hertfordshire and Bedfordshire. It is interesting to note the vast area the family must have traveled entirely on foot to have had children baptized in several counties.

Brickmaking at Hoo

What kind of work were Robert and his family employed in? Robert was described as a chair mender (1844), basket maker (1846), licensed hawker (1866), and skewer maker (1881). These were typical Gypsy occupations. He was also described as a labourer (1846), agricultural labourer (1856) and general labourer (1861). This probably included work such as fruit, vegetable and hop picking. At the time of his death in 1890 Robert was described as a greengrocer, an occupation that was also followed by his son James. Robert may also have worked on the Kent brickfields (hence the reference to 'hods' in our title). Many Patemans were born on or near brickfields. You will recall that Harriet Pateman (1825-1894) married Thomas Henry Wood, who was a brickfield labourer. You will also remember that, among the commercial traders mentioned in the Kelly's Directory for Hoo St Werburgh were the 'Wilson Brothers, brick makers'.

In addition to agriculture, Hoo St Werburgh was also well known for brick building. During the nineteenth and early twentieth century, Hoo was a local centre for the manufacture of bricks. This was in the days before the growth of the massive brick making companies. In Hoo, brick earth was dug from close to the Medway, and the finished product was exported out of Hoo by barge. The British Museum was built with bricks made in Hoo. In all, there were three brick making companies in Hoo, which were in the proximity of Hoo Creek. Hoo's association with brick making continued into the 1930's. In 1858 Mr. Coles was given permission by the Vestry to construct a tunnel under Stoke Road (then High Street) 'providing a proper arch is formed' and 'the existing tramway is removed from across Stoke Road and all expenses are paid.' This facility was needed to convey the brick earth via the tramway to the brick kilns on the south-side of the road. During the course of the excavations a small quantity of gravel was found and extracted.

One brick field with kilns was in the area which is still appropriately known as the Pit, between Bell's Lane and High Street. A tunnel under the road connected the Pit with what is now the garden of Myrtle Cottages; before they were built there was a kiln on that land. Baker's Terrace and Wilson's Cottages were built of bricks made in Hoo, but many more were taken by horse and cart to Swanley and Bexley to help in the ever increasing spread of bricks and mortar of outer London. More extensive remains (including the brick chimney) are to be seen down near the river where John Wilson had his brickfield (this is now a caravan site). It would probably surprise some of the members of the now considerable caravan colony on the old site, to realise the origin of some of the banks and grassy enclosures which provide their homes with some shelter from the north east wind that sweeps across the creek.

John Wilson was not only a brick master but a businessman. On or near the site of the present Hundred of Hoo Sailing Club (formed 1953) were built six Thames barges – *Susan, Emily, Emma, Mary Ann* (all in 1862), *Elizabeth* (1863) and *Polly* (1864). All of them were built and owned by John Wilson and used for carrying bricks round by water to London. It is interesting to note that in 1905 when Beluncle was sold, the auctioneer's prospectus specially mentioned 'Underlying portions of the land are extensive beds of brick and tile earth and gravel which might be profitably and inexpensively developed'. The next year when Burnt House Farm was on the market, and Messrs Cobb, again the Auctioneers, the 'extensive beds of brick earth and cement clay' and 'frontage on to the river affording excellent sites for the erection of commercial waterside premises' were among the attractions of the freehold property. But instead of expanding, the local brick and clay industry gradually declined and Beluncle and Burnt House remain farm properties as they have been for generations. Wilson Brothers brickworks at Hoo closed in 1903.

Hoo St Werburgh in Old Picture Postcards has a picture of the Hoo brick works: 'Hoo St Werburgh was the local brick making centre for several decades up to the 1930's. The necessary materials were dug from local sites and the 'pits' remaining as evidence can be seen between the Church and the River. The Hoo Brick Company was one of three firms manufacturing bricks (another was John Wilson) which were dispatched in Sailing Barges loaded at the nearby wharf in West Hoo Creek.' One of these barges, the *Henry* is shown on another postcard. There is also a postcard showing a group of Hoo Brick Company workers taking a beak from their labours in preparing bricks for the drying sheds. The same photo, dated 1872, appears in *The Times of Hoo St Werburgh*. There is also a photograph of labourers loading a barge on the River Medway. And there is a map from 1909 indicating the Brick Works.

The brickmaking industry at Hoo depended on the local deposits of brick earth, as did the earthenware subsidiary of pots and tiles. The deposits were found in the area roughly between the beacon at Chattenden to the west, Abbots Court to the east and the A228 to the north. The main workings were close to the church on either side of Vicarage Lane. Some of the works were immediately behind the vicarage, which was then in Vicarage Lane. That site would be in Butt Haw Close. It is recorded that the Rev. P.G. Benson complained about the fumes from the kilns making life unbearable. However by 1929 most of the works had been disposed of. Along Stoke Road there were 'pug-mills' where the clay was mixed.

Solomon J. Brice owned the Hoo Lodge Brickworks whilst those which caused the vicar's complaint were owned by the Broad family. Another brickworks to the east of Vicarage Lane was in the hands of the Wilson's, who also built barges in which the bricks were shipped away to building sites, especially to those in the south-east. The Hoo bricks were deep red in colour when fired and were moulded with the name in the 'frog' (the recess on top of the brick). The barges were built with rectangular holds and could carry as many as 40,000 bricks. The brick earth was also used for making earthenware pots of all kinds, and for making tiles. In *Kellys Directory* of 1858, George Leeder and Ben Baker are listed as potters. J. Roberts, one of the tile-makers, lived in Upnor Lodge, situated at the top of Elm Avenue, with his works on the riverside at Lower Upnor.

All that now remains is the name of the Pottery cottages. Here a family, Ted Baker and his sons made flower pots, drain pipes and ornamental bowls and even small pottery crosses for holding flowers. But the succeeding generation were muddlers and the business collapsed; the family left Hoo and took other employment, but now once again there are three generations of the Baker family making pottery over at Rainham.

Bricks were also made at Allhallows, Hoo. The field by the shore west of Bells is called Brickfield. In 1508 it appears to have been called – or mispelt – Brakefield. Not long since a quantity of red bricks were unearthed near the small pond, and there is a tradition that it is here that these bricks were made. Traditions being scarce in Allhallows, we may as well make the most of this one.

The Kentish Brick Maker

Brick making was traditionally a rural industry and until the introduction of the brick making machine, which became common by the mid nineteenth century, all bricks were moulded by hand. In the past when a building of any significant size was to be built, the brick makers would search out local pockets of suitable clay and brick-earth so that bricks could be moulded and fired in clamps as near as possible to the site. Thus many buildings built prior to the great expansion of the brick works in the last century, directly reflect the geology of the area. We do not know what part, if any, Robert Pateman played in the brick making process: grafting, moulding, drying or firing.

Traditionally most work stopped in the autumn but a few men were retained to dig enough clay for the next season. They used narrow-bladed spades, called *grafts*, and piled the clay in large heaps for rain and frost to weather it. In April, they turned it over, tempered it with water, then kneaded it with bare feet. From the pit the clay was taken to the pugmill – a vertical tub of wood or iron with a shaft from which projects a spiral of horizontal knives. A horse, harnessed to the end of a long beam joined to the shaft head, circled the mill. Clay was fed into the top, kneaded by the knives and extruded from the bottom. Children were often employed to carry or barrow the clay to the moulding bench.

The moulder would nail a stock board to his bench. A raised block or kicks was fixed to the stock to form the frog or recess in the bottom of each brick. The moulder dusted his mould with sand and set it on the stock. Sprinkling more sand on the bench, he rolled sufficient clay in it to form a rectangular clot or warp, smaller and deeper than the mould. This he threw hard into the mould so that it filled every corner. He cut the excess clay from the top with a wire bow and threw it aside for the next clot, then smoothed the surface further with his strike, a stick moistened with water. He lifted the mould off the stock and turned the brick out on to a pallet board for his bearer off to remove on a hack barrow to be set or pitched on the hack or drying platform to dry. This process produced sand-faced bricks. Between 1820 and 1850 inventors patented 109 brick making machines and kilns. Some of these were displayed at the Great Exhibition of 1851.

Bricks must be thoroughly dry before firing unless they are sufficiently hard and dry after forming and the firing allows for removal of residual moisture. The bearer off would remove the bricks from the hack barrow between two pallet boards, and set them on edge, about half an inch apart, in two rows up to eight courses high, on the hack. This was a slightly raised timber platform, protected either by moveable wooden hack caps or permanent open-sided sheds, with loo boards at the sides to repel driving rain. He set one course at a time to allow the bricks to stiffen before he added the next. When hardened, the bricks were skintled – set diagonally and further apart to speed up the drying, which took three to six weeks according to the weather. Early in the nineteenth century, hot-floor dryers were introduced, heated by under floor flues piping hot air from a furnace or steam from the works engine. Bricks were set on end in a single layer on the hot floors.

To change dried mud into stone the bricks must be burnt at a bright red heat. This took place in a clamp. Setters skillfully stacked the bricks, spaced apart to allow the fire gases to circulate, and formed fire channels in the base, finally covering the whole with turf and old bricks. The burner then lit and tended the fires. Clamps were later superceded by kilns. James Gibbs and Thomas Ainslie patented multi-chamber kilns in 1841 and 1843 respectively, but the best known continuous kiln is named after Friedrich Hoffmann, who designed it in 1856.

Although there are large and efficient brick making plants in Kent today, perhaps surprisingly brick making has not quite been mechanized into history, for handmade bricks are still made in Kent in much the same way as they were moulded in medieval times. Handmade bricks are much in demand. Because each brick is made individually the texture often shows the folds of the clay, thus enhancing the individuality of the finished brick.

1871 Census

From the 1871 census, those not in houses were to be recorded by name and entered in sequence, i.e. in the street or lane in which they were encountered. Gypsy families in tents or wagons were still commonly entered at the end of each district, so it is possible to search a wide area and find a reasonable proportion of the Gypsy entries by scanning through the records and checking the end of each district. A complete search of the area is always best.

On 2 April 1871 Robert (55, Luffner) was living with his wife, Mary Ann (52, Somerset) and their children, Alice (27, Wimbledon), John (23, Cliffe), James (21, Cliffe), Mary Ann (20, Westwood), William (19, Rainham), Elizabeth (16, Burham), Anne (15, St Mary), Walter (12, Stockbury) and Louisa (10, Hammersmith) in an old stable, at Becks Lane, Beckenham, Kent. This stable was located on a brickfield, which provides another link between Robert and brick making.

When vagrants were on the road they slept in the open air or lodged in alehouses or more usually a barn, outhouse or stable. Some barns were well known haunts for travelling people, such as a barn in Wingham and the Personage Barn at Aylesford, which was also known as the 'Travellers House' or 'Beggars House'.

We assume that Robert's wife, Mary Ann, died sometime between 1871 and 1881 because in 1881 Robert described himself as a widower. At the time of the 1881 census Robert was living in a tent on Mitcham Common. He was recorded as Robert

Bateman (60, Skewer maker, Hoo) and he was living with his sons, Walter Bateman (21, Skewer maker, Bembery) and Robert Bateman (13, Skewer maker, Bearsted).

Walter Pateman's age matches that of the Walter who appeared on the 1871 Census. We assume that Bembery is Pembury, which is close to Stockbury. But we are not sure who Robert Pateman (junior) was. If he was 13 in 1881 he would have been born in 1868, but we have no record of his birth, and he did not appear in the 1871 Census. It is possible that Robert Pateman did not register the birth of Robert junior.

Robert's daughter, Louisa Pateman (20, skewer maker, Notting Hill), was living in a neighbouring tent on Mitcham Common, with her husband Charles Lee (21, skewer maker, Rochester).

Where was the rest of Robert's family in 1881? We do not know where Anne or Noah were living, or if they were still alive. We do not know where Walter was living, but we know he was alive because he died in 1943.

Alice Bateman (boarder, 29, farm servant, Wimbledon) was living at 10 Lawrences Yard, St Mary Cray, Kent. John Pateman (34, Agricultural labourer, Rochester) was living at Orpington Lane, Farnborough, Kent.

James Pateman (29, bricklayer's labourer – another connection to bricks - Cliffe) was living at Bastard Green, Farnborough, Kent, with his wife, Jane Reynolds (20, St Mary Cray) and their daughter Betsy (4 months, St Mary Cray).

William Patenan (22, Beehive Maker, Dartford) was living in a van on the side of Orpington Lane, Farnborough, Kent, with his wife Mercy (25, Crockenhill) and their children Mary (5, Crockenhill) and Henry (1, Crockenhill).

Mary Pateman (28, Hoo) was living in a van in Piggendens Lane, Farnborough, Kent, with her husband George Reynolds (25, Highton, Kent) and their children John (6, Farnborough), George (4, Bromley), James (2 Farnborough) and Thomas (9 months, Sidcup).

Elizabeth Pateman (26, hawker, Maidstone) was living with her husband, Henry Taylor (27, hawker, Malden) at Acre Road, Kingston on Thames, Surrey, with their son, Henry Taylor (1, Oakingham, Surrey).

Some time between 1881 and 1890, Robert Pateman joined his sons John, James and William, who were living at Farnborough Kent. John died in 1883 and so it is likely that Robert lived his final years with James and William. In 1881 they were living in vardos on Tugmutton Common, Farnborough, but by 1890 they had moved into cottages at Tugmutton and Farnborough village.

So it seems possible that Robert Pateman, who had spent his life on the road, may have died in a house. Robert was living in a tent in 1844 and 1846 when John and James were born at Cliffe and Cooling; in 1861 Robert was living in a van that Louisa and Thomas were born in at Latimer Road, Hammersmith; in 1871 Robert was living in a barn at Beckenham; in 1881 Robert was living in a tent at Mitcham.. But he probably spent his final days in bricks and mortar, either at 5 Tugmutton (James) or Stow Cottages (William).

Robert Pateman died on 15 June 1890 at Farnborough of pleurisy and bronchitis. His given age was 77, a greengrocer by occupation and the informant, present at the death, was his son James Pateman. Robert was buried on 19 June 1890 at St Giles, Farnborough, Kent. He lies with his son James (buried 1926) and his grandson George (buried 1921).

John Pateman (1821-?)

John Pateman (1821-?) = Matilda Sheriff (1830-1908)
- Esther (1844-?)
- John (1848-?)
- Matilda (1851-?)
- William (1855-1940)
- Alice (1857-?)
- Elvey (1859-?)
- Thomas (1862-1902)
- Annie (1862-?)
- Ruth (1867-?)

According to the 1861 Census John Pateman was born in Kent, Hoo, in 1821. According to the 1881 Census John was born in 1821 at Luton, Beds. Like his brother Robert, we are not quite sure if John was born in Kent or Beds / Herts. John's wife was Matilda Sheriff, from Kingsey Buckinghamshire. Kingsey is in between Aylesbury and High Wycombe and in a part of the country that many Patemans lived in at this time. Matilda was born in 1825 (1861 census), 1824 (1881 census), 1823 (1901 census) or 1830 (death certificate). It is possible that John was a twin brother of Robert Pateman, who was also born at Hoo in 1821. As was noted above, John could have been baptised on 22 October 1826 at Toddington, Bedford, along with his brother Robert and sister Mary. John and Robert certainly seem to have travelled around a similar circuit of stopping places, either together or separately, as evidenced by the birth of their children. John's first and last children were born in 1844 and 1867; Robert's first and last children were born in 1840 and 1866. Robert had twins in 1861 (Thomas and Louisa); John had twins in 1862 (Thomas and Annie).

John's first child, Esther, was born at Wimbledon in 1844; Robert's daughter, Alice, was born at Wimbledon in 1842. John's second child, also John, was born in the Hundred of Hoo, Kent, in 1848; Robert's sons, John and James, were born in the Hundred of Hoo in 1844 and 1846.

John's third and fourth children – William and Matilda – were born in Wiltshire, in 1851 and 1855. The family may have been travelling to Bath, Somerset, where Robert's wife, Mary Ann, was born. John's fifth child, Alice, was born at Bearsted, Kent in 1857; Robert's son, Walter, was born at nearby Stockbury in 1859. Walter was baptised at Claygate on 3 July 1859 along with Elvey Pateman, daughter of John and Matilda. Robert's son, Robert, was born at Claygate in 1860. The family may have been travelling to Hammersmith, Middlesex, where Robert's twins, Louisa and

Thomas, were born in 1861. They may have travelled on into Essex, for the birth of John's next two children, Thomas and Annie. Thomas Pateman was born on 27 April 1862 at 5pm in a van on the roadside at Great Maplestead, Essex. His father was a basket maker and his mother was Matilda Pateman, formerly Sheriff. The informant was John Pateman, father, Hoo, Kent. Annie Pateman was born on 27 April 1862 at 5.30pm.

John's last child, Ruth, was born at Crayford, Kent in 1867; Robert's last child, Noah, was born at nearby Bromley, Kent, in 1866.

At the time of the 1861 Census, John Pateman (40, travelling mat maker) was living in a 'Traveller's van' at Stanbrook, Thaxsted, Essex, with his wife Matilda (36), and their children Esther (15), John (13), William (10), Matilda (10), Alice (6) and Elvey (2). All of these children appear on the 1881 census apart from Matilda, who may have died, got married, or moved away from her family.

In 1871 Matilda Bateman (45, travelling chair mender) was living in a caravan in Epping Forest with her children John (24), Esther (27), Matilda (19), William (19), Alice (16), Thomas (9), Elvey (12),Phoebe (6) and Ruth). John was in another caravan and he was described as John Robinson (50, travelling chair mender, Bedford, Luton).

On 3 April1881, John Bateman (60, licensed hawker) was living in a caravan at Peel Road, Woodford, Essex, with his wife Matilda (57, licensed hawker) and their children Esther (37, licensed hawker), John (33, tinman and brassier), William (30, labourer), Alice (24, licensed hawker), Alva (21, licensed hawker, lunatic), Thomas (18, licensed hawker, cripple), Ruth (14, scholar). Also living with them was Rose Ann Rich (20, daughter in law, Peckham, Kent) the wife of William Pateman.

It is interesting to note that John Pateman was a tinman and brassier. This introduces another trade to the Pateman family, in addition to tanners and brick makers, and the typical Gypsy occupations of hawking, chair mending and basket making. Thomas was described as a cripple and Alva was a lunatic. Discovering the presence of an ancestor with mental health problems, or at least what our forebears considered as mental health problems, is more common than perhaps some people think. That's because census returns from 1871 onwards, in the final column, record if a person was deemed to be a lunatic, an imbecile or an idiot. The first was someone who was prone to losing his or her reason though experienced moments of clarity; the second was someone who was judged to have fallen into a state of insanity in later life; while the third suffered from congenital mental problems. If you discover any of these terms used in relation to an ancestor, bear in mind that they were not applied scientifically or even with that much rigour, and that some methods of diagnosis seem antediluvian: women who had suffered post natal depression, for example, were seen as suffering from a form of mania, which is why it is not exceptional for a woman with a new born to be recorded as a lunatic.

Having a lunatic ancestor is nothing to be ashamed of. It is reasonably likely that that person was not mad: slightly eccentric was enough to alert the authorities in the past, and there is every chance they might have been suffering from some form of physical or mental handicap. A lack of knowledge and medical study led to many disparate mental health problems being lumped together under one label, with the tragic consequence that many people with different needs and types of problems were gathered together in the same asylum and offered similar treatments. Before 1800 it is likely that their own family looked after any mad ancestors, though if the family could not afford it the poor unfortunate might have been sent to the local workhouse. The Lunatics Act of 1845 ushered in the biggest change. By law, every county was required to build and run an asylum for poor lunatics.

We do not know what happened to Alva and whether she ended up in a lunatic asylum or not. Coming from a Gypsy family this is unlikely, in the same way that few Gypsies were sent to workhouses: Gypsy families tended to look after their own. It is to be hoped that Alva did not go into an asylum because they were terrible places and some people remained in asylums for much or all of their lives.

We do not know when or where John died and we do not know much about his children. William Pateman was born in 1855 at Redlynch, Wilts, and married Rose Ann Rich (born Malling, 1861) at Tonbridge, Kent in 1881. They had had fourteen children: Selina Elsie (1882-1907), Edith Rose (1883-1940), Charlotte Ruth (1884-1964), Phoebe (1885-?), Esther Matilda (1886-1907), William George (1888-?), Ernest Herbert (1889-?), Florence Phoebe (1890-1915), May Elizabeth (1894-1963), Wilfred (1894-?), Ethel Maud (1896-?), Leonard Hubert James (1898-1900), Lilian Alice (1899-?) and Gladys Victoria (1901-1926)

William Pateman was buried on 4 October 1940 at Star Lane cemetery, St Mary Cray. Rose Ann Pateman was buried on 1 February 1918, also at Star Lane. For more information about this branch of the Pateman family see *Corkes Meadow: the life and times of Noah Pateman and his family*.

In the 1901 Census Thomas Pateman (son, single, 39, Essex, cripple from birth) was living at 2 Sutton's Cottages, North Cray, Kent with his mother Matilda (head, married, 75, Kingsey, Bucks) and his sister Ruth (daughter, single, 34, field worker on farm, Crayford, Kent). Matilda is not described as a widow but as she is described as the head we assume that her husband John was dead. Thomas probably did not get married or leave home because of his disability. Ruth may have stayed at home to care for her elderly mother and disabled brother. Thomas Pateman died on 12 May 1902 at 2 Sutton's Cottages, North Cray, Kent. He was a 'shoe mender' aged 39 years and the informant was 'Ruth Pateman, sister, present at the death, 2 Sutton's Cottages, North Cray.' Matilda Pateman died on 14 June 1908, aged 78, at Jubilee Cottages, North Cray. She was the widow of John Pateman, a general labourer. The cause of death was broncho pneumonia and exhaustion. J. Hasell was the person who caused the body to be buried.

5. Wimbledon Common

- Mary Ann Pateman (1840-1844)
- Alice Pateman (1842-1892)

In this chapter our history moves from Kent and the Hoo Peninsula to Surrey and the London Commons. We do not know when or why Robert traveled from Kent to Surrey; it could have been part of a journey back to Bedfordshire / Hertfordshire, where Robert and/or his brother John may have been born. Or it might have been part of the seasonal pattern of Gypsy migration. In common with other counties in the south east of England, Surrey had a particularly high population of Gypsies and Travelers during the nineteenth century. Casual agricultural work was an important part of the rural economy, although there was a small amount of mechanization on the farms most work still relied on horse and hand. This farm work was seasonal and the first opportunity of the year was offered by the hop growers. Large areas of Surrey as well as neighbouring Kent, Sussex, and parts of Hampshire were under hops and when the first shoots appeared in spring they had to be started on their journey up the poles and strings. Hop training or 'twiddling' required a considerable workforce which couldn't be provided by the local communities who were already fully occupied at this busy time of year. From then on Travelers would move from farm to farm picking soft fruit throughout the summer as each crop ripened, strawberries, cherries, blackcurrants all had to be quickly harvested as soon as they were ready. Vegetables also needed picking including beans, peas and brassicas. After the round of summer harvesting, hop picking lasted for most of September followed by soft fruit which lengthened the working season into the autumn.

With the onset of winter the towns offered better prospects for making a living and Gypsies would head for the urban fringes where they could seek temporary casual work amongst the sedentary population. The commons of south and south west London provided ideal stopping places within easy access of the city and its population. Wimbledon, Putney, Wandsworth and Mitcham Commons all provided stopping places for Travelers, particularly during the winter months. This cycle of Gypsy agricultural work was described by William Howitt in the *Rural Life of England* (1844): 'About London, in April, May, and June, they get work in the market gardens. In July and August they move into Sussex and Kent for harvest-work, where they continue. Through September, great numbers of them find employment in the hop districts of those counties, and of Surrey. They constantly encamp on the commons near London. On Wimbledon Common, at Christmas 1831, there were no less than seventy of them.'

A postcard of London and Area (from a hand coloured map of Middlesex, Surrey, Essex and Kent, printed privately in 1822 by J & G Cary) shows Wimbledon and Wimbledon Common. Compared with those of today, transport and communications in 1822 were slow and unsophisticated, relying solely on the sea, rivers or canals, or horses, carts and carriages which depended on crude and poorly maintained roads. Few people traveled any great distance from their place of birth. Wandsworth, Clapham, etc, were just villages outside London.

Robert Pateman probably traveled from Kent to Surrey by horse and cart on difficult roads. He was one of those who did travel great distances from his place of birth. And he was not alone. The 1822 map shows the close proximity of Wimbledon to Wandsworth, just three miles down the road. Wandsworth was home to one of the 'Metropolitan Gypsyries' described by George Borrow in *Romano Lavo-Lil* (1874):

'What may be called the grand Metropolitan Gypsyry is on the Surrey side of the Thames. Near the borders of Wandsworth and Battersea, about a quarter of a mile from the river, is an open piece of ground which may measure about two acres. To the south is a hill, at the foot of which is a railway, and it is skirted on the north by the Wandsworth and Battersea Road. This place is what the Gypsies call a no mans ground; a place which has either no proprietor, or which the proprietor, for some reason, makes no use of for the present. The houses in the neighbourhood are mean and squalid, and are principally inhabited by artisans of the lowest description. This spot, during a considerable portion of the year, is the principal place of residence of the Metropolitan Gypsies, and of other people whose manner of life more or less resembles theirs.

During the summer and autumn the little plain, for such it is, is quite deserted, except that now and then a wretched tent or two may be seen upon it, belonging to some tinker family, who have put up there for a few hours on their way through the metropolis; for the Gypsies are absent during summer, some at fairs and races, the men with their cocoa-nuts and the women busy at fortune telling, or at suburban places of pleasure – the former with their donkeys to ride upon, and the latter as usual dukkering and hokkering, and the other travelers, as they are called, roaming about the country following their particular avocations, whilst in the autumn the greater part of them all are away in Kent, getting money by picking hops.

As soon, however, as the rains, the precursors of winter, descend, the place begins to be occupied, and about a week or two before Christmas it is almost crammed with the tents and the caravans of the wanderers; and then it is a place well worthy to be explored, notwithstanding the inconvenience of being up to one's ankles in mud, and the rather appalling risk of being bitten by the Gypsy and traveling dogs tied to the tents and caravans, in whose teeth there is always venom and sometimes that which can bring on the water-horror, for which no European knows a remedy. The following is an attempt to describe the odd people and things to be met with here; the true Gypsies, and what to them pertaineth, being of course noticed first.

On this plain there may be some fifteen or twenty Gypsy tents and caravans. Some of the tents are large, as indeed it is highly necessary that they should be being inhabited by large families – a man and his wife, a grandmother, a sister or two and half a dozen children, being, occasionally found in one; some of them are very small, belonging to poor old females who have lost their husbands, and whose families have separated themselves from them, and allow them to shift for themselves. During the day the men are generally busy at their several avocations, cutting the stick for skewers, making pegs for linen lines, basket-making, tinkering or braziering; the children are playing about, or begging half pence by the road of passengers; while the women are strolling about, either in London or the neighbourhood, engaged in fortune-telling or swindling. These Gypsies are of various tribes, but chiefly Lees, Boswells and Coopers, and Lees being by far the most numerous.

The furniture is scanty. Like the Arabs, the Gypsies have neither chairs nor tables, but sit cross-legged, a posture which is perfectly easy to them, although insufferable to a Gorgio, unless he happens to be a tailor. When they eat the ground serves them for a board, though they occasionally spread a cloth upon it. Of pots, pans, plates, and trenchers, they have a tolerable quantity. Each grown up person has a knife with which to cut food. Spoons are used by them generally of horn. They have but two culinary articles, kettle and boiler, which are generally of copper, to which, however, may be perhaps added the kettle-iron, by which the kettle and boiler are hung over the fire. As a fireplace they have a large iron pan on three legs, with holes or eyes in the sides, in order that the heat of the fire may be cast around. Instead of coals they use coke, which emits no flame and little smoke, and casts a considerable heat. Every tent has a pail or two, and perhaps a small cask or barrel. At the further end of the tent is a mattress, with a green cloth, or perhaps a sheet spread upon it, forming a kind of couch, on which visitors are generally asked to sit down. They have a box or two in which they stow away their breakable articles and whatever things they set any particular value upon. Some of them have feather-beds, and they are generally tolerably well provided with blankets.

The caravans are not numerous, and have only been used of late years by any of the English Gypsy race. The caravan or wagon-house, is on four wheels, and is drawn by a horse or perhaps a couple of donkeys. It is about twelve feet long by six broad and six high. At the farther end are a couple of transverse berths, one above the other, like those in the cabin of a ship; and a little way from these is a curtain hanging by rings from an iron rod running across, which, when drawn, forms a partition. On either side is a small glazed window. The most remarkable object is a stove just inside the door, on the left hand, with a metal chimney which goes through the roof. This stove casts, when lighted, a great heat, and in some cases is made in a very handsome fashion. Some caravans have mirrors against the sides, and exhibit other indications of an aiming at luxury, though in general they are dirty, squalid places, quite as much as or perhaps more than the tents, which seem to be the proper and congenial home of the Gypsies.

The mode of life of these people may be briefly described. They have two regular meals – breakfast and supper. The breakfast consists of tea, generally of the best quality, bread, butter, and cheese; the supper of tea and a stew. In spring time they occasionally make a kind of tea or soup of the tender leaves of a certain description of nettle. This preparation is highly relished by them. They get up early, and go to bed betimes. After breakfast the men sit down to mend chairs or make baskets; the women go forth to hawk and tell fortunes, and the children to beg, or to go with the donkeys to lanes and commons to watch them, whilst they try to fill their poor bellies with grass and thistles. These children sometimes bring home hedgehogs, the flesh of which is very sweet and tender, and which their mothers are adepts at cooking.'

It is possible that Robert Pateman may have stayed in or passed through this Gypsyry on his travels.

Mary Ann Pateman (1840-1844)

According to the 1871 Census Robert Pateman was born in 1816 and his 'wife', Mary Ann Enis, was born in 1819. In 1840, when their child Mary Ann Pateman was born,

Robert would have been 24 and his wife 21; it is possible that they may have had other children before Mary Ann.

Mary Ann Pateman was born on 19 May 1840 in South Hanningfield Parish, in the registration district of Chelmsford, in the sub district of Ingatestone in the County of Essex. South Hanningfield is between Chelmsford and Billericay and close to Ramsden Heath. This is interesting as I later lived on the Ramsden Estate in Orpington. Her father was 'Robert Pateman, basket maker' and her mother was Mary Ann Pateman, 'formerly Heinus'. Her surname was probably spelt this way because of the way it was said to and heard by the registrar. This suggests that Mary Ann Enis may have had a strong regional accent (possibly Irish) which made her pronunciation of Enis sound like Heinus. We do not know what Robert was doing in Essex in 1840 but he could have been traveling to or from Hertfordshire, Buckinghamshire or Bedfordshire, where many Patenmans lived at this time.

We have not found a record of Mary Ann's baptism. Writing in 1885 Morwood noted that 'During the last few years Gypsies have attended much more to baptism than their ancestors were wont to do. For more than a hundred years after their introduction into England the Gypsies paid very little regard to this religious rite'.

Although some Gypsy births were registered as early as the 1840s, registration was frequently avoided, and some families were still failing to register births as late as 1900. Fortunately, it was normal practice to have the children baptized. Gypsy baptisms took place in many parishes, and the only way to locate all entries for the family of interest is to search all registers over the likely area of travel. So the search continues!

Large numbers of traveler baptisms took place each September in the hop growing parishes of Hampshire and Kent. Baptism was frequently delayed until the annual gathering at the hop fields, and it was not unusual for a dozen or more traveler baptisms to take place in one place on a single Sunday. Gypsy families traveled considerable distances to these events. Fairs presented money making opportunities for Gypsies and the registers of parishes where large fairs were held can sometimes contain Gypsy baptisms.

Some churches were used for baptism at all times of the year by Gypsies who frequented nearby heaths and commons. Most Gypsies were baptized in Anglican churches, but occasionally entries can be found in the registers of other denominations. Sometimes only the mother's name appears in a baptism entry even if she had a stable partner. Occasionally the forenames of both parents are entered, but the surname used is the mother's. The place given under 'abode' may be the place where the family was encamped, a place which the family regarded as a base, or the birthplace of the father.

Morwood: 'Under the old poor law every child of unmarried Gypsies belonged to the parish in which it was born, and in times of poverty the parents were liable to have their children taken from them and sent each to its own parish. Under the new poor law, however, the child belongs to its mother's parish. Crabb says that Gypsies are now very careful to have their children baptized in the church of the parish to which they belong, with the idea that thereby they can lay claim to a little parochial relief, which they usually term 'settling the baby'. The sponsors are generally members of the same family, and are always treated with great respect. But even to this rule we know of the following exception.

On a chilly morning in winter several mothers had taken their children to the parish church of a small town in Gloucestershire to be baptized, the infant daughter of the rector being there for the same purpose. Another clergyman, however, was to perform the ceremony, and as it was about to begin a Gypsy woman of the Lock family, with an infant girl on her arms, pressed eagerly towards the font. Some of the other women eyed the Gypsy mother with disdain, and stepped aside as if afraid they would be contaminated by her touch. Gently to reprove them, the rector of the parish spoke kindly to the Gypsy, and told her to present her child, which was baptized the first, and for which he stood as sponsor; then followed the baptism of his own child, and then that of the children of the mothers referred to.'

Mary Ann Pateman died on 13 October 1844 at Stockbury, Kent aged four years and five months. On her death certificate she was described as the 'daughter of Robert Pateman, pedlar', who signed with a mark as being present at her death from whooping cough. We do not know where Mary Ann was buried or what kind of funeral she had.

Gypsies were normally buried in churchyards; there is little evidence to support reports of road side burial. Burials are more difficult to locate than baptisms, though burial indexes are now being compiled for several counties. Burial entries frequently give no information other than name and age, making identification difficult. Deaths after 1837 were usually registered. Some Gypsies ended their days in the workhouse and were buried in the workhouse parish.

Gypsies were sometimes commemorated on tombstones. Relevant inscriptions can be located by visits to churchyards and cemeteries, or by reference to the many monumental inscription transcripts prepared by family history societies. Gypsy funerals were sometimes reported in a local newspaper, as was the case with Paul Ayres in the *Surrey Advertiser*, on the 21 and 28 November 1891.

There are a number of customs surrounding Gypsy deaths and burials. Leland, in his work *English Gipsies*, was given to understand 'that when Gypsy men or women die, their friends don't care to hear their names again – it makes them too sad; so they are changed to other names.' The same author also refers to a form of respect for the departed among Gypsies, to the effect that they bury some object of value with the corpse. He was informed that in the coffin of one Gypsy a new beautiful pair of shoes were put; also 'that three thousand pounds were hidden with one of the Chilcotts'; and that 'some of the Stanley's were buried with gold rings on their fingers.'

Another story, told by Morwood, concerns the burial of a Gypsy under a wide spreading yew tree standing in the churchyard: 'In choosing this place of internment, the idea of the Gypsies appears to have been that the yew tree would afford partial protection to the departed from the cold and storms of winter, as well as a cooling shade from the intense heat of summer.'

On 15 May 1869 John Cussans reported the following account of a Gypsy burial: 'A labourer told me that, about forty years ago, an old Gypsy woman died near Littlebury, Essex. The body was swathed in clothes, and laid upon trestles by the encampment. Over the head and feet two long hazel twigs were bent, the ends thrust into the ground. From these hung two oil lamps, which were kept burning all night, while two women, one on either side of the corpse, watched, sitting on the ground. The following day the uncoffined body was buried in Littlebury churchyard by order of the local authorities; not, however, without great opposition on the part of the deceased's friends, who wished to bury her elsewhere.'

Stockbury

According to the *Post Office Directory* of Kent: 'Stockbury is a village and parish in the Mid and East Divisions of the county, Holingbourn union, Eyhorne and Milton hundred, lathes of Ayleford and Scray, Maidstone county court district, Sittingbourne rural deanery, Maidstone archdeaconry, and diocese of Canterbury, two and a half miles south from Newington station, six and a half miles north east from Maidstone, and on the road to Sittingbourne.

The church of St Mary Magdalen is a cruciform building in the Early English style, the columns and arches of which are of Bethersden marble: it consists of chancel, nave and transepts; the chancel is kept in repair by the Ecclesiastical Commissioners as owners of the great tithes; the southern transept, which belongs to L. Ruck esq. is in a very dilapidated condition, the rest of the church being in perfect repair. The register dates from the year 1653. The living is a vicarage, yearly value £350, in the gift of the Dean and Chapter of Rochester, and held by the Rev. Thomas Cobb, M.A. of Sidney Sussex College, Cambridge. There is property which has been bequeathed to this parish for the education of three boys and three girls, and there are other charities of £13 yearly. There are National schools in connection with the church and a small place of worship for Bible Christians. Edward Leigh Pemberton, esq. M.P. is lord of the manor, and also the principal landowner. The soil is stony and clay; subsoil, chalk and clay. The chief crops are corn and hops. The area is 2,951 acres; rateable value £3,858; and the population in 1871 was 590.'

There was a post office - letters arrived from Sittingbourne at 10am and were dispatched at 5pm. The nearest money order office was at Newington. There was a baker, grocer, two publicans (*Three Squirrels* and *Harrow*), shoe maker, blacksmiths, draper, wheelwright, farmers and hop growers. You will note that Stockbury was not far from Newington, which has already appeared in this history. You will also note that the chief crops were corn and hops – which might have attracted Gypsies like Robert Pateman into the area.

Today the Stockbury Viaduct, which carries the M2 over the dry valley through which passes the A249 that links Maidstone with the Isle of Sheppey, is as much a local landmark now as Stockbury's old St Mary Magdalene's church.

But the church is higher, seeming to crane its neck to see past the viaduct to the Swale and the Medway estuary beyond. Near the church are the remains of a Norman motte and bailey castle which must once have frowned down upon the surrounding countryside. Pevsner thought Stockbury's church was one of the most interesting in

Kent. It is actually a little way out of the village centre, it's only near neighbour the adjoining farm. But the grassed churchyard is well-tended and surrounded by old trees and the view from its two-tier burial ground, over surrounding farm land and orchards, has a gentle peacefulness about it that subdues the ceaseless activity of the main roads on two sides.

The entire village is a memorial to St Simon Stock, from whom it takes its name. He lived in a hollow tree hereabouts before he became the head of the Carmelite Order in England at their Aylesford Priory.

It is a small Downland village with a post office and store, and ancient and modern houses clustered around a modest triangle of village green, where the village sign features the church, three squirrels and a harrow. The *Three Squirrels* is the name of an inn below the village alongside the A249 and the *Harrow Inn* overlooks the green. It has pictures painted on the wall showing Stockbury in spring, summer, autumn and winter.

Modern day Stockbury, with its church, post office, store and two pubs has changed very little from when Robert Pateman was living in the area. He may well have gone into the *Three Squirrels* or *The Harrow* for a few pints after labouring all day in the fields and the hop gardens.

Some time between the birth of Mary Ann in 1840 and the birth of his next child, Alice Pateman, in 1842 Robert traveled from Kent to Surrey. We don't know how Robert carried out this journey, but throughout most of the nineteenth century the Gypsies preferred to travel in their traditional way with light horse drawn carts and on foot. Life was simply led, there were virtually no financial overheads and the only possessions apart from the tent, horse and cart were clothes and any simple tools that were essential to life.

In the countryside the Gypsies were perfectly capable of living off the land, small creatures like rabbit, hedgehog or perhaps some cleverly acquired game or the occasional chicken provided the basis for meals. Herbs and plants or some vegetables garnered from the edge of a field would fill out the stew pot and when in urban areas the returns from sales of crafts or odd jobs would be sufficient to provide enough to feed the family. It was a hand to mouth, day to day existence with little that needed to be planned too far in advance.

Alice Pateman (1842-1892)

We do not know when Robert Pateman arrived in Wimbledon. As he does not appear on the 1841 Census for Wimbledon Common, we assume that he arrived some time after 6 June 1841, when the census was carried out. We do not know where Robert was living at the time of the 1841 census – he could have been in another part of Kent, or in Surrey, Middlesex, Bedfordshire or Hertfordshire. We do not know exactly when in 1842 or where in Wimbledon his second child, Alice Pateman, was born; she may have been born in Wimbledon Village or on Wimbledon Common.

The following description of Wimbledon in 1838 gives a good account of what Wimbledon was like at the time when Robert Pateman and his family were living in the area:

'Wimbledon Park may have been in danger of completely disappearing in 1913, yet 75 years earlier it had been the scene of a Grand Fete to celebrate the young Queen Victoria's coronation. Though still owned by Earl Spencer it had been leased to the Duke and Duchess of Somerset. They used the house and grounds as a summer retreat and in 1837 had already invited the Queen (shortly after her accession) to a garden party on the lawns. Victoria drove there from London with her uncle, the Duke of Sussex, and when they got near the house, local people un-harnessed the horses and pulled her to the front porch.

At the Coronation Fete a year later one of the guests was Mrs. Stevenson, wife of the United States Ambassador. In her memoirs she described the occasion as 'the affair of the season'. The Queen arrived at about six o'clock and 'promenaded the grounds where the company had assembled on rich carpets, with sofas and chairs.' Meanwhile Tyrolean minstrels, Russian dancers, Alpine singers and Highland pipers provided entertainment. Then the Duke and Duchess led the Queen into dinner in a 'very beautiful marquee, its roof supported by twelve columns, the interior lined with crimson stripes.' Four hundred and fifty guests sat down to a large meal, while a military band played light music. At the end of the dinner 'the extremely pretty illuminations' were set off and 'the ball commenced in the tent'.

Mrs. Stevenson chose this moment to 'make my escape.' She went to see a fellow American, Mrs. Charlotte Marryat, now one of Wimbledon's leading personalities. A month earlier she had spent a week at the Marryat home, Wimbledon House Parkside, recovering from illness. She had been impressed with the house, 'one of the most beautiful villas in England', with its garden, 'quite a showplace', and with her hostess, 'now a widow, employing herself in good works'.

Mrs. Marryat had been married to a wealthy businessman and Member of Parliament, but in 1824 he had suddenly collapsed and died. She had since devoted herself to her large family (including Frederick, a captain in the navy and famous novelist), to her garden where she introduced new plants including rhododendrons, and to 'good works'. A keen Evangelical, she presided at family prayers every evening, went on Sundays with other ladies to the Gypsy encampment in Caesar's Camp to read them the Bible and held a fair in her grounds to raise money for new Almshouses to replace the old Workhouse in Camp Road.

Suppression of Wimbledon Fair

The Almshouses, so important if poor elderly people in the village were to escape the dreaded new Union Workhouse in Kingston, were opened in 1838 shortly before the Coronation Fete. But already Mrs Marryat was aiming at another 'moral improvement.' She strongly disapproved of the Fair held in the High Street every Easter Monday as it attracted, according to Earl Spencer, 'all sorts of London blackguards'. So, helped by the Curate at St Mary's, the Reverend Mr. Edelman, she lobbied the members of the vestry and finally in 1840 secured its suppression on the grounds that 'its moral effect on the people was so bad.'

Only one member of the Vestry, Major-General Sir Henry Murray, was strong-minded enough to oppose her. Son of the Earl of Mansfield and a soldier who had distinguished himself leading a cavalry charge at Waterloo, he lived at Wimbledon Lodge, a fine 'Greek revival' house on Southside. He argued strongly that the Fair was an old village custom, one of the few festivals 'which the labouring classes have the opportunity of enjoying'. His speeches had little effect, except to impress his fellow Vestrymen with his character. Two years later when he had to leave Wimbledon for a time to serve on the Staff in Ireland, they unanimously thanked him for his 'advice and urbanity', added that his 'politeness and kindness' had made him 'highly respected' and hoped he would soon return.

These members of the Vestry who ran local affairs included some of the leading villagers: James Courthorpe Peache, a timber merchant from Lambeth, who had recently bought (and named) Belvedere House; Adam Hogg, a colonel in the East India Company's Army, who lived in Holme Lodge, one of the two houses later united as Southside House; Thomas Mason, the leading High Street grocer and local Postmaster; George Croft, a builder and timber merchant of West Place, who owned forty two cottages; and Richard Blake, who had recently taken over Cowdrey Farm near the Wandle.

In the late 1830s they were very concerned about the state of the Common – the dangerous condition of the gravel pits, obstructions in the horse rides and the 'decreasing salubrity of the air arising from the number of stagnant pools'. The two Colonels, Murray and Hogg, were deputed to see Earl Spencer, but with no practical result. At the same time the Vestrymen were also concerned at the 'very limited number of parishioners' who were able to 'join in the service of Almighty God' as St Mary's only had room for a congregation of about seven hundred. So they resolved to increase its capacity, first by trying to rearrange the sittings and when that failed by the more drastic method of pulling down the Georgian nave and commissioning Gilbert Scott and William Moffit to build a new one – a move strongly opposed by General Murray. The result, however, was an impressive Victorian church with a distinctive spire and large nave, which the Archbishop of Canterbury consecrated in 1843.

The chief concern of the Vestry in 1838, however, was law and order. After a 'dangerous attack' had been made 'upon a gentleman on Wimbledon Common', they appointed two special constables, David Penner and Thomas Dann, the miller. Dann was chosen as his Windmill overlooked a favorite spot for duels, 'a lawn-like land with a small stream running through it (the site of the later Queensmere). In August 1838, John Mirfin, a young linen draper, was killed in a duel there with another young man, Francis Elliott, after their carriages had collided when driving to London (an early Victorian example of 'road rage'). Dann had not then been able to intervene, but two years later he arrived on the scene just after the Earl of Cardigan had shot his opponent, Captain Harvey Tuckett, in the chest. He arrested Cardigan and escorted him to Wandsworth police station, while his wife dressed Tuckett's wounds. Cardigan was tried by the House of Lords and acquitted. But his behaviour seems to have discredited dueling and so the Vestry had one less problem to give them concern, especially as they now had their first professional policeman, Sergeant Pinegar, who lived at 1, Brickfield Cottages on the Ridgway (now 1 Oldfield Road).

Two very different opinions of the village they tried to manage were given in contemporary reference books. *Pigot's New Commercial Directory* of 1834 described it as 'a beautiful and highly genteel village which is surrounded by the seats of the nobility and gentry.' Yet *The Railway Companion* of 1839, describing what could be seen on a journey from Nine Elms, dismissed it as a mere 'hamlet', though it had 'a number of elegant villas', while at its two inns there was 'abundant accommodation and entertainment'.

Wimbledon may have been a hamlet in medieval times, but by 1838 it had become a sizeable village with over four hundred 'inhabitable houses' and a population of around 2,500, a thousand more than at the start of the century. There were still plenty of poor families living just off the High Street, especially near the *Dog and Fox*, where Beehive Buildings, Mutton Alley and Carter's Alley consisted of rows of small cottages, built back to back, housing farm labourers, gardeners and laundresses. Yet in the High Street itself and in Church Lane there were plenty of small thriving shops, including four grocers, three bakers, dairymen, tailors and boot and shoe makers, two butchers and 'fruiterers', a hairdresser (appropriately John Barber) and even the first fishmonger, William Frost.

There was also real choice among the tradesmen: several builders, carpenters (who also acted as undertakers), plumbers, and blacksmiths (one describing himself as a 'veterinary surgeon'), along with a rat catcher and well borer. Finally along with *The Dog and Fox* and *The Rose and Crown*, there were now four 'Beer Retailers' and two brewers. Yet if all these businesses suggest crowds regularly thronging the streets, a revealing story about the village stocks at the corner of Church Lane and the High Street shows how fairly deserted they often were. Old folk remembered seeing a man sitting in the stocks about the year Victoria became Queen, but added that there was 'no one to see him; there might not be more than half a dozen people passing that way in the whole day.'

Among those who most certainly would not have passed that way, except on Sundays when going to church, were the nobility and gentry who lived in the 'elegant villas' round the Common. Notable among them were two individuals who have given their names to houses or districts of present-day Wimbledon: the Duchess of Cannizzaro and Charles Pepys, Earl of Cottenham. The Scottish Duchess and her Italian husband have been described as 'two most colorful characters'. They had married in 1814, she apparently because he was 'good looking, intelligent and of high birth' (a Sicilian Count and later Duke), he mainly for her money – she was a 'beautiful heiress, totally uneducated, but full of humor.' Three years later they leased Warren House (the later Cannizaro) as a country retreat, and there entertained many famous people, including Mrs. Fitzherbert, the real wife of George IV, Countess Esterhazy, wife of the Austrian Ambassador, and the great Duke of Wellington.

But in 1833 the rather incongruous marriage broke up. The Duke went off to Italy with a Mme Visconti, and the Duchess consoled herself with her 'all absorbing interest', music. She was a great patron of musicians, built up her own valuable music library, and fell in love with 'a strapping young Italian singer.' Then in 1841, as suddenly as they had erupted into the life of Westside, they disappeared. They both died within a few months of each other and when William Mason, acting as enumerator for the census that summer, called at the house he found only servants there. So on his form, with no owner to record, he gave the place a name – 'Cannazerro House'. The name somehow stuck in local directories, finishing in 1874 with the present spelling 'Cannizaro'.

Charles Pepys, Earl of Cottenham, gave his name not merely to a house, but to a road and a whole district in West Wimbledon. In 1831 he bought Prospect Place and its 250 acre estate between Copse Hill and Coombe Lane with grounds 'improved' by Humphry Repton thirty years earlier. He wanted it to be a real home where he, his wife and their fifteen children could have peace and quiet in beautiful surroundings. Though a successful barrister, an able judge and from 1836 to 1841 Queen Victoria's first Lord Chancellor, he cared little for society and, when his work at Westminster was finished for the day, drove straight home for 'his hour of peace and joy when he went up to the nursery to sing his little ones what he called Chinese songs'. Such a man would hardly welcome the appearance of noisy, dirty trains on his estate.

The idea of building one of the new railways to link London and Southampton had first been put forward in 1830, before the Earl had moved to Wimbledon. But the survey of a possible route, made by Francis Giles, a leading canal engineer, came just after his arrival and met with his total opposition as it ran right across the southern part of his estate. So Giles was forced to move the line south of Worple Lane into 'the lowlands' where the chief landowner, Caroline Phillips, the only legitimate child of Benjamin Bond-Hopkins, was ready to sell blocks of fields to the railway company. But the change meant the creation of a long, high embankment (using earth from the cutting at Surbiton) to keep the gradient level for the early trains, and the building of bridges and tunnels to preserve old rights of way.

The line was thus not ready to be opened (and then only as far as Woking) until May 1838. Heavy rain damaged the early embankment, local contractors were inefficient and Giles showed little drive. In 1837 he was replaced by Joseph Locke, a pupil of George Stephenson, inventor of the Rocket. He promptly sacked all the contractors and gave the work to Thomas Brassey, who later made his name building railways all over the world. He transformed affairs and a year later was able to hold two trial runs from the terminus at Nine Elms near Vauxhall to Woking. The train went at the astonishing speed of thirty miles an hour and the journey was said to have been 'smooth and easy'. It was watched 'on every eminence along the line' (such as Wimbledon Hill), by 'admiring rustics who gathered in thousands to cheer the trains.' So on Monday 21 May when the line was opened to the public, people flocked to use it – except at Wimbledon.

The small new station, labeled 'Wimbledon and Merton' because it was half way between the two villages, was right out in the country where it could only disturb the cows and a few farm workers. Round it were just three buildings. On the Merton side of the new iron bridge over the tracks was the home of the stationmaster, Ben Bradford along with a cottage where lived the railway policeman (who also acted as signalman and ticket collector). On the other side was *The Mansel Arms*, a new railway pub which acted as a ticket office and where passengers had to go down a steep flight of stairs to reach the small platform to the west of the bridge. There they might have to wait two to three hours – unless they had seen one of the tiny time tables – as there were just five trains a day each way.

It is therefore hardly surprising that at first most Wimbledonians were not very eager to use the railway. As late as 1845 the average number of passengers boarding one of the trains at the station was about a hundred a day. One of those who did travel up to London shortly after the line was opened was Edward Rayne, the owner of West Barnes Farm, who had himself helped to bring gravel and rails for the track. He was obviously pleased with the speed of the journey, recording in his diary: 'I went and returned from town by the railway and was home again by noon.'

Nonetheless, even after the railway opened, four of the old short stage coaches continued to ply every day between the village and London. They cost about double the first class train fare to Nine Elms, but took passengers all the way to the City. In Church Lane there were also two 'flys', open front cabs which could be hired for journeys from door to door. The post, however, was still fairly primitive. There was only one 'letter carrier', John Culverwell, who lived in Almshouse Lane (later Camp Road). He had to collect the letters from Thomas Mason, 'Letter Receiver' (as well as grocer) at the top of the High Street. He then had to walk to Putney with them, collect the letters for Wimbledon at the Post Office there and on his return to the village deliver them to addresses he had to remember from the names of the householders as there were no street numbers'.

Wimbledon Common

The early settlement of Wimbledon in prehistoric times can probably be attributed to the geology of the common. The earliest archaeological remains are worked flints used by people of the Neolithic Age (c. 3000 BC to 1000 BC). The origin of Wimbledon Common probably lies in Saxon times but its first explicit mention in a document was not until 1461 when the records (or Rolls) of the Manor Court begin. The heyday of the Common was between 1461 and 1641. After this date the Common gradually declined over a period of some 200 years.

Wimbledon and Putney Commons, as they were transferred to the Conservators in 1871, were what remained of the waste of the manor of Wimbledon, land too poor to be brought under the plough. Nearly all we know of their history before the middle of the seventeenth century comes from the manor court rolls and relates to the control of the use of common by the tenants of the manor. Custom, as recorded in the rolls and in the memory of the 'homage' or jury, determined how many animals each tenant might turn out to pasture at different times of the year and how much firewood might be cut. The court heard complaints of infringement of the rules and fined offenders. The system lived on in Wimbledon until the middle of the nineteenth century when, with the coming of the railway, the village began to grow rapidly into a town – from 2,693 in 1851, the population rose to 4,644 in 1861 and 9,087 in 1871. Expansion began earlier and went faster in Wandsworth, which then, as later, included Putney for purposes of local government.

Long before the growth of London suburbs started to link up the villages into a continuous frame of built-up streets around them, Wimbledon Common and Putney Heath had been found useful for many purposes. Here, as on Hampstead Heath and Blackheath, within a few miles of London, was a wide expanse of open ground, uncultivated, where large crowds could assemble, horses could be raced, troops could be exercised and reviewed, duels could be fought and highwaymen prey on the increasing traffic along the Portsmouth Road.

There are plentiful references to duels on Wimbledon Common over nearly two centuries. Two of these involved local residents: William Pitt, then Prime Minister and living at Bowling Green House on Putney Heath, fought George Tierney MP there in 1798, without injury to either party and in 1807 Sir Francis Burdett fought and wounded James Paull, an encounter Gillray celebrated in a satirical cartoon.

Before the last recorded duel, in 1840, the railway had reached Putney and Wimbledon and the character of both villages was being transformed. It was and still is a good place to live and the rising professional men of the early Victorian era made their homes around the Common, replacing aristocratic tenants or owners or building themselves new homes.

Among those who left recorded comments on the character of the common were Silas Neville in 1769, John Constable who in 1812 'enjoyed the view' while walking with his friend Thomas Stothard, a collector of butterflies, and Leigh Hunt who wrote a lyrical essay about the common in 1846. 'The Common was noble and the air and the green country delightfully fresh' was W.M. Thackeray's comment in that same year.

The movement for the preservation of commons was one part of the Victorian's heroic struggle to humanize town life in industrial society. The 1851 census revealed that for the first time half the population of England was living in the great towns. Most town dwellers then were immigrants from the villages and living conditions in the unplanned, newly built urban settlements inspired them with a nostalgic longing for open spaces under an open sky, the companionship of birds and beasts, a way of life closer to nature, 'where man belongs'.

The Gypsies' Ring

There is a drawing of a Gypsy Camp on Wimbledon Common, c.1856. One of the reasons so much of the Common's history has been forgotten is the fact that modern maps do not always show the old landmarks. And so it was with the Gypsies' Ring. The map shows it between White Cottage and Caesar's Well. The Gypsies also used Caesar's Camp which until 1875 had not been leveled and would have made an ideal and secluded spot for their temporary home.

In the nineteenth century Gypsy travelers on their way to Wandsworth Common would stop here every year and set up camp. Surprisingly they were tolerated and welcomed by the local people. Charlotte Marryat of the grand Wimbledon House would come out and read the Bible to them on Sunday afternoons. One of the Gypsies, Mignonette Lee was converted to Christianity and attended St Mary's church in the Village. One writer also speaks of the excitement in the Village when the Gypsies came.

The Gypsy families that came back to Wimbledon Common year after year were the Lees, the Coopers, and the Smiths. They collected heather on the Common and used it to make brooms to sell to the villagers. The Gypsies also drew the attention of various well-known writers of the day, such as Theodore Watts-Dunton, Charles Leland, and most notably George Borrow, all of whom wished to learn more of the Gypsy way of life. Borrow and Leland both studied and wrote about the Romany language and culture. Watts-Dunton was known to receive Gypsy visitors at his Putney home, the Pines.

It is not known when the Gypsies first came to Wimbledon, but they had been known in England since the sixteenth century when they arrived from the continent. One story, perhaps apochryphal, which mentions Gypsies on the Common in the early eighteenth century is that of Daniel Watney. Born in 1705, the first known ancestor of the famous brewing family was said to have been found on Wimbledon Common soon after his birth by a local farmer named Acres. The baby was thought to have been left by Gypsies after they moved camp. The farmer and his wife brought the boy up and could not decide a name for him. Their discussions on what name to call the child are said to have resulted in 'Watney' as a corruption of 'what name'. Daniel Watney married the farmer's daughter, Mary at St Mary's church on 23 August 1730.

It was very rare for a Gypsy family to abandon a baby or child; it was more common for the reverse to happen – a new born baby would be left in the woods by a scared servant girl, for example, and the Gypsies would take the child in and raise it as one of their own. There is a photograph of 'Gypsy families in Wandle Bank c1905-1910.'

Prize Fighting

To this day Gypsies are well known for bare-knuckle prize fighting. Videos of these fights can be seen playing and for sale at most large gatherings of Gypsies, such as at the horse fairs at Appleby and Stow on the Wold, and at the Epsom Derby. Along with Coombe Wood, Coombe Warren and Molesey Hurst, Wimbledon Common was one of the most famous venues for bare-knuckle prize-fighting in the eighteenth and early nineteenth centuries.

The sport had been declared illegal in 1750 but continued to flourish, often patronized by the nobility. The Duke of Clarence, later to become King William IV, allowed Bushy Park Estate to be used for prize-fighting bouts. Because of this, fights here and in the surrounding area often had a blind eye turned to them by the authorities.

There were at least seventeen bare-knuckle fights on Wimbledon Common between 1788 and 1823, and many more at neighbouring Coombe Wood and Coombe Warren. In fact, the fights were sometimes moved from one venue to another on the occasions when the authorities did attempt to stop them.

Some of the more notable fights on Wimbledon Common were: Belcher vs. Gamble on 22 December 1800; Tom Jones vs. Elias the Jew (also known as Dutch Sam) on 15 July 1801; and Henry 'Game Chicken' Pearse vs. Edward Bourke on 24 January 1804.

The latter match, for a £100 purse, lasted well over an hour and totaled 28 rounds, and was one of the matches moved several times to evade the authorities. The organizer, Thomas Owen, was prosecuted and imprisoned for three months for riot and conspiracy. The *Morning Advertiser* reported that there was a crowd of 1,500 watching the fight, and that Owen, in his defence, said that if he was guilty then so were the noblemen and others in attendance.

A fight at nearby Coombe Warren reported in *The News* of 11 February 1816 gives a flavor of the rough and ready bouts which took place. The contest, on Tuesday 6 February was between Carter, and a 'black named Joseph'. The purse was 25 guineas – more than a year's wages for an agricultural labourer at the time.

The betting was two to one on Carter, and the men had two 'seconds' each, indicating that there was at least some semblance of organization. The fighting itself however included what would now be regarded as foul play. This of course was fifty years before the Queensberry rules were introduced in 1867.

Carter won the fight and betting was pretty feverish throughout the bout, with odds changing as it progressed, and it is easy to imagine the passions aroused not just by the fighting itself but by the ebb and flow of money riding on it. There was a second bout that day between a fighter named Ballard and an unnamed Jewish sailor.

Fights on the Common were still being organized as late as 1830 when a match was being planned between William Perry and Barney Dogherty. However, once the authorities got wind of it the venue was switched to Mortlake, only to be changed twice more to avoid prosecution. Although the bare-knuckle fights came to an end, Wimbledon had played an important part in what was the forerunner to the modern sport of boxing.

Fatal Fight on Wimbledon Common

A report appeared in *The Times* newspaper on 21 March 1831 with the headline Fatal Fight on Wimbledon Common: 'On Saturday afternoon an inquest was held at the workhouse, at Putney, before Mr. Carter, the coroner for Surrey on the body of Jeremiah Taylor, aged 47, whose death was occasioned under the following circumstances.

It appeared from the evidence, that the deceased was a basket maker, and traveled about the country with his family, consisting of his wife and six children. He belonged to the Gypsy tribe, but he was a very industrious hard working man. For some time past a rancour had existed between the deceased and a man named William Falkner, a clothes peg maker, and one of the same tribe. About a fortnight ago the parties pitched their tents on Wimbledon Common. On Wednesday last the deceased challenged Falkner to a fight, but he refused. The following day (Thursday) the deceased was employed the whole of the day making baskets. About 4 o'clock in the afternoon, Falkner, who had been from his tent all day, returned in a state of intoxication. He shortly afterwards went to the tent of the deceased man and muttered something to himself. The deceased asked him if he was talking about him, and Falkner replied that he was, and said that he could beat his master's master. The deceased asked him what in; when Falkner replied, in manhood.

The deceased then got up from his work and pulled off part of his clothes, and they both commenced fighting. Several persons endeavored to part them, but they insisted on fighting it out. Once during the fight the deceased offered to shake hands with his opponent, but he refused. The battle lasted nearly three quarters of an hour, and in the last round they both fell to the ground in consequence of Falkner treading on the stocking of the deceased, which hung about his foot. The deceased fell under most, he never spoke afterwards, and died about 4 o'clock the following morning.

From the evidence of Mr. Charles Shillitoe, a surgeon, at Putney, it appeared that the death of the unfortunate man had been occasioned by the rupture of a blood vessel in the head, caused by a blow, a fall, or through violent exertion. Several witnesses were examined, and said that they saw nothing unfair on either side during the fight. Falkner, who was in custody, was called into the inquest room, and asked if he wished to say anything, the Coroner cautioning him at the same time not to say any thing to criminate himself. Falkner replied that he was intoxicated at the time, and should not have fought if the deceased had not challenged him on the previous day. He appeared to be very much bruised about the face, and his collar bone had been put out during the fight.

The Coroner briefly addressed the Jury, and, after a short consultation, they returned a verdict of 'manslaughter' against William Falkner; and the Coroner issued his warrant for his committal to Horsemonger-lane gaol.'

Enclosure

By the end of the nineteenth century Gypsies were seen less frequently on Wimbledon Common, when the authorities started to clamp down on them and reduce the number of sites available for setting up camp. It was claimed that the Common 'was no easy matter to cross by day or by night' and that it harbored 'Gypsies, vagrants and trespassers', and so offended the growing number of famous or wealthy people who lived in the big houses around its perimeter. None were more anxious to improve matters than successive lords of the manor. One tried to enclose the Common in 1807 without adequately consulting the inhabitants and was forced to withdraw his bill.

The communities of Gypsies on the commons inevitably had their opponents and in the late 1850's and early 1860's the Lord of the Manors of Putney and Wimbledon, the 5th Earl Spencer, was being petitioned by local residents complaining about their presence. At the time there were about 150 Gypsies living on a corner of Wimbledon Common and Earl Spencer replied to one complainant:

'I regret that the Gypsies on Putney and Wimbledon Manors should again be troublesome. I assure you that it is not the first time that this question has been brought before me. It has given me great trouble and annoyance because whatever I do my powers are so limited that I cannot take effectual means to get rid of the nuisance. The defect in my powers lies in the difficulty of conviction, and the facility that exists for the Gypsies to escape before the summons can be executed. The position is an extremely harassing and difficult one for my common keeper.

I assure you that it is my earnest wish to do all I can for the neighborhood in this respect: and my orders are strict to lessen the nuisance as much as possible. I am willing to adopt any effectual way of putting down the Gypsies. It is curious that at this very time last year I annoyed a friend of Lady Spencer's by refusing to comply with her request, which was just the contrary to yours, that the Gypsies might be allowed to stay on the common in order that their children might go to school.'

When Earl Spencer wanted to enclose the Common in 1864 he cited the Gypsies as one of the reasons for taking action. 'Besides being immoral characters, they bring contagious diseases and do not submit to sanitary and other regulations, commit depredations, and in other respects are not desirable neighbors to the houses that are now found near here.' The Rev. Dr. Biber, Incumbent of Roehampton, accused the Gypsies of 'things so atrocious that it had been impossible to put them on paper' in a memorial to the police signed by 'every person, gentle and simple, through Roehampton and the neighbourhood.'

At a meeting held in the Lecture Hall of the Village Club in November 1864, the Earl put forward his plan to restore control. He would turn the largest part - Wimbledon Common or 'the waste' south of Portsmouth Road – into a public park 'for the enjoyment and recreation of the inhabitants', and to pay for its upkeep (and for a new manor house which he intended to build on the site of the Windmill) and would sell the rest – Putney Heath – to developers. To disarm opposition he promised to drain the swamps, to construct a new road across the Common to make access easier, to get rid of the Gypsies and to keep the fence round the new park as small as possible with plenty of gates 'so that the common would be practically open as it is now'.

He won considerable support for his plan but there were also powerful interests against it. At the meeting in the Lecture Hall, Sidney Smith, who lived on Parkside rejected the Earl's claims that the swamps were 'prejudicial to health' and that the Gypsies caused 'inconvenience'. The problem thus remained unresolved as any fencing or enclosure that would be effective against the travelers would also prevent the local commoners from gaining access. In spite of opposition from residents the common remained accessible and available as stopping places for Gypsies and travelers.

After long negotiations, the Earl and his opponents agreed on a compromise which was embodied in the Wimbledon and Putney Commons Act of 1871. In return for an annual payment of £1,200 (commuted for a lump sum of £22,500 in 1958), Earl Spencer ceded his 'entire interest' in the Commons to a Board of Conservators, who have since looked after the Common so that it could be used 'for purposes of exercise and relaxation', and remain 'for ever open and unenclosed and unbuilt on.'

The enclosure of common land posed a serious threat to the traditional Gypsy way of life. It denied them access to camping grounds which they had used for centuries. It was part of the gradual process which eventually forced them off the roads altogether. Enclosure (when all the sophistications are allowed for) was a plain case of class robbery, played according to fair rules of property and law laid down by a parliament of property owners and lawyers. What was at issue was a redefinition of the nature of agrarian property itself: the social violence of enclosure consisted precisely in the drastic, total imposition upon the village of capitalist property definitions.

Enclosure was the culmination of a long secular process by which men's customary relations to the agrarian means of production were undermined. It was of profound social consequences because it illuminates the destruction of the traditional elements in English peasant society. But enclosure was not just about the greed of landowners: a new argument was added for general enclosure – that of social discipline. The commons, 'the poor man's heritage for ages past', were now seen as a dangerous centre of indiscipline. They were described as a breeding ground for 'barbarians', 'nursing up a mischievous race of people.'

By the early twentieth century the Gypsies no longer came to Wimbledon Common, but they had left behind them another little piece of Wimbledon history.

St Mary Cray

We do not know where Alice was at the time of the 1851 and 1861 census – presumably she was traveling with her family in Kent, Middlesex and Surrey. On 18 February 1861 Alice Pateman was in attendance at the death of her younger brother, Thomas, who died aged 11 days, 'in a van on the common, Latymer Road', Hammersmith, Middlesex.

On 2 April 1871 Alice Pateman (27, Wimbledon) was living with her family in an old stable on a brickfield at Becks Lane, Beckenham. Some time after 1871 Alice left her family and became a farm servant in St Mary Cray, a Kentish village not far from Beckenham. On 3 April 1881 Alice Bateman (boarder, 29, farm servant, Wimbledon) was living at 10 Lawrence's Yard, St Mary Cray, Kent. We do not know where Alice was at the time of the 1891 census, but we assume she was still living in St Mary Cray.

The village of St Mary Cray took its name from the church of St Mary The Virgin, once surrounded by a prosperous farming community. The present building dates from around 1250 and was restored between 1861 and 1895. It is believed that the church is built on the site of a Roman encampment and Roman tiles and pottery have been found in the lower portion of the bell tower. The church has many treasures, a notable one being the fifteenth century Italian oak screen separating the chancel and the Hodsoll chapel, named after a local farming family. The church is also known for its seven brasses, the earliest of which is the Avery brass of 1568.

Until the reign of Edward 1 the village was known as South Cray. In 1281, Edward gave rights for a weekly market to be held here and a substantial area was given over for this purpose. A small patch of green known as Market Meadow is all that remains today but, until the early eighteenth century, St Mary Cray had a market house on this plot of land.

Hasted described St Mary Cray as a 'handsome and populous village' with the river being always central to the life and industry of the inhabitants alongside the Cray. The river's course has been altered by developments over the centuries, often being hidden in narrow culverts. In the nineteenth century, it was renowned for the purity of its water due to the proximity of its underground source and it was once famed for its trout. The village has long been recognised in more recent times as an industrial area with a population, until the late nineteenth century, larger than Orpington. However, the whole area was surrounded by orchards; apple, cherry, pear and plum and there were also hopping and strawberry fields with most of the produce from all these enterprises going to Borough Market. The produce was usually taken by horse and cart late at night; a journey taking several hours but, later, it was transported by rail.

Milling was the oldest established industry in St Mary Cray. In the eighteenth century one mill produced paper. Milling became a thriving industry as the village's close proximity to London guaranteed raw material and a market for the finished product. In 1833 William Joynson took over the mill and turned to the production of high quality security paper used for bank notes and stamps, amongst other uses. As the century progressed, rail became used for transport and so increased opportunities to obtain new raw materials. In the 1930s it made hygienic food wrapping and other industrial papers and was later taken over by the Wiggins Teape group when it produced vegetable parchment. With the growing use of plastics in the food industry in the 1970s the mill became obsolete and was eventually demolished.

The railway viaduct of nine arches was built in 1858 to link the Chatham and Dover routes and was one of the probable Nazi targets during the bombing raids of 1941. It remains a distinctive landmark today. The lake in St Mary Cray, known locally as the Blue Lagoon, was part of a planned garden estate and open-air swimming pool, opened in 1933, which attracted many day trippers from London who came down by train at weekends. Jack Doyle, the boxer, trained here during some of the winters in the 1930s. Badly damaged in the war it is now used for private fishing.

Star Lane

We do not know what bought Alice Pateman to St Mary Cray, but the local Romany population is believed to be the largest in England. They were attracted to the area by the wide variety of seasonal agricultural work, fruit picking and hopping. Many of them settled in the area during the winter months, and a large Gypsy encampment was developed at Corke's Meadow (near Sevenoaks Way gas works). When this site was cleared for development, many of the displaced families were rehoused in the Star Lane area. Romany funerals are commonly held in the parish church and it is quite a sight to observe a long procession of mourners and masses of floral tributes as they approach Star Lane cemetery.

The first meeting of the St Mary Cray burial board took place at the Vestry Room, St Mary Cray, Kent on Monday 14 July 1879. At their meeting on 18 March 1880 the burial board considered two options for the development of a grave yard in St Mary Cray: a one and a half acre site in Star Lane which was on sale for £800; and a piece of land known as Dippers Slip off Poverest Road. The owner of Dippers Slip 'did not consider any land on his estate suitable for a cemetery but if the board were able to suggest a site it should receive attention. The board having regard to the pressing and urgent necessity for the immediate provision of a burial ground and to the fact that all their efforts to obtain another site have failed, have determined to submit to the vestry the desirability of negotiating for the purchase of the Star Lane site.' It was estimated that the total cost would amount to £2,200 and 'the board accordingly made application to the vestry for power to borrow the same.'

This decision was not popular and became a local electoral issue. A poster was produced pointing out several reasons why a cemetery should not be located in Star Lane, including its proximity to a railway line:

'St Mary Cray Cemetery : hints to voters. If you wish to have a cemetery with a bad approach VOTE FOR STAR LANE SITE!

If you wish for funerals to be checked in a narrow lane by passing vehicles VOTE FOR STAR LANE SITE!

If you wish for the noise of the train and the whistle of the engines to disturb your burial service VOTE FOR STAR LANE SITE!

If you wish to run the risk of the sparks from the engines falling in your cemetery and perhaps causing a fire among the graves VOTE FOR STAR LANE SITE!

If you wish for a thoroughly bad site at an extravagant price, namely £800 for one and a half acres VOTE FOR STAR LANE SITE! and remember the rates.
If on the other hand you believe that a better site may be and ought to be found, then let the responsibility of the purchase rest on those who want to force the site upon you and record your VOTE AGAINST STAR LANE SITE !!

Every householder has a vote! Let it be given without fear. Remember the Poll opens at three o'clock on Wednesday next, and closes at nine. Do not fail to come and VOTE AGAINST STAR LANE SITE !!!"

This campaign was effective because, at their meeting on 7 June 1880, the burial board considered further correspondence concerning the land at Dippers Slip. The final decision appears to have been purely financial. At their meeting on 14 June 1880 the burial board had full costings for the Dippers Slip site (£3,135) which were £709 more than the Star Lane site (£2,426). This would produce a rate in the £ of four pennies and a farthing for Dippers Slip and three pennies and three farthings for Star Lane. So, in order to keep local taxation at a minimum, the Star Lane site was chosen.

In addition to the purchase of the site (£800) there were: legal expenses and stamp duty (£21), erection of fences and boundary wall (£50), making and draining roadway, planting and laying out ground (£100), making a plan of the ground showing grave spaces (£5.5s), erection of lodge for superintendent and gates (£250) and erection of chapels (£1,200). The attractive but redundant cemetery chapel of 1881 is now in the care of the local authority.

Alice Pateman died on 22 January 1892 at Fulcher's Square, St Mary Cray. She was 50 years old and her occupation was 'field woman'. The cause of death was broncho pneumonia and the informant was 'Mary Reynolds, sister, present at the death, Tugmutton, Farnborough'. Mary Reynolds was Alice's younger sister, Mary Pateman (born in 1851) who married George Reynolds. Alice Pateman was buried on 29 January 1892, aged 50, in Star Lane Cemetery, St Mary Cray.

There are eight other Patemans buried at Star Lane Cemetery: Walter Pateman (1943, Alice's brother); Betsy Pateman (1897, daughter of Alice's brother, James); William Pateman (1940, son of John and Matilda Pateman), his wife Rose Ann (1918) and two of their children, Edith Rose (1940) and Leonard (1900); a still born child (1954, child of Dorothy and Arthur Pateman, Robert's great grandson); and Ivy Pateman (1966.)

6. The Dickens Connection

- John Pateman (1844 -1883)
- James Pateman (1846-1926)

Robert returned to the Hoo Peninsula some time between the birth of Alice in 1842, and the birth of his next child, John, at Cliffe in 1844. The Hoo Peninsula is one of the hidden corners of Kent, often overlooked by travelers visiting the main attractions of the county. It is a largely unspoilt region with over 155 miles of public rights of way from which to explore this empty landscape so beloved of Charles Dickens.

Charles Dickens spent most of his life in and around North Kent and used many of its buildings as models for his stories. Rochester appears in four of Charles Dickens novels, as itself in *Pickwick Papers* and *Great Expectations*, as Dullborough Town in *The Uncommercial Traveller* and as Cloisterham in *Edwin Drood*. The Ship and Lobster pub in Denton, Gravesend, was a key watering hole for the writer and also mentioned in *Great Expectations*.

Charles Dickens was born in Portsmouth on 7 February 1812 and was five years old when his father, John Dickens, came to work in the Navy Pay Office in Chatham. They lived at No.2 Ordnance Terrace, Chatham, and Charles often played in a hayfield opposite which later became Chatham Railway Station. It was during this time that he met many of the people who would later appear as characters in his novels. His babysitter, Mary Weller, would become Peggotty in *David Copperfield*; a neighbour, Mrs. Newnham, who lived at No. 5, is thought to be the old lady in *Our Parish*; and at No. 1 lived George Stroughill, who was his greatest friend at that time and later would be used as a model for Steerforth in *David Copperfield*.

In 1821 the family moved to 18 St Mary's Place, next to a Baptist Chapel where the Reverend William Giles officiated. His son, William, (Mr. Feeder BA in *Dombey and Son*) taught at a school in Chatham that Charles and his sister attended. The young Charles continued to gather images in his mind. The rope makers, block makers and anchor smiths at Chatham Dockyard, the convict hulks in the Medway and the view of Rochester cathedral and castle at sunset all appeared in his later novels.

It was in 1857 that Dickens, already a wealthy and successful author, decided to move from London to the locality he had coveted as a boy and in a letter to a friend he described the events leading up to the move: 'Down at Gad's Hill near Rochester is a quaint little country house of Queen Anne's time. I happened to be walking past a year and a half or so ago with my sub editor of *Household Words* when I said 'You see that house. It has a curious interest for me because when I was a small boy down these parts I thought it the most beautiful house ever seen. And my poor father used to bring me to look at it and used to say that if ever I grew up to be a clever man perhaps I might own the house.'

We came back to town and my friend went out to dinner. Next morning he came in greatly excited and said 'It is written that you are to have Gad's Hill Place. A lady has told me that her father was the rector and lived there for many years. He has just died and left it to me but I want to sell it.' Charles Dickens bought the house for £1,790 and knew he had found his spiritual home. He wrote in 1860: 'This is Falstaff's own Gad's Hill and I live on top of it'. He arranged weekend parties for his literary friends - Wilkie Collins was a frequent visitor and so was Hans Christian Andersen who stayed for several weeks

Gad's Hill House was built in 1780 for the then Mayor of Rochester, Thomas Stephens. It was immortalized by Dickens in *A Christmas Carol*, where he described it as 'a mansion of dull red brick with a little weather-cock surmounted Cupola on the roof and a bell hanging on it.' It was here at Gad's Hill Place that Dickens was perhaps at his happiest; it was here he wrote much of *A Tale of Two Cities*, *Great Expectations*, *Our Mutual Friend* and the unfinished *The Mystery of Edwin Drood*.

Dickens took long walks in the countryside: it seems that despite his early 'delicate' constitution he later thought nothing of walking twelve miles or so at a 'cracking' pace. Given the remote location and sparse population of the Hoo peninsula, it is not entirely inconceivable that Dickens could have met or passed Robert Pateman and members of his family during his peramabulations around the area. They could have featured among the characters in 'Tramps', one of seventeen essays that were published in *The Uncommercial Traveller* (1860).

Tramps

Dickens was enchanted by Gad's Hill, the surrounding countryside and 'the tramps whom I perceived on all the summer roads in all directions.' Dickens used Gad's Hill as a place to relax, a place where he could be the country squire, interesting himself in country matters - haymaking, tramps, trees and gardens. One day Dickens was working when he heard the noise of a tremendous row going on outside: 'Ours being a country constantly infested with tramps, I looked upon the disturbance at first as merely one of the usual domestic incidents of tramp life arising out of some nomadic gentleman beating his wife up our lane, as was quite the common custom'.

'Tramps' catches the feel of Gad's Hill and its vicinity; the reader is invited to sit with Dickens at his desk in the library and look out with him across the lawn:

'Whenever a tramp sits down to rest by the wayside, he sits with his legs in a dry ditch; and whenever he goes to sleep (which is very often indeed), he goes to sleep on his back. Yonder, by the high road, glaring white in the bright sunshine, lies, on the dusty bit of turf under the bramble-bush that fences the coppice from the highway, the tramp of the order savage, fast asleep. He has no occupation whatever and has no object whatever in going anywhere'.

Dickens had strong feelings on the subject of begging and mendacity, and reveals knowledge of the ploys used by tramps and beggars to extract donations from other pedestrians:

'The slinking tramp is of the same hopeless order, and has the same injured conviction on him that you were born to whatever you possess, and never did anything to get it; but he is of a less audacious disposition. He will stop before your gate, and say to his female companion with an air of constitutional humility and propitiation - to edify anyone who may be within hearing behind a blind or a bush –

'This is a sweet spot, ain't it? A lovelly spot! And I wonder if they'd give two poor footsore travellers like me and you, a drop of fresh water out of such a pretty gen-teel crib?'

There is another kind of tramp, whom you encounter this bright summer day. As you walk you descry in the perspective at the bottom of a steep hill up which your way lies, a figure that appears to be sitting airily on a gate, whistling in a cheerful and disengaged manner. As you approach nearer to it, you observe the figure to slide down from the gate, to desist from whistling, to uncock its hat, to become tender of foot, to depress its head and elevate its shoulders, and to present all the characteristics of profound despondency.

Towards the end of the same walk, on the same bright summer day, at the corner of the next little town or village, you may find another kind of tramp, embodied in the persons of a most exemplary couple whose only improvidence appears to have been, that they spent the last of their little All on soap. They are a man and woman, spotless to behold - John Anderson attended by Mrs. Anderson. This cleanliness was the expiring effort of the respectable couple, and nothing then remained to Mr. Anderson but to get chalked upon his spade, in snow-white copy-book characters, HUNGRY! And to sit down there.

Another class of tramp is a man, the most valuable part of whose stock in trade is a highly perplexed demeanor. He then produces from under his dark frock a neat but worn old leathern purse, from which he takes a scrap of paper. On this scrap of paper is written, by Squire Pouncerby, of The Grove, 'Please to direct the Bearer, a poor but very worthy man, to the Sussex County Hospital, near Brighton' - a matter of some difficulty at the moment, seeing that the request comes suddenly upon you in the depths of Hertfordshire.

But the most vicious, by far, of all the idle tramps, is the tramp who pretends to have been a gentleman. This shameful creature lolling about hedge taprooms in his ragged clothes, now so far from being black that they look as if they never can have been black, is more selfish and insolent than even the savage tramp.

The young fellows who trudge along barefoot, five or six together, their boots slung over their shoulders, their shabby bundles under their arms, their sticks newly cut from some roadside wood, are not eminently prepossessing, but are much less objectionable. There is a tramp-fellowship among them. They generally talk about horses.

Bricklayers often tramp, in twos and threes, lying by night at their 'lodges' which are scattered all over the country. Bricklaying is another of the occupations that can by no means be transacted in rural parts, without the assistance of spectators. Sometimes the 'navvy,' on tramp, with an extra pair of half boots over his shoulder, a bag, a bottle, and a can, will take a similar part in a job of excavation, and will look at it, without engaging in it, until all his money is gone.

Who can be familiar with any rustic highway in summer-time, without storing up knowledge of the many tramps who go from one oasis of town or village to another, to sell a stock in trade, apparently not worth a shilling when sold? Shrimps are a favorite commodity for this kind of speculation, and so are cakes of a soft and spongy character, coupled with Spanish nuts and brandy balls.

On the hot dusty roads near seaport towns and great rivers, behold the tramping Soldier. Much better the tramping Sailor, although his cloth is somewhat too thick for land service. But why the tramping merchant-mate should put on a black velvet waistcoat, for a chalky country in the dog-days, is one of the great secrets of nature that will never be discovered.'

If the Canterbury Pilgrims came up Gad's Hill, as they assuredly did, they must have done what other travelers did for years to come - pause at the top. Dickens has attested to this:

'I have my eye upon a piece of Kentish road, bordered on either side by a wood, and having on one hand, between the road-dust and the trees, a skirting piece of grass. Wild flowers grow in abundance on this spot, and it lies high and airy, with a distant river stealing steadily way to the ocean, like a man's life. To gain the milestone here, which the moss, primroses, violets, blue bells, and wild roses, would soon render illegible but for peering travelers pushing them aside with their sticks, you must come up a steep hill, come which way you may. So, all the tramps with carts or caravans - the Gypsy-tramp, the Show-tramp, the Cheap Jack - find it impossible to resist the temptations of the place, and all turn the horse loose when they come to it, and boil the pot. Bless the place, I love the ashes of the vagabond fires that have scorched its grass! What tramp children do I see here, attired in a handful of rags, making a gymnasium of the shafts of the cart, making a feather bed of the flints and brambles, making a toy of the hobbled old horse. Here, do I encounter the cart of mats and brooms and baskets - with all thoughts of business given to the evening wind - with the stew made and being served out - with Cheap Jack and Dear Jill striking soft music out of the plates that are rattled like warlike cymbals when put up for auction at fairs and markets.'

This was the Old Dover Road on which stood 'a delightfully old fashioned roadside inn of the coaching days which no man possessed of a penny was ever known to pass in warm weather.' This was, and is, the *Sir John Falstaff,* a hostelry on the north side of the road a little below Dickens' house:

'Within appropriate distance of this magic ground is a little hostelry. This is a house of great resort for haymaking tramps and harvest tramps. Later in the season, the whole countryside, for miles and miles, will swarm with hopping tramps. They come in families, men, women and children, every family provided with a bundle of bedding, an iron pot, and a number of babies. They crowd all the roads, and camp under all the hedges and on all the scraps of common land, and live among and upon the hops until they are all picked, and the hop gardens, so beautiful through the summer, look as if they had been laid waste by an invading army. Then there is a vast exodus of tramps out of the country; and if you ride or drive around any turn of the road, at more than a foot pace, you will be bewildered to find that you have charged into the bosom of fifty families, and that there are splashing up all around you, in the utmost prodigality of confusion, bundles of bedding, babies, iron pots, and a good humored multitude of both sexes and all ages, equally divided between perspiration and intoxication.'

Dickens was troubled by the condition of many of the poor folk who came down to Kent for the annual hop picking. 'Hop picking is going on', he wrote to a friend, 'and people sleep in the garden, and breathe in at the keyhole of the house door. I have been amazed, before this year, by the number of miserable lean wretches, hardly able to crawl, who go hop picking. I find it is a superstition, that the dust of the newly picked hop, falling fresh into the throat, is a cure for consumption. So the poor creatures drag themselves along the roads, and sleep under wet hedges, and get cured soon and finally.'

In 1864 a miniature Swiss Chalet presented to Dickens was erected in the garden at Gad's Hill (it can now be seen at the Dickens Museum in Rochester) and it was here that he wrote the last chapters of *Edwin Drood*. Dickens died on 9 June 1870, following a stroke the previous evening. He had always wished to be buried in Rochester but his family decided to have him interred at Westminster Abbey.

Henry Pye

The other major character on the Hoo Peninsula at this time was Henry Pye, who transformed the area and may well have employed Robert Pateman and his family. In 1845 the roads through the Hundred were in a disgraceful condition. All that was done in the way of mending them was to throw down loose stones which were rolled in by the wheels of any traffic that happened to be passing – and suitable stone for road making and mending was hard to come by on the Peninsula.

Marsh ague, a form of malaria, had been endemic in the Hundred for long enough. There was a cynical saying that no young husband 'down on the marsh' need despair if he fell too quickly out of love with his bride. Provided she had come from some other part of the county she was almost certain to die within the year. Malaria certainly accounted for the considerable drop in the Hundred's population during the seventeenth and eighteenth centuries.

Agriculture, the Peninsula's staple industry, was at a low ebb. The land was heavy, unlimed and undrained. The excellent grazing on the marsh was spoilt by the fact that the ditches and outlets to the river were choked and uncared for. The Peninsula was a backward and poverty stricken corner of a rich and prosperous farming county when Henry Pye became the tenant of the Dean and Chapter of Rochester at St Mary's Hall Farm, round about the year 1845.

Today the Hundred contains some of the best land and some of the best farms in Kent, a change which is due in a very large measure to the revolution in farming methods and practices effected by Henry Pye. Marsh ague had disappeared by the turn of the century, and there were enormous improvements in the Hundred's roads. There is a stained glass window to his memory in Hoo St Werburgh Church and he is buried in the churchyard there.

Henry Pye was a tough, enterprising, self-opinionated, stubborn, progressive, outspoken, kind-hearted man, with a zest for work and sport and people. And he was a wonderfully good farmer. He had a gift and a taste and an inherited aptitude for farming, because he was prepared to put a lot of money into his farms in order to get a lot of money out, because he was progressive and eager to strike out on a new line, because he was a pioneer in mechanization, because he treated his men well, because, all his life, he was convinced that he was the best farmer in Kent and therefore in the world, and because he never allowed his tremendous capacity for hard work to interfere with his pleasures and amusements.

He operated in the Hundred on a very big scale. At one time or another he farmed St Mary's Hall, Swigshole, Ross Farm, Hopper's, Turkey Hall Farm, New Barn Farm, and Clinch Street Farm. In addition, he managed a number of farms for other people, often refusing any payment for his trouble. Farming was a passion with him. He collected farm tenancies and farm managements as another man might collect company directorships. He introduced a number of innovations to farming practice in the Hundred.

He drained the land that he farmed, putting in an elaborate system of irrigation. He chalked all his fields, carrying the chalk from a pit at Cooling. He was the first man in west Kent to own and operate steam ploughing tackle and steam threshing tackle. He cleaned out the ditches and the river outlets on the marsh and kept them clear – it was this which proved to be the answer for malaria. When he first went to live at St Mary's Hall he kept a stock of quinine for his workers and their families.

He took advantage of the absence of frost in the Peninsula – thanks to its nearness to the sea – to grow early potatoes for the London market. He grew as good wheat as any in Kent. He grew hops at Turkey Hall. But his most notable contribution to the Hundred's prosperity was his establishment of seed growing as a large-scale industry. He obtained contracts with the leading wholesale seedsmen of Covent Garden and the supply of seed – particularly radish, wurzel and pea seed – for this market formed the backbone of the Peninsula's farming economy until it was killed by imports from overseas.

He was a great man for sheep and bullocks. At Swigshole he had six hundred acres of pasture and he rented a further two hundred acres of fattening graze on the Cliffe Marshes for the tegs that he bought each May at the Maidstone fair. He was a pioneer in the use of artificial fertilizers. He had only to go and look at the crop, and if he saw that it was not doing well he knew what had to be done. All his neighbors used to come to him when they got into trouble.

He was strict with his men, allowing no smoking on the farm, and one of his employees, who started work under him as a boy, got a thrashing from his master for running along a potato clamp. But if he was free with his stick he was always ready to give any boy that came to him a start – he was a noted trainer of sheep-shearers – and with the older men he was quick to encourage enterprise. He believed in picking good men as working bailiffs and giving them a fairly free hand. One of the best of them, he used to declare, was a man who could neither read nor write. He was feared, for he had his bad days, but he was trusted. He farmed the area for an incredible 64 years and died in 1909.

John Pateman (1844-1883)

Robert's first son, John Pateman (named after his grandfather and great-grandfather) was born on 23 June 1844 'in a tent in the parish of Cliffe'. His father's occupation was given as a chair mender.

Cliffe

According to *Kelly's Directory* (1845): 'Cliffe at Hoo, sometimes called Bishops Clive, is a parish in the Lathe of Aylesford. It lies partly at the edge of extensive marshes, bordering on the Thames. It is 8 miles north of Rochester and 9 miles east of Gravesend. Its area is 5400 acres and its population in 1841 was 540. Cliffe was anciently an important place'. A later *Post Office Directory* notes that 'Here are whiting and Portland cement works and chalk quarries. The chief crops are corn, potatoes and fruit. There are 80 acres of hops.'

When Cliffe was first established as a settlement it stood, like nearby Cooling, at the water's edge, as evidenced by Wharf Lane. The marshes were gradually reclaimed from the twelfth century onwards by the monks of Christchurch, Canterbury. By the mid fourteenth century the present day coastline had been more or less established leaving Cliffe considerably further inland. The sea-walls have been progressively extended and heightened since then, partly to reclaim more land for use as pasture and partly as a sea defense.

The Saxon Shore Way is a long distance footpath of some 140 miles from Gravesend to Rye. It follows the line of the ancient coastline, as it existed in Roman times before much of the Kentish marshlands were reclaimed. By following its course through the Hoo Peninsula it is possible to form a picture of how the landscape once looked, when much of what is now lush meadow at river level was under water.

Cliffe has the only church in Kent dedicated to St Helen, legend stating she was the daughter of Coel, Colchester's 'Old King Cole' of the nursery rhyme. St Helen's church is quite out of proportion to anything a casual inspection of the village might suggest was needed there. The thirteenth century banded flint and ragstone (a familiar feature in this area) building has many additions including a double storey porch and a fifteenth century tower. Inside various architectural periods are clearly seen and the fourteenth century south windows are of particular note. The remaining wall paintings indicate some of the magnificence of the medieval church and are worth a moment's study.

The church dominates the village, which clings to the very fringes of the North Kent marshes where the Hoo Peninsula sticks out its thumb of land into the Thames and Medway estuary. On the seaward side, there is a kind of melancholy about the barren windswept acres beloved of wildfowl and their watchers, but inland the landscape is more garden like, the richly fertile soil hosting orchards and crops and vegetables and cereals.

During the sixteenth century, Cliffe was a considerable town and may well have declined by then from earlier even greater size and importance. If this really was the Cloveshoo (or Cloveshoh) of Saxon times (and despite the often repeated assertion that it was, there is no proof of it) then it was here that no fewer than seven Saxon councils were held between the years AD 742 and 824 and here that synods drew up the rules for better government of the Church, providing a framework for centuries to come. It is claimed too that Magna Carta was drafted here in 1215 before the final document was taken to Runnymede for King John to sign.

Early in its career, Cliffe village was a farm of the monks of Christ's Church at Canterbury, with a fourteenth century population of about 3,000 people. Until a fire in 1520 Cliffe was an important port on the Thames having links with the kingdom of Essex across the river. The great fire marked the beginning of a decline. The waterways were silted up, the sea walls decaying and the increasing incidence of malaria was persuading the population to move away.

In 1840 a survey of tithes in the Cliffe parish was made following an act of parliament enacting that tithes should be paid in money and varied according to the average price of corn over the seven preceding years. In 1840 the price of wheat was seven shillings per bushel, barley 3s.11d and oats 2s.9d. The whole of the Cliffe parish was included in the tithe payments and details show a large number of owners and tenants holding land in small acreages, the largest being between 60 and 80 acres, land being divided into arable, marsh, woodland and numerous cottages.

A government survey of the same date (1840) recorded the fact that Cliffe had no nonconformist gatherings. The Enclosure Commissioners in 1860 made an award giving enclosure rights to occupiers on Great Mead (Redham Mead) and Rye St. common, all of which were of small acreage and presumably the awards were made to the regular users of the common. A coastguard station was in existence on Redham at this date, while large ponds existed at Ponds Hill and Allens Hill. In 1845 the population had dropped to 877 with only agriculture and sheep farming providing employment. A visitor in 1860 described it as 'An old, old village with an old world air about it, and an old church, and some dingy fishermen gathered on the river path, and a rubicund Boniface smoking his pipe at the door of an inn which affords but scant accommodation to man and horse', apparently referring to the *Black Bull Inn* and Pond Hill.

The digging of the Higham to Strood canal brought labourers to Cliffe from far and wide and for a time there was no shortage of work for able bodied villagers. Although the canal project flopped rather badly, all that digging was not wasted, because the same line was used by the South Eastern Railway, which opened in 1845 and brought a branch line to Cliffe in 1882. The branch line came to meet the demands of the cement works which had brought another string to the bow of village prosperity during the nineteenth century.

The first cement factory was built there in 1868 and after an explosives factory was built nearby in 1901 the population soared again to over 3,000. The remains of several cement works can be seen in the area. The works at Salt Lane opened in 1909 and closed as recently as 1970. West of the village are a series of lagoons dating from 1934 created by clay extraction for the area's cement manufacture, cement from works here being used to construct the Eddystone, Needles and Lizard light houses. During excavations several interesting archeological finds were made. These lagoons now support a rich variety of wildfowl and waders. The Black Road, a prominent local feature, takes its name not from the present tarmac covering, but from the deposits of black silt excavated from clay workings.

Begun as a result of a Royal Commission of 1860, Cliffe Fort was intended to be co-ordinated with Shornmead, Coalhouse and East Tilbury forts to defend the lower Thames. In 1885 an experimental torpedo station, designed by Louis Brenan, was constructed in the fort. General Gordon is said to have complained about fumes from a nearby cement works affecting the health of his troops and about a loading jetty being prejudicial to his plans for defense. Cliffe Fort was virtually abandoned in the 1920's but saw service again when a detachment of Home Guard was based there during 1939-1945. Guns remained in position at the fort until after World War Two. The interior is dangerous and strictly private, but it can be viewed from the sea wall.

Cliffe Fort is an ideal place to view the river scene. The wooden hulk of a Norwegian vessel called *Hans Egede* can be seen; this was being towed from Ramsgate to Thames for a refit when it sprang a leak off Egypt Bay and sank. To prevent it becoming a danger to shipping the Port of London Authority beached it where it now lies. Although shipping activity on the Thames has declined considerably in recent years, it is still the busiest river in the country, much of the traffic being modern container vehicles. In 1991 for example more than 13,000 cargo ships passed through the Port of London.

Cliffe Marshes

In *Great Expectations* (1861) Dickens draws heavily on the landscape of the Hoo Peninsula. The atmosphere of the marshland, with its isolated churches and remote villages, was well suited to the mysterious events of the book. It is to the damp mound of the Cliffe Battery, all that remained of a Tudor fortification on the river bank, that Pip makes his tremulous way to carry provisions and a file to the fugitive Magwitch. Later in the book Pip is lured by Orlick to an old sluice gate hut on the banks of the canal near the lime works. In Dickens's day there were still lime kilns at Cliffe from which the prepared lime was transported down the canal to the river and into Thames barges:

'It was a dark night, though the full moon rose as I left the enclosed lands, and passed out upon the marshes. Beyond their dark line there was a ribbon of clear sky, hardly broad enough to hold the red large moon. In a few minutes she had ascended out of that clear field, in among the piled mountains of cloud. It was another half hour before I drew near to the kiln. The lime was burning with a sluggish, stifling smell, but the fires were made up and left, and no workmen were visible. Hard by, was a small stone quarry. It lay directly in my way, and had been worked that day, as I saw by the tools and barrows that were lying about.

Coming up again to the marsh level out of this excavation – for the rude path lay through it – I saw a light in the old sluice house. I quickened my pace and knocked at the door with my hand. Waiting for some reply, I looked about me, noticing how the sluice was abandoned and broken, and how the house - of wood with a tiled roof – would not be proof against the weather much longer, if it were so even now, and how the mud and ooze were coated with lime, and how the choking vapor of the kiln crept in a ghostly way towards me.'

Astonishingly, after the Second World War, the Cliffe marshes were suggested as the site for the third London airport, the Victory Airport. It was intended to combine large passenger carrying seaplanes using a Cliffe terminal on the Thames, in which no doubt Shorts Brothers, seaplane makers at nearby Rochester, would have been commercially interested. Land passenger carrying aircraft would have used runways constructed on the north Cliffe marshes. Although this went no further than being a plan, the idea was resurrected in 2003 when the Cliffe marshes were once again put forward as an option for a new London airport.

Today there is little enough to suggest that Cliffe was once a town of some size and importance. The High Street is still picturesque with weatherboard houses, despite a lot of new building elsewhere. The shops and houses in Church Street include *Longford*, which is an especially good example of 'Kentish' weatherboarding with the overhang. Above *Longford* are cottages and shops which together create a 17th century atmosphere. There are several medieval houses hiding behind later facades. Allens Hill farmhouse situated in Bucklands Road is a late fifteenth century timber framed building clad in brick and weatherboarding. The area was a popular smugglers haunt and some of the houses, particularly in Wharf Lane, had deep cellars in which to hide contraband.

An open space called The Buttway is an ancient recreation area for sport and games and archery practice. A three day fair is permitted under the authority of a twelfth Century Charter. The School, overlooking the Buttway, was a National (Church) School built in 1854, about the same time as other village schools on the Peninsula.

The old St Jame's Day (25 July) tradition of blessing the apples in churches has lapsed now and so has the apparently purely local tradition, referred to by Edward Hasted, that required the rector to distribute every year a mutton pie and a loaf of bread to as many as chose to demand it, at a cost of about £15 a year. Remembering what a mutton pie and a loaf of bread would have cost in Hasted's eighteenth century, we can assume that rather a lot of the local people turned up at the rectory to claim their hand out.

Born in a tent

John Pateman was 'born in a tent'. The tents that Gypsies lived in were constructed by pushing flexible hazel rods into the ground and bending them over to create a dome shape. This was then covered with sailcloth or other heavy material which was then held in place with large pins or skewers. These 'bender' tents were flexible in their construction, they could simply be small domes for one person to sleep in or else far more sophisticated structures. Some had a number of small 'rooms' which opened into a central area which was open at the top so that smoke from the fire could escape. These tents were described by Borrow (1874):

'The tents are oblong in shape and of very simple construction, whether small or great. Sticks or rods, between four and five feet in length, and bending towards the top are stuck in the ground at about twenty inches from each other, a rod or two being omitted in that part where the entrance is intended to be. The bends serve as supporters of a roof, and those of the side rods which stand over against one another are generally tied together by strings. These rods are covered over with coarse brown cloths, pinned or skewered together; those at the bottom being fastened to the ground by pegs. Around the tent is generally a slight embankment, about two or three inches high, or a little trench about the same depth, to prevent water from running into the tent in time of rain.'

Chair mending

Robert Pateman was a 'chair mender', a typical Gypsy occupation. Robert may well have repaired chairs all the way along the journey from Wimbledon to Cliffe. The chair mender's craft was described by Charles Dicken's in 'Tramps':

'Then there are the tramp handicraft men. Are they not all over England, in this Midsummer Time? Where does the lark sing, the corn grow, the mill turn, the river run, and they are not among the lights and shadows, tinkering, chair mending, umbrella mending, clock mending, knife grinding ? Very agreeable, too, to go on a chair mending tour. What judges we should be of rushes, and how knowingly (with a sheaf and bottomless chair at our back) we should lounge on bridges, looking over at osier beds! Among all the innumerable occupations that cannot possibly be transacted without the assistance of lookers on, chair mending may take a station in the first rank. When we sat down with our backs against the barn or the public house, and began to mend, what a sense of popularity would grow upon us! When all the children came to look at us, and the tailor and the general dealer, and the farmer who has been giving a small order at the little saddlers, and the groom from the great house, and the publican, and even the two skittle players (and here note that, howsoever busy all the rest of the village human kind may be, there will always be two people with leisure to play at skittles, wherever village skittles are), what encouragement would be on us to plait and weave!'.

There is a well known painting of *The Old Chair Mender* by M.B. Foster (1825-1899). The picture shows the old chair mender (with a Gypsy diklo or handkerchief tied on his head) in the foreground, mending a chair from a bundle of reeds which lies next to him. A small child is passing him the reeds. They are being watched by a group of four children – one of them holds a broom and another has a basket, both of which were also made by the Gypsy. At a cottage door the chair mender's wife is hawking baskets. It is an idyllic rustic scene, suggesting health and plenty. The reality of rural England in 1844 may have been very different.

On 2 April 1871 John Pateman (23, Kent Cliffe) was living with his family in an old stable on a brick field at Becks Lane, Beckenham, Kent. Some time after 1871 John left his family and settled in the area of Farnborough, Kent, with his two younger brothers, James and William. On 3 April 1881 John Pateman (34, lodger, agricultural labourer, Rochester) was living at Orpington Lane, Farnborough, Kent. He was one of five lodgers in the house of Robert Rudd and his family.

John Pateman died on 26 June 1883 at Broad Street Green, Farnborough, Kent. He was a 38 year old labourer and he died of a 'prostatic disease' (prostate cancer?). His death certificate contains 'the mark of George Reynolds, brother in law, present at the death, Broad Street Green, Farnborough.' George Reynolds was the husband of John's sister, Mary (born 1851). John Pateman was buried in St Giles Churchyard,

Farnborough, Kent. For more information about the Tugmutton Gypsies see *Tugmutton Common – the life and times of William Pateman and his family*.

James Pateman (1846-1926)

James Pateman (1846-1926) = Jane Reynolds (1861-1939)
- Betsy Pateman (1880-1881)
- Emmie Pateman (1882-1956)
- Phillis Pateman (1883-1902)
- Hannah Pateman (1884)
- Robert Pateman (1885-1960)
- Mary Ann Pateman (1886-?)
- Charlotte Pateman (1887-?)
- Phoebe Pateman (1889-?)
- Jane Pateman (1890-?)
- Celia Pateman (1892-1894)
- John Pateman (1893-1900)
- Polly Pateman (1894-1900)
- Betsy Pateman (1896-1897)
- Elvy Pateman (1897-1950)
- George Pateman (1899-1921)
- Daisy Pateman (1901-1975)
- Rose Pateman (1903-1993)
- William Pateman (1904-1966)

Sometime between the birth of John Pateman on 26 June 1844 and the death of Mary Ann Pateman on 13 October 1844, Robert Pateman moved to Stockbury. Robert then moved back to the Hoo Peninsula for the birth of his next son, James Pateman, on 17 July 1846 'in a tent on Cooling Common, Cliffe'. Robert's occupation was given as 'labourer', rather than agricultural labourer, which suggests that he may have been employed in non agricultural manual work such as canal or railway building?

Cooling

According to *Kelly's Directory* (1845): 'Cooling, or Cowling, is in the Lathe of Aylesford, 6 miles north of Rochester and 4 miles from Higham Station on the Rochester Railway. This ancient village lies high, but the greater part of the parish is marsh, extending to the Thames. The area is 2000 acres and the population in 1841 was 144'. A later *Post Office Directory* notes that 'In the marshes are osier beds. The chief crops are grain.' The osier beds would be used to provide the reeds for basket making and chair mending, two traditional Gypsy crafts. From general farming in the eighteenth century, a change to hop growing took place only to be replaced by market gardening when transport became available to the London markets. Hop picking was another Gypsy occupation. The wildness of the marshes and distance from the kind of law enforcement found in larger villages and towns, might have also made this a more trouble free place for Gypsies to live and work.

The village of Cooling lies on the marshes and is probably the smallest village, in population terms, on the Hoo Peninsula but with a considerable history. It is closely connected with the Cobham family and the aristocracy, although Jack Cade (a campaigner for higher wages for peasants and laborers) was well supported here, and smugglers were familiar with the 'lie of the land'. From Cooling Road, which twists and turns through rich farm land and neatly planted orchards, a splendid panorama of marsh and river can be enjoyed. One can easily imagine days when, without a complete sea wall, small ships would quietly creep up the creeks and fleets for lawful and other kinds of activity. The straight line drainage system and the sea wall were largely completed in the nineteenth century.

'Cowling is an unfrequented place, the roads of which are deep and miry, and it is as unhealthy as it is unpleasant'. So wrote the Kentish historian Edward Hasted in the 1770s when Cooling, situated at the back end of the Peninsula and Hundred of Hoo, must have been a very bleak and lonely place. Today it is still a small and scattered rural community, its population over the past two centuries having fluctuated between 100 and 200 people.

Great Expectations

In September 1860 Dickens began to write *Great Expectations* (1861), perhaps his greatest novel. Dickens used Cooling church as the setting for the opening scene which begins unforgettably in a twilit and overgrown churchyard on the eerie Kent marshes: 'My father's family name being Pirrip, and my Christian name Philip, my infant tongue could make of both names nothing longer or more explicit than Pip. So, I called myself Pip, and came to be called Pip.

I give Pirip as my father's family name, on the authority of his tombstone and my sister – Mrs. Joe Gargery, who married the blacksmith. As I never saw my father or my mother, and never saw any likeness of them (for their days were long before the days of photographs) my first fancies regarding what they were like, were unreasonably derived from their gravestones. The shape of the letters on my father's, gave me an odd idea that he was a square, stout, dark man, with curly black hair. From the character and turn of the inscription 'Also Georgiana Wife of the Above', I drew a childish conclusion that my mother was freckled and sickly.

Ours was the marsh country, down by the river, within, as the river wound, twenty miles of the sea. My first most vivid and broad impression of the identity of things seems to me to have been gained on a memorable raw afternoon towards evening. At such a time I found out for certain, that this bleak place overgrown with nettles was the churchyard, and that Philip Pirrip, late of this parish, and also Georgiana wife of the above, were dead and buried; and that Alexander, Bartholomew, Abraham, Tobias, and Roger, infant children of the aforesaid, were also dead and buried; and that the dark flat wilderness beyond the churchyard, intersected with dykes and mounds and gates, with scattered cattle feeding on it, was the marshes; and that the low leaden line beyond was the river; and that the distant savage lair from which the wind was rushing, was the sea; and that the small bundle of shivers growing afraid of it all and beginning to cry, was Pip'.

In those days this churchyard must have been a wonderfully wild and eerie place (and it still is!) and just the right setting for Magwitch, the escaped convict, to appear out of the mists and terrify the young Pip. We can imagine the road as a rutted track, hardly a house to be seen and two miles of marshes to the muddy foreshore of the Thames estuary. Today it is less wild, although not always less windy, and has more signs of civilization. Where Pip looked across bleak marshes, we now look across meadows to the Thames. He would have seen the same distant hills of Essex but not the oil refineries and terminals at Thames Haven and Shell Haven, the sprawl of Canvey Island and, to the east, the distant tower blocks of Southend on Sea.

To the south of the church tower is the handsome chest tomb of John Comport, of Cooling Castle, who died in 1827. Nearby is a worn headstone, with 13 little body stones, marking the last resting places of 13 children, from two families, all of whom died in infancy. To the west of the headstone are Ellen (1854, aged 5 months), Sarah (1837, aged 3 months), and John (aged 1 month), the children of John and Sarah Rose-Baker, the son and daughter in law of Michael Comport of Decoy House. The row of ten graves east of the headstone, include seven Comport children, all born at Cooling Court or Cooling Castle. These are William (died 1771, aged 8 months), William (1773, aged 7 months), James (1777, aged 4 months), Francis (1775, aged 1 year and 5 months), William (1779, aged 8 months) and Elizabeth (1779, aged 3 months). Beside these are Sarah Elizabeth, daughter of George Comport of Gattons (died 1779, aged 3 months), Thomas, son of Michael Comport of Decoy House (1880, aged 3 months) and Mary, daughter of Michael and Jane Comport of Cooling Court, who died in infancy in 1767. It is Michael and Jane who are commemorated on the now illegible headstone. These are now known far and wide as Pip's Graves. Although there is no documentary proof and, despite the fact that Dickens reduced their number to fit his story, many people believe that it was these little graves that prompted his hero, Pip, to relate:

'To five little stone lozenges, each about a foot and a half long, which were arranged in a neat row beside their grave, and were sacred to the memory of five little brothers of mine - who gave up trying to get a living exceedingly early in that universal struggle - I am indebted for a belief I religiously entertained that they had all been born on their backs with their hands in their trousers-pockets, and had never taken them out in this state of existence.'

Some literary historians claim that the churchyard in *Great Expectations* was that at Lower Higham or Hoo St Werbergh. It seems likely that Dickens used a combination of features from all three graveyards. The classic 1945 film version of *Great Expectations* was filmed on the Hoo Peninsula.

Hulks

Dickens described the convict hulk from which Magwitch escaped 'lying out a little way from the mud of the shore, like a wicked Noah's Ark'. Prison hulks were a common sight on the River Medway. During the French Wars of 1793 to 1815, for example, it was to be the fate of a large number of British warships to end their days as prison hulks. These were the vessels that were no longer deemed fit for sea service. Instead, they were allocated permanent moorings away from the more active vessels of the fleet, their decks crammed full of captured enemy seamen. For the government it was an obvious solution. Such ageing vessels had no real future and a massive number of captives had to be housed somewhere. While purpose built accommodation could be (and eventually was) constructed, this was always the more expensive option. Unfortunately, of course, there was a down side to the process. Use of such vessels, ageing and rotting as they were, had a deleterious affect upon the health of those who occupied these vessels.

From the outbreak of war in 1793 until 1810, the *Hero* served in this miserable role, moored permanently in Gillingham Reach on the River Medway. For those who were dispatched to the *Hero* prison ship, life was far from pleasant. Rarely holding less than 400 captive soldiers and sailors, these luckless individuals spent most of their day in the cramped confines of the orlop and gun decks. It was here that they ate, slept, and entertained themselves. The only natural light available was that which was provided by the barred but unglazed ports that ran the length of the two gun decks. Even in winter, with so little ventilation, the heat and stuffiness of these two decks was often unbearable.

Adding to the distress of the prisoners was the location of the hulks. Alongside Gillingham Reach, both to the north and south east, were mosquito infested marshes. Some of these mosquitoes were mere irritants, feeding on the blood of sleeping prisoners and leaving their bite marks to fester and bleed. Others, however, the anopheline variety, were malaria carriers, passing on a mild English form of the disease. Throughout the autumn period of each year those brought down with malaria would be weak and highly susceptible to additional diseases. As a result, the death rate at this latter end of the year was always horrendously high.

A page from the *Hero's* muster book, shows the name of prisoners arriving and of their later disposal; a map of Gillingham Reach shows the mooring points used by prison hulks during the late eighteenth century; a painting of the River Medway during the mid eighteenth century shows a hulked warship in the foreground; Turner's famous view of the River Medway in 1832, shows a prison hulk immediately beyond the parish church. By this date such hulks were used to house civilian convicts employed in the dockyard.

Cooling Marshes

The marshes round Cooling are a haven for wildlife and there are some wonderful walks to be had across them. Though developments have taken place over large areas of the South East of England the marshes at Cooling remain as untouched as they were in the days of Charles Dickens. The sea remains an ever present threat even though nowadays it is difficult to believe it once came so close to the village. It was not until the floods of 1953 that people began to realize that some stories of the past which now seem far fetched might well be true.

What today is known as Eastborough Farm Cottages is reputed to have been called 'Elizabeth Nell'. This was where Queen Elizabeth I was supposed to have once landed in her Royal Barge perhaps on her way to Dover with her favored suitor, the Duke of Anjou in 1582. Such a landing did not seem feasible until the floods of 1953 when the water came within 100 yards of them. Photographs taken at the time show the GPO station at Cooling and the two houses opposite Cooling Castle surrounded by water.

Bewick Swans, White Fronted Geese, Hen Harriers and Merlins know a good thing and regularly winter on the marshes along with Wigeon, Teal, Shovelar, Pintail and Gadwall. Flocks of Golden Plover can be seen feeding and the mudflats are ideal for many winter waders such as Dunlin and Knot. Shelduck are frequently seen on the mudflats at low tide and swimming on the river when the tide is in. Apart from these there are many other birds in residence such as Long and Short Eared Owls who hunt over the marshes along with the Hen Harriers who hunt in the ditches.

Snow Buntings feed along the sea wall, Lapland Buntings are found on the higher grazing land together with Corn Buntings. Bearded Tits are sometimes seen in the late autumn and in the spring Little Grebes nest along the ditches with ducks such as Pochard and Garganey along with other smaller birds such as Meadow Pipits, Skylarks, Yellow Wagtail, Reed Warblers, and Redshanks.

As the whole area has many open ditches and gullies it attracts many water loving plants such as common reeds and spike rush and fennel pondweed which is relished by the duck population. It also attracts many other forms of wildlife such as dragon and damselflies and numerous butterflies and moths such as the Common Blue, Meadow Brown and the Painted Lady. Grasshoppers and Roesel's Bush Cricket are to be heard everywhere and to be seen if you look carefully, as too is the Marsh Frog.

Basket making

James and John Pateman were baptized together on 26 July 1846 at St Helen's Church, Cliffe. Their father's occupation was given as basket maker. Cliffe being a peculiar of the Archbishop of Canterbury the Rector was exempt from all visitations except from the Archbishop in person. Rectors were appointed by the Archbishop with promptings from the Pope. Cliffe being a rich living, the appointments were given to prominent churchmen, most of whom had other livings and did not reside in the parish. The rector at the time of James and John's baptism was Canon James Croft, who was Rector from 1818 until 1869. Croft was Archdeacon of Canterbury and Rector of Saltwood. One of his curates was Edward Aefree who later became Vicar of St Swithins Cannon Street and incorporated the stone which marked the centre of Roman London in his church wall for its protection. An Ecclesiastical Commission set up in 1839 diverted money away from the Canterbury officials to the repair and upkeep of churches and admonished the officials for neglect and spending too much time in 'belly cheer'; the number of canons was reduced from twelve to six.

The art of basket making was developed at an early stage of man's evolution. In Britain oak, hazel and willow provided material for making the strong rigid containers necessary in everyday life. Fences and houses, too, were built from wickerwork or wattles. Early baskets were probably much like those found on the farms of highland regions until the second half of the twentieth century. 'Frame' baskets were constructed with wild materials on simple but time consuming principles, and in these areas basket making mostly remained a seasonal job reserved for the dark days of winter. In lowland Britain the weaving of willow, using different techniques, developed into a profession and ultimately a sizeable industry. The number of craftsmen employed and the output of their labors must have been immense, but such are the temporary nature of willow and the humble status of the basket maker that the evidence of the scale of production has all but disappeared.

In practically every instance where today one needs cardboard, plastic or plywood for packing material, two hundred years ago this need would have been met by wickerwork. Fruit and vegetables were gathered from the fields into baskets; fish, poultry and dairy produce were all packed into wicker for the journey to the town markets. Jobs requiring the transport of bulky materials such as manure or rubble needed baskets, and not only were rural items such as animal muzzles, bird traps and beer strainers made of willow, but so were the traveling trunks, hat boxes and umbrella holders of the well to do.

The distribution of workshops depended on local demand and favorable conditions for growing willows. In certain counties these factors combined to create a concentration of makers, often within a small area of several villages. At the beginning of the twentieth century East Anglia and the East Midlands, the plain of York, Worcestershire, Gloucestershire, Kent, Bedfordshire and the Thames Valley supported a fair number of country workshops, making for the most part simple agricultural baskets. A greater variety of produce was to be found in the important centers of Lancashire, Somerset and the Trent Valley (Nottinghamshire and Leicestershire), while the largest and most sophisticated workshops were found in the towns. Guilds of basket makers were formed. Records show that the Worshipful Company of Basketmakers of the City of London was established before 1469. This company was eventually granted a royal charter by George IV in 1937, but by then its old responsibilities had long since been taken on by the trade unions. The basket maker wore a bowler hat, a status symbol that put the skilled craftsman in a class above the laborer.

Decline of the basket trade continued throughout the twentieth century for many economic reasons. An economy in which time has much value and quality very little has no place for a durable product that is extremely labor intensive. Moreover, where the use of wicker has still been viable, the cheapness of foreign labor has often led to basket importation. British basket makers, as members of an industrially advanced country, started to experience the undermining of their trade in the second half of the nineteenth century. Imports from the Netherlands, Germany and France severely affected the makers of agricultural work up to 1939. Wartime renewed the demand for baskets but since then competition in the domestic market has continued from the products of Spain, Poland, and the Far East.

Between 1945 and 1980 the number of 'twiggies' (as some makers call themselves) fell from seven thousand to about five hundred, of whom two hundred were blind and working under subsidized conditions. Today accomplished basket makers are few. The blind workshops still produce articles of a robust nature superior in strength to importations, although not necessarily very refined. In comparison many other makers, in attempts to beat importation on the same ground, have taken short cuts and generally lost the merits and quality of traditional willow work.

Willow must have been cultivated for almost as long as it has been used for basket making. Until the nineteenth century willow garths, or withy beds, were collections of mixed varieties in which the growing plants were cut off at several feet allowing a head of shoots to spring from a single stem or stool. The shoots are cut off and are known as osiers, withies in the West Country, or simply rods. Towards the end of summer growth stops at a height around seven feet and the wood matures. Cutting can begin after leaf fall, which is usually in early November following frost. Many willows are still cut by hand, a skilled and laborious task that can last all winter.

The crop is hauled to the yard for sorting into suitable sizes. The bark is then removed by peeling or stripping which provides a material altogether different and more refined. The willows are then spread out against a fence to dry in the wind, or put in drying sheds, especially in winter. The dried rods are tied up into bundles, called bolts. The basket maker requires very little equipment – a small collection of tools and enough room to work a seven foot willow are the only real essentials. Baskets are made on a plank - wooden boards resting on the ground to provide a level and dry workplace. The basket maker sits at one end, with perhaps his tool box or cushion to lean upon, so he is almost at ground level. On the floor each side are his rods; his tools are to his right, while the basket in front is inclined away from him on the lapboard. This position enables him to keep the willows neat and ready at hand. The essential tool kit consists of a shop knife, secateurs or shears, a beating iron for knocking down the weaving, and a steel bodkin for piercing holes. Willow is stored dry but to be made pliable it must be soaked in water. In order to start the day with well prepared material, the basket maker usually soaks up his stuff the evening before. This involves putting the rods in water for about an hour, then removing them to lie and mellow. This takes several hours; overnight is ideal. In the morning the rods are damp, cool and sweet smelling but not wet or slippery.

The processes used in making a round general purpose farm basket, of the sort sold nowadays for logs, include: tying the slath, pairing, staking up, upsetting, siding up, bordering off and handling. The basket maker would use the beating iron to knock down the weave for a tight uniform finish. Another type of basket was the five bushel hop tally basket which was used in the hop gardens of Kent until the last days of hand picking in the 1970's.

In Kent the basket maker was in much demand, for baskets were required for virtually any commodity that had to be picked or carried. Baskets were used for flint gathering, cement carrying, for picking potatoes, apples, pears, plums, cherries and so on. In the towns in comparatively recent years basket makers were required for making laundry baskets, bakers' bread baskets, post office baskets, etc. The osier beds are no longer commercially managed in Kent today, although place names such as Osier Field, Osier Meadow still remain. Several attempts have been made to revive the industry, but possibly because of the neglected osier beds together with cheap imported basket ware these ventures have not been successful.

The Packman family of St Mary Cray made baskets for generations and had a shop in the High Street, backing onto the river Cray. Orpington local historian Bill Morton has conjectured that Packman could be a variation of Pateman; Bill has also suggested that the origin of the word Packman could be associated with a man who had a pack on his pack and traveled the roads – which would fit with the Gypsy Patemans.

Gypsy crafts

Until the 1960s the gaily painted horse-drawn Gypsy wagons were a common feature of the Kent countryside, especially in the fruit and hop picking season. When no farm work was available Gypsies would concentrate on their own traditional crafts and many of them were extremely competent craftsmen. They maintained their wagons, many of them carried out their own harness and saddlery repairs, together with the traditional Gypsy crafts of chair mending, basket weaving, broom making and so on.

Until the introduction of the plastic spring type clothes pegs, thousands of Gypsy made pegs were sold, especially in rural areas, every year. Willow was the favorite wood for pegs, hazel was sometimes used, and the metal strip was cut from food cans. A good peg maker could produce a gross of pegs in less than two hours. Many country folk would buy the Gypsies' imitation flowers which were usually made from shaving off thin strips of elder. The flowers were dyed in vivid colors.

On 2 April 1871 James Pateman (21, Kent Cliffe) was living with his family in an old stable on a brick field at Becks Lane, Beckenham, Kent. Sometime after 1871 James left his family and 'married' Jane Reynolds. According to the 1881 census Jane Reynolds was born in St Mary Cray, Kent, in 1861; the 1891 census states she was born in Sittingborne in 1856; and the 1901 census claims she was born in 'Lidden' (Lyde?), Kent in 1859; her death certificates says she was 78 when she died in 1939, which would give a birth year of 1861. So we can assume that she was born in Kent some time between 1856 and 1861.

Jane was the daughter of George Reynolds and Charlotte Busby. There were close links between the Patemans and Reynolds, another Gypsy family. Jane's brother, George Reynolds (1853) was married to James Pateman's younger sister, Mary (1851). Jane's sister, Mercy Reynolds (1855-1940), was married to James Pateman's younger brother, William (1856-1921). So three siblings of the Reynolds family married three siblings of the Pateman family:

James Pateman = Jane Reynolds
Mary Pateman = George Reynolds
William Pateman = Mercy Reynolds.

As no marriage certificates can be found for any of these weddings, we suspect that they all 'jumped over the broomstick' or underwent a similar Gypsy ceremony, possibly at the same time. Between 1880 and 1904 James and Jane had 18 children (which we know of). Their first child, Betsy, was born at Star Lane, St Mary Cray on 22 November 1880. James and Jane lived in this area, which had a large Gypsy population, before they moved to Farnborough in 1881.

On 3 April 1881 James Pateman (29, bricklayer's labourer – another connection to bricks - Cliffe) was living at Bastard Green, Farnborough, Kent, with his wife, Jane Reynolds (20, St Mary Cray) and their daughter Betsy (4 months, St Mary Cray).

On 5 April 1891 James Pateman (45, potato dealer, Cliffe) was living at Tugmutton, Farnborough, Kent, with his wife Jane Reynolds (35, Sittingbourne) and their children, Emmie (8, Farnborough), Phyllis (7, Farnborough), Robert (6,

Farnborough), Mary (5, Farnborough), Charlotte (Farnborough), Phoebe (2, Farnborough) and Jane (1, Farnborough).

On 31 March 1901 James Pateman (48, greengrocer, Kent, Cliffe) was still living at Tugmutton with Jane (42, Kent, Lidden), Robert (16, greengrocers apprentice, Kent, Farnborough), Mary Ann (15, Farnborough), Charlotte (14, Farnborough), Phoebe (13, Farnborough), Jane (11, Farnborough), Elvy (3, Farnborough) and George (2, Farnborough).

As can be seen from these census returns, James settled with his family in Farnborough, Kent, in 1881. At first they were living in tents and 'house carts' on Tugmutton Common. Later they moved into little cottages in Willow Walk, which fringed Tugmutton Common. James Pateman's address was given as Tugmutton in the *Strong Directory of Farnborough* in 1890 and in the *Bush Directory of Farnborough* from 1894 to 1900. In 1901 the address changed to 5 Tugmutton until 1908. In 1909 the address changed again, this time to Willow Walk, until 1914, when the *Bush Directory* stopped publication (presumably because of the Great War).

In 1911 James Pateman (60, married 32 years, greengrocer, Kent, Cliffe) was living at 5 Willow Walk, Farnborough, Kent) with his wife Jane (51, assisting in the business, Kent, Sittingbourne) and their children Emily (14, school, Farnborough), George (13, school, Farnborough), Daisy (10, Farnborough), Rose (8, Farnborough) and William (6, Farnborough).

James Pateman's occupation was variously described as hawker, bricklayer's labourer, labourer, greengrocer, pedlar, potato dealer, general labourer, general hawker, potato merchant, potato salesman, salesman and general dealer.

James Pateman died on 29 May 1926 at 5 Willow Walk, Farnborough. He was a 79 year old general labourer. He died of 'senile decay' and the informant was 'F. Pankhurst, son in law, present at the death, 5 Willow Walk, Farnborough.' Frederick Pankhurst was the wife of Phoebe Pateman. James was buried on 5 June 1926 at St Giles Churchyard, Farnborough, in the same grave as his father, Robert Pateman (1890) and his son George Pateman (1921).

Jane Pateman died on 25 March 1939 at 5 Willow Walk, Farnborough. She was the 78 year old widow of James Pateman 'a greengrocer master'. She died of myocardial degeneration and chronic bronchitis (she smoked a clay pipe for much of her life). The informant was 'R.Pateman, son, 1 Colegate Cottages, Farnborough'. This was Robert Pateman (1885-1960). Jane was buried on 1 April 1939 at St Giles Churchyard, Farnborough, in the same grave as her daughter, Phyllis Pateman (1902).

James Pateman was part of a significant community of Gypsies who lived at Tugmutton, Farnborough. For many years James lived at 5 Tugmutton / Willow Walk. His next door neighbours were Levi and Urania Boswell, the 'King and Queen' of Kent Gypsies. The full story of the Tugmuttton Gypsies is told in the next volume of this family history – *Tugmutton Common : the life and times of William Pateman and his family*.

7. Gypsies of Kent

- William Pateman (1851-1921)
- Mary Ann Pateman (1851-1929)
- Elizabeth Pateman (1852-1916)
- Henry Pateman (1856-1858)

At the turn of the nineteenth century Kentish folk began to manifest some curiosity about the exotic strangers who had sojourned so long in their midst. They were astonished to discover how close a connection Gypsies had with Kent. There were more Romany to be found in the county than in the whole of Scotland, exclusive of the Borders.

The Romanies were certainly not new arrivals in Kent. Popular belief dated their arrival in the county to 1511. A generation later they were made the victims of very severe enactments. The Statutes of 1st and 2nd Philip and Mary and 5th Elizabeth menaced anyone: 'importing' gypsies with a fine of £40. Any 'Egyptian' who remained a month in the kingdom, or any English person joining their band for a month, was threatened with 'felony without benefit of clergy'. Gypsies did suffer the death penalty in parts of England, some of them in large numbers, but not, apparently, in Kent.

William Harman, an Elizabethan justice and writer, congratulated himself that in his day they had well-nigh disappeared. Another contemporary writer disagrees with him. 'Notwithstanding, all would not prevail, but still they wandered as before, up and down, and meeting once a year at a time appointed, sometimes at Kidbrook, by Blackheath, or elsewhere as they agreed still their meeting.'

No one had shown a great deal of interest in the Gypsies until they became the subject of scholarly investigation in the nineteenth century. Then about 1818 John Hoyland, a minister of the Society of Friends, 'being struck with commiseration for their condition, began to inquire into their real character'. Hoyland traveled with them and stayed in their winter camps. Like William Harman, he felt that they were on the verge of extinction, which was all the more reason for investigating them.

Enclosures, and the severity of magistrates, said Hoyland, had diminished their numbers. Probably many had left Kent for good. Why were these visitors to Kent so different from other folk? Where had they come from and what language did they speak amongst themselves? After considerable wrangling among the philologists, most became convinced that Romany, the language spoken amongst themselves by the Gypsies, was an Indian dialect.

But if the Gypsy language could be explained, it was a different matter to make sense of their strange customs. In a country where there was no national costume and everyone tried to dress in 'respectable' fashion as much as they could, the Gypsies persisted in their own style of dress.

'Their women's costume is unique,' wrote a Victorian observer, 'and pretty uniform: scarlet cloaks, black beaver hats, with broad slouching brims, or black velvet bonnets, with large wide pokes trimmed with lace, a handkerchief thrown over the head under the bonnet, and tied beneath the chin, long pendant ear-rings, black stockings, and ankle boots.'

Fortune telling

Gypsy women professed to be able to tell fortunes. 'A good day to you, sir,' they would say. 'Your honor is born to a fortune. I see that by the cast of your countenance. It was a right lucky planet that shone on your honor's birth!' They would then tell the stranger's fortune by 'crossing his palm', with a piece of silver that he gave them: the silver coin was used to sign his hand with the cross, so as to show no black magic was being used and then the Gypsy would peer intently at the lines on the palm.

'As o'er palm the silver piece she drew,
And traced the line of life with searching view,
How throbbed my fluttering pulse with hopes and fears,
To learn the color of my future years.'

Gypsies would sell love charms to those who wanted them. They would also undertake cures. The supposed psychic powers of Gypsy women may have resulted in the Romany being moved on and molested less frequently than they would otherwise have been. 'Nobody will live long who is cursed by the old woman,' a Gypsy told S.L. Bensusan.

Alone amongst English folk, the Gypsies were divided into families which were really tribes. Gypsy names were distinctive: Boswell, Lovell, Kemp and Rossiter being four well known names. The tribe was headed by a king, or queen. The king might carry a scepter made from an oak cudgel with a twining snake carved on it, with a slouch hat carrying a pipe and a crow's feather as a crown. Weddings, christenings and funerals were the signal for great gatherings of the clans.

The Romanies had begun the nineteenth century suffering from a great weight of prejudice. Closer acquaintanceship with Gypsies would have removed at least some of this prejudice. That Gypsies were not morose and unfriendly could be seen from the way that their faces lit up when addressed in their own language. Accost a Gypsy with *Shau shau palla?* – 'How do you do, brother?' and you will see the effect.

Prejudice was often displayed by the Gypsy diet, the cauldron bubbling over the bright fire of sticks. 'Their kettles,' wrote an eye witness, 'were not filled with the produce of poaching, nor of thefts from a hen roost, still less with meat 'that had died of its own accord'. No, they used frequently to come back from the town with good joints honestly purchased.' Outsiders, such as the girls who would sometimes steal to their tents, sure of a savory regale, could never see how they could either bake or roast. 'Better a great deal than in your poor pinched in grates' was the reply. A Victorian observer reports that when baking, the items would be placed in a pan of fireproof ware, covered with another, then set deep in a bed of glowing ashes and covered with more such ashes to a depth of about a foot or eighteen inches.

Gypsy women had always maintained themselves, and their families, by hard work. They had produced brooms, baskets and wicker work chairs to be found in every cottage. Their men folk had often been unjustly shunned as work shy, but they too had done the few jobs they could find. While many mended pots, pans and kettles, some made pottery or ground and sharpened knives. Others turned their pugnacity and love of animals to good account by becoming pugilists, horse traders or jockeys.

Traveling Showmen

The Industrial Revolution did much to help the Gypsy get accepted by his fellows. England as a whole, and Kent in particular, had become avid for mass entertainment. At the big fairs of Deptford and Greenwich, Gypsy men were able to join the ever moving life of the fair, or the circus. They went from fair to fair as horse dealers, hawkers of baskets or tin ware, workers of lucky bag stalls, knife and snuff box shies, fortune tellers, and proprietors of drinking and dancing booths.

Nothing could make the life of the traveling showman (like Henry Taylor, who married Elizabeth Pateman) comfortable or secure, but it at least ensured the Gypsy a livelihood. At last he was able to find a profitable outlet for his wanderlust. There can be no greater contrast between the Gypsies observed by early nineteenth century investigators and those described by traveling showman 'Lord' George Sanger. The early Victorian Gypsies slept in wretched tents, and traveled with nine horses or more, for whom they had to find grazing somehow. The later Gypsy's trim and new caravan had horses to match. Showmen's caravans grew so large and heavy that they needed to be hitched up to a traction engine. The Gypsy showmen of the end of the century were 'clad in shining velveteens, spangled with buttons of gold, silver and pearl. Buckles of silver and glittering paste adorned their clog shoes, and peeping from the black, well oiled locks might be seen enormously thick gold earrings. They made a brave show I can tell you.'

Gypsies have shown great ingenuity and perseverance in trying to adapt to the Kent of the late twentieth century. It has never been an easy task. Horse coping and horse dealing have thrived more now that every girl wants a pony. But gathering wild flowers, a traditional Gypsy livelihood, is more difficult now that many species are protected. Fortunately it is still possible to gather wild fruits and mushrooms. The herbal lore of Gypsies is still in demand. Not only are they prepared to prescribe for all equine diseases (with mallow as a favorite remedy) but they are great alternative medicine providers for human patients as well. Juliette de Bairacli Levy, who has studied them at close hand, describes some of their herbal remedies – mallow, plantain and dock for wounds and bruises; coltsfoot for coughs; yarrow and sorrel for fevers, and that great healing herb, comfrey.

Peg making still thrives and some Gypsies also make artificial flowers out of wood. Many Gypsies still find work in fruit orchards. Readiness to undertake temporary seasonal agricultural work has often earned Gypsies a plus from an officialdom that is sternly disapproving of all other aspects of Gypsy life. Juliette de Bairacli Levy even met one baby who had been born in a Kent strawberry field where her mother was at work!

Some Gypsies have become notable achievers, building up fortunes in the scrap metal, car repair and garaging businesses. Such successes have often been won at the expense of abandoning the traditional mode of life. Sadly, those who still hold to the old ways and persist in fleeing what Matthew Arnold called 'this strange disease of modern life' often find as little comprehension and toleration among non Gypsies as their forefathers did when they first entered Kent in Henry VIII's time.

William Pateman (1851-1921)

William Pateman (1851-1921) = Mercy Reynolds (1855-1940)
- Mary (1876-?)
- Henry (1878-1961)
- Noah (1883-1949)
- Walter (1886-1917)
- Alice (1889-?)
- Phoebe (1892-?)
- William (1894-?)
- Amy (1896-?)

Robert Pateman travelled to Stanwell in Middlesex for the baptism of his next child, William Pateman, on 6 July 1851 at St Mary the Virgin. Robert and Mary Bateman were described as 'trampers.' Robert returned to Kent and travelled around the Rochester area.

Rochester

Post Office Directory: 'Rochester is a city and parliamentary borough on the south bank of the navigable river Medway. The city is paved, well lighted with gas, and supplied with water from a reservoir at Gillingham: it is straggling, and extends for a considerable distance along the bank of the Medway. The bridge connecting Rochester with Strood, is a handsome and substantial iron structure of three arches, erected in 1856, at a cost of £200,000. Rochester cathedral was founded in 604; in 1840 the whole interior was repaired and restored and has been very much improved. Rochester had formerly four parish churches, but the site of St Mary's is unknown: St Margaret's church was built in the fifteenth century; St Nicholas' church is a Gothic building, erected in 1421; St Clement's church has been demolished; St Peter's is an ecclesiastical parish, founded in 1860. The Cathedral Grammar School was founded in 1544. William's Free Mathematical School was founded in 1601. The Guildhall was erected in 1687 and the Corn Exchange was rebuilt in 1870. Markets are held for corn on Tuesdays and for cattle on the fourth Tuesday in each month. A fair is held at Rochester on 18 May, and at Strood on 26, 27 and 28 August. There is a Gaol and Gasworks. The County Court Office was built in 1862. The Theatre is principally supported by the garrison and its officers. Fort Pitt is now used as a military hospital. Rochester Castle is an ancient edifice, of Norman Architecture, near the bridge, with very thick walls of Kentish rag stone. The keep is one of the finest castellated ruins in the kingdom; the grounds around the castle have been laid out as a place for public recreation. The population in 1871 was 18,352.'

Charles Dickens spent five idyllic childhood years here from 1817 to 1822. He was a national legend when he returned for the last thirteen years of his life, dying at Gad's Hill in 1870. There is hardly a place in and around the City of Rochester upon Medway that does not feature somewhere in Dickens' books. From its earliest appearance as Great Winglebury in *Sketches by Boz*, to its role as the setting for his masterly *The Mystery of Edwin Drood*, Rochester is everywhere. And the counter parts of the characters who move through the pages of his books can be recognized, even today, in the streets and the countryside beyond.

Only three of the major novels were written largely in Rochester: *The Tale of Two Cities* and *Our Mutual Friend*, neither of which feature the city, and *The Mystery of Edwin Drood*, in which it plays such an important role. It lives too in *Pickwick Papers,* briefly in *David Copperfield, Seven Poor Travellers, The Uncommercial Traveller* and in *Great Expectations*. The ancient magic of Rochester cathedral and its castle, in particular, inspired Dickens and repeatedly cast their spell over his stories. He longed to be buried within their protection in the old cemetery of St Nicholas, once part of the castle moat:

'What a study for an antiquarian!' were the very words which fell from Mr. Pickwick's mouth, as he applied his telescope to his eye. 'Ah, fine place!' said the stranger, 'glorious pile – frowning walls, tottering arches – dark nooks – crumbling staircases.'

According to William Hughes in his *A Week's Tramp in Dickens Land,* Dickens always took his friends to see the castle and wrote most movingly of it in *Household Words* in 1851:

'I climbed the rugged staircase, stopping now and then to peep at great holes where the rafters and floors were once – bare as toothless gums now – or to enjoy glimpses of the Medway through dreary apertures like sockets without eyes; and, looking from the Castle ramparts on the Old Cathedral, and on the crumbling remains of the old Priory, and on the row of staid old red brick houses where the Cathedral dignitaries live, felt quite apologetic to the scene in general for my own juvenility and insignificance.'

'Old Cathedral too' said Mr. Jingle, in Pickwick Papers, 'earthy smell – pilgrims' feet worn away the old steps – little Saxon doors – confessionals like money takers' boxes at theatres – queer customers those monks.' The formidable strength of the castle is also described by the lawyer, Mr. Grewgious, in *The Mystery of Edwin Drood*. He peers inside:

'Dear me', said Mr Grewgious, peeping in, 'it's like looking down the throat of Old Time.' Old Time heaved a mouldy sigh from tomb and arch and vault and gloomy shadows began to deepen in corners; and damps began to rise from green patches of stone; and jewels, cast upon the pavement of the nave from stained glass by the declining sun, began to perish.'

Sketches by Boz

The *Sketches by Boz* (from 1836) were a series of journalistic essays looking at the world around Dickens. They were sometimes reflective, sometimes humorous, usually perceptive, although Dickens himself wrote critically of these first attempts at authorship: 'I am conscious of their being often extremely crude and ill considered and bearing obvious marks of haste and inexperience.'

In *The Great Winglebury Duel*, Alexander Trott is trying to avoid a duel with his rival in love, Horace Hunter. Rochester High Street, the proposed site of the duel, is described much as it is today as a 'long straggling, quiet High Street, with a great black and white clock and a small red town hall half way up – a market place – a cage – an assembly room – a church – a bridge – a chapel – a theatre – a library – an inn – a pump and a post office.'

Pickwick Papers

Published in parts from March 1836 in the *Monthly Magazine*, these were a publishing sensation. They chronicle the adventures of Samuel Pickwick who sets out from London on a journey of scientific and cultural investigation. First stop is the Medway towns and their adventures begin at the *Bull Inn* in Rochester. 'Good house – nice beds'. Originally this eighteenth century coaching inn was called the *Bull on the Hoope* but was renamed the *Royal Victoria and Bull* after the future Queen Victoria stayed there before her coronation:

'It was a long room with crimson covered benches, and wax candles in glass chandeliers. The musicians were confined in an elevated den. Two card tables were made up in the adjoining card room, and two pairs of old ladies, and a corresponding number of old gentlemen, were executing whist therein.' The ballroom, with its chandelier, remains and the Rochester Pickwick Club still meets for dinner upstairs.

The medieval stone Rochester Bridge of Mr. Pickwick's day was far removed from the road/rail constructions in existence today. This was then still the only way over the Medway into Rochester and the views it offered were spectacular; many of Dickens' characters paused upon the bridge. Mr. Pickwick:

'On either side, the banks of the Medway, covered with corn fields and pastures, with here and there a wind mill, or a distant church, stretched away as far as the eye could see, presenting a rich and varied landscape. The river reflecting the clear blue of the sky, glistened and sparkled as it flowed noiselessly on; and the oars of the fishermen dipped into the water with a clear and liquid sound.'

The new Rochester bridge, designed and built by William Cubitt, was opened on 13 August 1856 when a procession of mayors and wardens walked across the new superstructure accompanied by a Royal Marine band. This was followed by a dinner at the Corn Exchange when plans were outlined for the removal of the old bridge which had stood for hundreds of years. This was achieved in the most dramatic fashion – not by time but by gun powder. Colonel Sandham, commanding officer of the Royal Engineers, decided he would assist in the demolition by experimenting with his mining and blasting techniques. After much preliminary work by Sappers and Miners, 500 pounds of powder was deposited at the base of each pier, arch and abutment and, with a bugler sounding the signal, several thousand tons of masonry came crashing into the river. Barges were on hand to remove the surplus stone and material.

Mr. Pickwick also visited Fort Pitt (the remains of Napoleonic fortifications), The Lines, Chatham (a massive fortified network of tunnels, walls, batteries, forts and ditches, started in 1756 to protect Britain from the French), and the *Leather Bottle*, Cobham: a 'clean commodious village ale house'; the timber framed inn where Dickens stayed on several occasions. Today it has changed very little and is rich in Dickensiana.

David Copperfield

Published in 1849, this is Dickens' self-acknowledged autobiography in which David visits the City of Rochester, briefly, on his journey to Aunt Betsy Trotwood.:

'I see myself, as evening closes in, coming over the bridge at Rochester, foot sore and tired, and eating bread that I had bought for supper. One or two little houses, with the notice 'Lodgings for travelers' hanging out had tempted me; but I was afraid of spending the few pence I had, and was even more afraid of the vicious looks of the trampers I had met or over taken. I sought no shelter, therefore, but the sky; and toiling into Chatham – which in that night's aspect is a mere dream of chalk and drawbridges, and mast less ships in a muddy river, roofed like Noah's Arks – crept at last upon a sort of grass grown battery over hanging a lane, where a sentry was walking to and fro. Here I lay down near a cannon, and happy in the society of the sentry's foot steps slept soundly until morning'.

In Chatham, David tries to sell his jacket to raise funds for food. Charley, the second hand clothes dealer was an unforgettable character, known to Dickens as a boy. David also goes to St Mary's church, Chatham. Dickens sometimes attended this church as a child. His aunt Fanny was married here and there is a Weller buried in the graveyard.

Dullborough Town

Published in *All the Year Round* on 30 June 1860, *Dullborough Town* is almost a contemporary description of Rochester at the time when William Pateman was born there. In fact Dullborough is a composite portrait of the Medway Towns of Chatham, Strood and Rochester, which Dickens knew as both child and adult. Dullborough Town features in several other of his stories including 'Nurses Stories' (*All the Year Round*, 8 September 1860) and 'Birthday Celebrations' (*All the Year Round*, 6 June 1863).

In *Dullborough Town* (reprinted in *The Uncommercial Traveller*), Dickens makes the painful discovery that nothing matches the memory of the child. He meets the old greengrocer who had figured so largely in his young life – to find that his hero has long forgotten him: 'I had no right, I reflected, to be angry with the greengrocer for his want of interest; I was nothing to him: whereas he was the town, the cathedral, the bridge, the river, my childhood, and a large slice of my life, to me.' He also returns to the cornfields where he had played, only to find:

'The station had swallowed up the playing field. I looked in again over the low wall at the scene of departed glories. Here, in the haymaking time, had I been delivered from the dungeons of Seringapatam, an immense pile (of haycock) by my countrymen, the victorious British (boy next door and his two cousins) and had been recognized with ecstacy by my affianced one (Miss Green) who had come all the way from England (second house in the terrace) to ransom and marry me. There was no comfort in the theatre. It was mysteriously gone, like my own youth.

Of course the town had shrunk fearfully since I was a child there. I had entertained the impression that the High Street was at least as wide as Regent Street, London, or the Italian Boulevard at Paris. I found it little better than a lane. There was a public clock in it, which I had supposed to be the finest clock in the world; whereas it now turned out to be as inexpressive, moon faced, weak a clock as ever I saw. It belonged to a town hall, a mean little brick heap, like a demented chapel, with a few yawning persons in leather gaiters, in the last extremity for something to do, lounging at the door with their hands in their pockets, and calling themselves a Corn Exchange!

Ah, who was I that I should quarrel with the town for being changed to me, when I, myself, had come back so changed to it! All my early readings and imaginations dated from this place and I took them away, so full of innocent construction and guileless belief, and I brought them back so worn and torn, so much the wiser and so much the worse.'

When Dickens was a boy Chatham Dockyard was brimming over with energy and action, for the Royal Navy was being overhauled and refitted for the great and glorious days of Victorian expansion.

Great Expectations

Published in parts from 1860, this book belongs almost entirely to Rochester. It was to the Guildhall in Rochester High Street that Pip came with Joe Gargery, to be articled as an apprentice:

'The hall was a queer place I thought, with higher pews in it than a church – and mighty Justices leaning back in chairs, with folded arms, or taking snuff, or going to sleep, or writing, or reading the newspapers and with some shining black portraits on the walls, which my unartistic eye regarded as a composition of hardbake and sticking plaster. There, in a corner my indentures were duly signed and attested, and I was 'bound'.

The timber framed building directly across the High Street from Eastgate House was the home of Pip's Uncle Pumblechook. The premises were, said Pip: 'of a peppercorny and farinaceous character, as the premises of a corn chandler and seeds man should be.' High up, between the window of Pip's attic where he complains of its 'sloping roof which was so low in the corner where the bedstead was, that I calculated the tiles as being within a foot of my eyelashes'.

The Satis House in Great Expectations is, confusingly, not the actual Satis House in Bakers Walk now used by the King's School, but the impressive red brick Restoration House in Crow Lane. Dickens, as he so often did, simply transposed the names. There is a small guest house recently re-named the *Blue Boar* on Rochester High Street. But when the young Pip was treated to a slap-up meal after being bound as an apprentice, it was the *Bull Inn*, now the *Royal and Victoria and Bull*, not the *Blue Boar* which Dickens described as the scene of their celebration.

The Mystery of Edwin Drood

Edwin Drood was conceived as a short novel to be published in twelve parts. Dickens had just written the last part of the sixth installment when he died in June 1870. The book is set in London and in Cloisterham – Rochester, where, at the time, one Edwin Trood was landlord of Dickens' local public house, the *Falstaff Inn* at Gad's Hill:

'An ancient city Cloisterham, and no meet dwelling place for any one with hankerings after the noisy world. A monotonous, silent city, deriving an earthy flavor throughout from its Cathedral crypt, and so abounding in vestiges of monastic graves that the Cloisterham children grow small salad in the dust of abbots and abbesses.

A brilliant morning shines on the old city. Its antiquities and ruins are surpassingly beautiful, with the lusty ivy gleaming in the sun, and the rich trees waving in the balmy air. Changes of glorious light from moving boughs, songs of birds, scents from gardens, woods penetrate into the cathedral, subdue its earthly odor, and preach the Resurrection and the Life.'

Eastgate House, 'a venerable brick edifice', is now the Dickens Centre. Dickens knew Eastgate House as a girl's school and in *Edwin Drood* it became the Nuns' House, Miss Twinkleton's Seminary for Young Ladies. Dickens renamed Minor Canon Row, Minor Canon Corner. It remains a backwater of nineteenth century terraced homes for church officials, sheltered behind the cathedral. It was here that the Reverend Septimus Crisparkle lived with his mother, celebrated for her wonderful home made pickles, jams, biscuits and cordials:

'Minor Canon Corner was a quiet place in the shadow of the cathedral, which the cawing of the rooks, the echoing footsteps of rare passers, the sound of the cathedral bell, or the role of the cathedral organ, seemed to render more quiet than absolute silence'.

The lopsided gatehouse, home to Mr. John Jasper, was one of the old monastery precinct gates. It is now known as Chertsey's Gate and is a private house. At other times it has been known as Cemetery Gate and College Gate. Neighbor to Mr. Jasper was Mr. Tope, chief verger and showman, 'accustomed to be very high with excursion parties.' His wife waited on Mr. Jasper and let out rooms in his house when they were needed. Tope's House is now a restaurant.

Dickens places the home of Auctioneer, Mr. Thomas Sapsea, 'the purest jackass in Cloisterham' in the same premises as Uncle Pumblechook in *Great Expectations.* Today it is an estate agents. Dickens commented that the building had been modernized over the years as people found that they 'preferred air and light to fever and plague.' Behind the Cathedral is The Vines. It was formerly a vineyard and is today a pleasant open space in the heart of the city. The path which intersects it with gates at either end is where Edwin sauntered with Rosa Bud as they discussed their future (or not) together.

The Seven Poor Travelers

Every year between 1850 and 1867 Dickens wrote a Christmas Story for *Household Words* and for *All the Year Round*. Of all the Christmas Stories, *The Seven Poor Travelers* has the greatest meaning for Rochester. Early in 1854 Dickens had visited Richard Watts Charity in the High Street and signed the visitor's book. The story he then wrote for the Christmas edition of *Household Words* describes the experience of a traveler arriving in Rochester on Christmas Eve.

The old building has barely changed from Dickens' own description of his stay there. The plaque above the door still reads: 'Richard Watts, Esquire, by his Will dated 2 August 1579 this Charity for Six Poor Travelers, who, not being Rogues or Proctors, May receive gratis for one Night Lodging, Entertainment, and Four pence each.'

Having decided that he was neither rogue nor proctor, the traveler knocks. The real life matron, Mrs. Clackett, described as 'a decent body of wholesome matronly appearance' was, according to William Hughes in his *Week's Tramp in Dickens-Land*, 'very much astonished' to find herself in the story. Dickens, the seventh poor traveler, writes:

'I found it to be a clean white house, of a staid and venerable air with choice little low lattice windows and a roof of three gables. I found the party to be thus composed. Firstly, myself. Secondly, a very decent man indeed, with his right arm in a sling, who had a certain clean agreeable smell of wood about him, from which I judged him to have something to do with shipbuilding. Thirdly, a little sailor boy, a mere child, with a profusion of rich dark brown hair, and deep womanly-looking eyes. Fourthly, a shabby genteel personage in a threadbare black suit, and apparently in very bad circumstances, with a dry suspicious look; the absent buttons on his waistcoat eked out with red tape; and a bundle of extraordinarily tattered papers sticking out of an inner breast pocket. Fifthly, a foreigner by birth, but an Englishman in speech, who carried his pipe in the band of his hat, and lost no time in telling me, in an easy, simple, engaging way, that he was a watchmaker from Geneva, and traveled all about the Continent, mostly on foot, working as a journeyman, and seeing new countries, - possibly (I thought) also smuggling a watch or so, now and then. Sixthly, a little widow, who had been very pretty and was still very young, but whose beauty had been wrecked in some great misfortune, and whose manner was remarkably timid, scared, and solitary. Seventh, and lastly, a Traveler of a kind familiar to my boyhood, but now almost obsolete, - a Book Pedlar, who had a quantity of Pamphlets and Numbers with him, and who presently boasted that he could repeat more verses in an evening than he could sell in a twelvemonth.'

The seventh poor traveler treated the other guests of Watts Charity to a first class Christmas dinner of roast turkey, beef and plum pudding, carried in procession up the High Street from *The Bull*.

Mercy Reynolds

On 2 April 1871 William was living with his family in an old barn on a brick field at Becks Lane, Farnborough, Kent. Some time after 1871, William 'married' Mercy Reynolds, who was baptized at All Saints church, Orpington, on 26 August 1855. Her father was George Reynolds and her mother was Charlotte Busby. Her brother, George Reynolds, was married to Mary Pateman; her sister, Jane Reynolds, was married to James Pateman.

William and Mercy's first two children, Mary (1876) and Henry (1880) were born in Crockenhill, Kent. It is likely that William was working on the land at Crockenhill, which was well known for growing peppermint. On 3 April 1881 William was living in a 'van on side of Orpington Lane, Farnborough, Kent' with Mercy and their two children. William's next child, Noah, was born in 1883 in a 'house cart' at Locks Bottom. William stayed in the Locks Bottom / Farnborough area for the birth of Walter (1886) and Alice (1889). In 1890 William is listed in the *Strong Directory* as living at Stow Cottages, Farnborough. The story of Walter Pateman has been told in *Seven Steps to Glory: Private Pateman goes to War* (2002).

On 5 April 1891 William was living at Church Road, Farnborough, with his wife and five children. His remaining children, Phoebe (1892), William (1894) and Amy (1896) were born at Stow Cottages. On 31 March 1901 William was living in Cobden Road, Farnborough, with his wife and five children. Also living with him were his son in law, Elias Lewis (married to Mary Pateman) and their four year old son, Charles Lewis. In the 1902 *Bush Directory* William is still listed as living at 4 Cobden Road. Sometime after 1902, William moved to Chislehurst Road, Orpington.

William was variously described as a pedlar, beehive maker, hawker, agricultural laborer, general laborer, laborer and farm laborer. 'Laborer' was a vague description and could refer to bricklayers, carpenter's assistants, agricultural workers or any casual employee. William Pateman died on 24 October 1921 at Chislehurst Road. He was a 65 year old general laborer and the cause of death was pleurisy and bronchitis. The informant was 'A. Lee, daughter, 4 Broadway, St Mary Cray'. This was Alice Pateman, wife of Jesse Lee. William Pateman was buried at All Saints churchyard, Orpington, on 29 October 1921: 'In Memory of William Pateman, Died October 24th 1921, Aged 65, At Rest.'

Mercy Pateman is listed in the *Kelly's Directory for Bromley* as living at Chislehurst Road from 1924 until 1928. From 1929 the address changes to 61 Chislehurst Road, where Mercy resided until her death. The Electoral Register for 1938-39 and 1939-40 lists Mercy Pateman and Tom Reynolds at 61 Chislehurst Road. Mercy Pateman died on 3 January 1940 at County Hospital, Farnborough, Kent. She was 84 years old and the cause of death was 'broncho pneumonia, following fractured ribs due to a fall in the street (9 days). No PM. Misadventure.' Mercy was buried on 9 January 1940 at All Saints Churchyard, in the same grave as William, although her name was not added to his headstone. The story of William Pateman and his life in Farnborough is told in the next volume of this family history - *Tugmutton Common : the life and times of William Pateman and his family.*

Mary Ann Pateman (1852-1929)

Mary Ann Pateman (1852-1929) = George Reynolds (1853-1937)
- John (1875-?)
- George (1877-?)

- James (1879-?)
- Thomas (1880-1964)
- Elvy (1888-?)

Robert's next child, Mary Ann Pateman, was born in 1852 at Westwood in Kent.

Westwood

According to *Kelly's Directory* (1852): 'Westwood is a very pretty village three and a half miles south of Gravesend, with a number of gentlemen's seats and private houses. Here are the noted gardens called Spring Head from which most of the market gardeners obtain water cresses for the London market. The place is much frequented by the visitors of Gravesend, being well supplied with fruit. The area of the parish is 2340 acres and its total population 667'. A later edition of *Kelly's Directory* (1866) added: 'This is a fruit growing district. The population in 1861 was 717'. So Robert may have been in the area for the fruit picking.

As we have said before, another typical Gypsy occupation was hop picking; on 26 October 1853 thirty hop pickers, including 16 from one family, were drowned when the wagon in which they were returning from a day's work in the hop gardens toppled over the side of a bridge into the River Medway at Hartlake near Tudeley. They were swept into the murky torrent, running exceptionally fast at the time because of heavy rains.

The wagon, drawn by two horses – one in front of the other – was fully loaded with pickers from London and Ireland. Some were sitting on the sides and back and others supported each other as it jolted towards the bridge in gathering gloom around 6pm. The lead horse went over the crest of the bridge and was nearing the steep gradient on the other side when the horse behind stumbled, causing a wagon wheel to swerve against the boarded side of the bridge. As the bridge gave way those sitting on the sides and back were able to jump off. The others, screaming frantically, were thrown into the river and swept down stream.

Customers at the *Bell Inn*, Golden Green, some distance away heard the cries for help and joined those who were already trying to rescue the victims with their hop poles. A few were saved in this way but of the 41 on the wagon there were only 11 survivors. All of those who died were 'strangers' – people who came 'hopping down in Kent' every year and took advantage of the cheap fares which were offered by the railway companies. They had been working at Cox's Farm on the Hadlow side of the Medway and after a long working day – it had begun at dawn – were returning to their seasonal camp on the Tudeley side.

The waggoner on this fateful journey was John Waghorn. Having collected up the ten bushel sacks of hops and taken them to the oast house to be dried, he returned for the pickers. First to travel were villagers who lived on the other side of the river; men who worked on the farm and those who enjoyed earning extra money during the picking season. He returned for the 'strangers'. As they reached the approach to the timber bridge at Hartlake, Waghorn knew that flood water lay some two feet deep so he climbed onto the back of the lead horse. The bridge, belonging to the Medway Navigation Company, had a three feet closed board fence on either side and metal rungs on the decking. It was in poor condition but nobody had bothered to report this to the Company.

The second horse slipped on the decking and the bridge just collapsed. All through the night people with lanterns looked in vain for more survivors. By first light in the morning they realised that 30 had died including 16 members of the Leatherland family from the Rosemary Lane area of London. Several others were Irish Gypsies. They were buried in Hadlow church yard and a memorial was later placed there to remember them

Cholera

Cholera, the 'terrifying visitor', returned to Kent with a vengeance in 1854 (it had last visited in 1832). Cholera, which killed so many soldiers in the Crimea, also swept through Canterbury, Greenwich, Sheerness, Maidstone, Sevenoaks, Milton and Tunbridge Wells. During a two month period 2,914 diarrhoea cases were treated by Chatham dispensary and there were almost 2,000 cases in the 30 parishes of the Eastry Union.

A London physician, Dr John Snow, believed cholera was spread by contaminated water and to prove his point he removed the handle from a public pump in Soho. No one could drink from that source and there were fewer fatalities in that part of London. Not everyone accepted his ideas. Most people believed that the disease had spread from the Orient killing tens of thousands in Europe alone.
The most telling outbreak in Kent was at Sandgate where, to the consternation of all inhabitants, improvements were made to drainage and water supply. Sanitary reformers discovered that the drainage system was deficient and drains were blocked and leaking. It appeared that all private water supplies were polluted.

Meanwhile, there were reports of more and more cases across Kent, including 170 in Tonbridge, which coincided with 900 cases of dysentery. Cholera also penetrated far into the Kent countryside to places as remote as High Halden and Staplehurst. The Canterbury dispensary took a lead by supplying free medicines. Folkestone gave out handbills to the poor urging them to accept free treatment.

On 2 April 1871 Mary Ann (20, Westwood) was living with her family in an old barn on a brick field at Becks Lane, Bechenham, Kent. In 1872 (according to the 1911 Census) she left her family and 'married' George Reynolds. As was noted in the previous chapter, there were close links between the Patemans and the Reynolds, another Gypsy family. George was the son of George Reynolds and Charlotte Busby. They had six children: John (1835), Alice (1843), Louisa (1846), Elvy (1847), George (1853, Ightham, Kent), Mercy (1855, who married William Pateman) and Jane (1856, who married James Pateman).

George Reynolds was born on 4 May 1853 at the Common, Ightham, Kent. His father was a hawker and his mother's name was given as 'Charlotte Reynolds, formerly Jones'.

Mary Ann and George had five children that we know of (given the long gaps between some of the births they may have had more children who were unrecorded or who died in infancy): John (1875, Farnborough, Kent), George (1877, Bromley, Kent), James (1879, Farnborough, Kent), Thomas, 1880 (Sidcup, Kent), Elvy (1888, Farnborough). This suggests that the family traveled around a relatively small part of northwest Kent.

On 3 April 1881 Mary Ann Pateman was were living in a 'van in Piggendens Lane, Farnborough, Kent'. William Pateman and George's sister, Mercy Reynolds, were living in a neighboring van. George's brother, John Reynolds, was living on Bastard Green, Farnborough, close to James Pateman and George's sister, Jane Reynolds.

On 5 April 1891 Mary Ann was living at Tugmutton, Farnborough, close to James Pateman and John Reynolds. William Pateman was living in Church Road, Farnborough.

On 31 March 1901 Mary Ann was still living at Tugmutton, close to John Reynolds and James Pateman. Another George Reynolds (son of John) was living at Worlegs Hole, Farnborough, with his wife Margaret (27, Somerset – which provides a link with Robert Pateman's wife, Mary Ann Enis, also born in Somerset) and their three children. William Pateman was living in Cobden Road, Farnborough.

In 1911 George Reynolds (64, general farm labourer, Farnborough) was living at 4 Willow Walk, Farnborough with his wife Mary Ann (65, Farnborough). They had been married for 39 years.

So Mary Ann and George made a similar journey to the rest of the Pateman and Reynolds families: after a life on the road, traveling, and living in tents and then vardos, they made the move into bricks and mortar in Farnborough, Kent at the turn of the twentieth century. By 1911 there were two groups of Patemans and three groups of Reynolds living in the Tugmutton area. Their story is told in the next volume of this family history, *Tugmutton Common: the life and times of William Pateman*.

Mary Ann Pateman died on 14 May 1929, aged 78 years, at 3 Willow Walk, Farnborough. She was the wife of George Reynolds, farm laborer. The cause of death was cerebral haemorrhage. The informant was E. Chisholm (Elvy), daughter, present at the death, 44 Magpie Hall Lane, Bromley. Mary Ann was buried at St Giles, Farnborough.

George Reynolds died on 28 October 1937, aged 84 years, at Farnborough Hospital. He was a general labourer of 3 Willow Walk, Farnborough. The cause of death was senility (myocarditis) and arthritis. The informant was G. Reynolds, son, 4 Willow Walk. George was buried in the same grave as his wife. Their son, Thomas Reynolds, died on 18 June 1964 aged 83 and was also buried in the same grave.

Elizabeth Pateman (1852-1916)

Elizabeth Pateman (1852-1916) = Henry Taylor (1854-1927)
- Henry (1880)
- Walter (1882-1938)

- Amy (1884)
- Caroline (1886-1951)
- Alice (1892)

Sometime after the birth of Mary at Westwood in 1851, Robert headed east, to Burham, where Elizabeth Pateman was born on 13 November 1852. On her birth certificate she was named 'Betsy Pateman', her father was a 'labourer', and her mother was 'Mary Pateman, formerly Enis'.

Burham

There is a very contemporary account of Burham in the 1855 *Kelly's Directory*: 'Burham is in the lathe of Aylesford, West Kent, on the banks of the navigable Medway and foot of the chalk range, 5 miles north west of Maidstone and south west of Rochester and 37 from London. Its area is 1,737 acres and its population 518.' A later *Post Office Directory* added: 'The Aylesford brick, tile and pottery works are partly in this parish. The chief crops are wheat, beans, barley and hops.'

Here we find hops and hods, both of which may have attracted Robert Pateman into the area – also cement. Burham moved inland about a mile during the nineteenth century, after whatever prosperity it had enjoyed stopped coming from its river frontage and began to be provided by chalk quarrying for the new cement works.

From very small beginnings, Burham grew rapidly to house a population of about 500 in 1851 and almost 2,000 by 1900. It was during this period of growth that the twelfth century waterside church of St Mary the Virgin became too small and too distant and a rather grand new one was built, for the 'new' village. It lasted less than a hundred years, however, and was declared unsafe and demolished in 1980. The old one, down by the waterside, is still standing and was restored in 1956 after being disused for many years.

Today, St Mary's church is officially 'redundant' and cared for by the Churches Conservation Trust and both Church of England and Methodist worshippers share the unobtrusive little nineteenth century church in Church Street. One of the curiosities of the old churchyard used to be a memorial stone, now lost, with a twisted face on it and the words:

'Behold Burham's Belle, a delight
With her curls asymmetric and tight;
Let us hope that her Biz
Was as straight as her Phiz
And she kept, like her nose, to the right.'

Great Culland House lasted from 1592 until 1953 and then it was pulled down. The French Ambassador to Elizabeth I stayed in it to be near his friend Sir Walter Raleigh, who was staying at nearby Aylesford Priory. The old house, though gone, is not forgotten, nor will it be while the great donkey powered wooden treadmill which used to draw water from the nearby well remains preserved outside Maidstone Museum.

A more recent memorial to a more ancient event is the rag stone monument on the bank of the River Medway close to the old church. The inscription reads: 'This stone commemorates the battle of the Medway, AD43, when a Roman army crossed the river and defeated the British tribes under Caractacus.' It was possibly the most decisive battle of the Roman invasion and opened the way for the Roman conquest of Britain. The idea of marking the spot in this way came from the author Nigel Nicolson of Sissinghurst Castle.

Henry Taylor

On 2 April 1871 Elizabeth, (16, Burham) was living with her family in an old barn on a brick field at Becks Lane, Bechenham, Kent. Some time after 1871 she left her family and married Henry Taylor, who was born at Malden, Surrey, in 1854. They had five children Henry (1880), Walter (1882), Amy (1884), Caroline (1886) and Alice (1892)

On 3 April 1881 Elizabeth (26, Maidstone) was living in Acre Road, Kingston on Thames, Surrey, with Henry and their son, Henry Taylor (1, Oakingham, Surrey). Elizabeth was 35 when she had her first child. Henry junior died sometime between 1881-91.

Amy Taylor was born on 14 April 1884 and was baptised on 17 May 1886 at Hillingdon, Middlesex, with her sister Caroline. Her father was a commercial traveller.

Caroline Taylor was born on 29 January 1886 and was baptised on 17 May 1886 at Hillingdon, Middlesex, with her sister Amy. Her father was a commercial traveller.

In 1891 Henry (32, general dealer, Surrey, Malling) and Elizabeth (37, Gravesend, Kent) were living in two caravans and a tent at Inwood Road, Isleworth with their children Walter (9, Egham, Surrey), Amy (7, Wanstead, Essex) and Caroline (5, Islington, Middlesex). Alice was born sometime after 1891.

Henry's father, Joseph (71, travelling showman, Bushey, Hertfordshire) was living nearby in 2 caravans with his son Albert Taylor (45, horse dealer, Putney, Surrey) and granddaughter Mary Clark (17, housekeeper, Norbiton, Surrey).

George Taylor (34, horse dealer, Egham, Surrey) was living with his wife Ellen (28, Middlesex, Brentford) in a nearby caravan.

In 1901 Henry (42, general hawker) and Elizabeth (43, Bromley, Kent) were living at White Bear Field, Heston, Middlesex with Walter (19), Amy (17), Caroline (15), and Alice (9). Henry's father Joseph (81, general hawker) was also living in White Bear Field, as was Henry's brother Alfred (42, general hawker, Stanmore, Middlesex) and his family.

In 1911 Henry (59, showman) and Elizabeth (59, assisting in the business, Dartford, Kent) were still White Bear Field but only Alice (19, assisting in the business) was still living at home. They also had 2 'traveller's servants'. Henry's son, Walter (30, travelling showman) and family were also living in White Bear Field as was Henry's brother Albert (61, showman) and his wife, and Henry's brother Alfred (51, traveller to all fairs showman) with his family.

Elizabeth Taylor died on 10 March 1916 aged 58 and was buried in Hounslow Cemetery.

Irene Colbert informed me that 'Henry Taylor was a son of my x2 grandfather Joseph Taylor who married Henrietta Ayres on 13 March 1871. Joseph was a son of Jeremiah Taylor (basket maker) and Sarah Fisher. Emma Taylor, Henrys sister, was my great grandmother. Emma's daughter Rose married Joseph Manning (of Manning's fairs).'

Irene sent me a copy of Caroline Taylor's birth certificate. Caroline was born on 29 January 1886 in a van in the Agricultural Hall, Liverpool Road, Islington. Her father was a hawker and her mother was Elizabeth Taylor, formerly Pateman.

Irene also sent me: a photo of her mum; photos of Henry's sisters Emma and Elizabeth; the marriage certificate of Joseph Taylor (basket maker) and Henrietta Ayres; the death certificate of Joseph Taylor (general dealer) who died on 2 March 1902 at White Bear Meadow, Heston, Middlesex. His son Henry was present at the death, caused by chronic bronchitis and gout.

In August 2011 Irene sent me a photo of the grave of 'Mary & Joseph Taylor, died 1889 & 1902. Proud to be born Travelling People. Chimney Sweep to Windsor Castle.' This small monument attracted my attention on a previous visit to Hounslow. Since then I have been told by descendants of Henry Taylor who still live on the site known as Station Estate Feltham this is Henry's parents Joseph and Henrietta Frances Ayres. My first thought was yes the date for Joseph's death is correct as per his death certificate. I know from Census Henrietta was alive on 1881 census and Joseph was calling himself a widow by 1891 so this ties in. Then the name Mary I know Henrietta was maybe not her real name I use it because it's the one on their marriage certificate I have found her known as Martha and Hannah in records. More difficult as the space for father is blank on marriage certificate. She always maintained on census born Alton Hampshire and I know Hampshire is where a great many Ayres family hail from. Then what of chimney sweep. When Jeremiah Taylor was killed in the fight on Wimbledon Common 1831 his wife Sarah (Fisher) and her children went straight into Putney Workhouse. I also knew she sent her son Plato Taylor to her family (chimney sweeps) in Bushey Herts. I have recently found these references on the Apprentice List for Surrey History Centre:

- Nathanial Taylor to Ed Childs Bushey 1823 (before the event)
- Plato Taylor to Thomas Fisher Bushey 1831
- Joseph Taylor to Thomas Keyte of New Windsor. 1832

Jeremiah and Sarah had children of these names. The small stone looks like it was an addition placed at sometime later. So maybe I am now looking at the name Mary. I have sent for a couple of death certificates both incorrect.'

Henry Taylor died on 12 February 1927, aged 73, at Hounslow Hospital, Heston. He was a Showman of 124 Bedfont Lane, Feltham. The cause of death was enlargement of prostate and pyelitis. The informant was Walter Taylor, son, present at the death.

Henry's obituary appeared on Saturday 26 February 1927 in *The World's Fair*, the weekly newspaper for fairground people. First published in 1904 and still going strong today, *The Worlds Fair* contains valuable biographical information in the form of birth, marriage and death notices and obituaries, useful pointers to when and where fairs were held plus 'business' news in the shape of articles and advertisements. Gypsy families who were associated with fairgrounds are often included.

A photo of Henry appeared under the caption 'Famous Showmen Pass Away': 'The late Mr Henry Taylor, whose death we reported last week, was one of the most popular showmen in the London district and at his funeral on Monday last remarkable expressions of sympathy were shown. An obituary notice and a report of the funeral will be found in this issue.'

Obituary

The obituary was by Tom Norman: 'Impressive scene at the funeral of Mr Harry Taylor. During the last 35 years I have been present at a considerable number of showmen and travellers funerals in all parts of the country but never yet have I been present at such a beautiful ceremony as I witnessed on Monday at the funeral of the last remains of my dear old much admired pal and friend of 45 years' standing Mr H Taylor. On alighting from the station at Feltham I was somewhat bewildered at the crowds of persons standing in silent respect outside their houses and shops along each side of the streets and at every other vacant space leading to the ground and home belonging to the deceased gentleman.

On arriving on the ground the sun shining beautifully with royal and spring like weather, I shall never forget the sight that I beheld, where hundreds of the best known men and women travellers were congregated together to pay their last tribute to one whom they had loved, admired and respected. Knowing my old pal and friend the long number of years I have done I knew that he was held in unquestionable high esteem and respect by all he ever came in contact with, but that respect was far from my comprehension which was evident by the hundreds of those present from miles around.

And what an impressive and sympathetic crowd it was. The arrangements for the funeral and the procession were most grand and well conducted in every detail. I counted no less than 14 carriages in the procession, each carriage being literally covered with floral tributes, which in the beautiful sunlit spring day has left an everlasting impression upon my mind. One floral emblem among the large number of others which impressed me as being a most touching and appropriate one for the occasion was a perfect model of a set of swings in beautiful flowers of various colours with our late friends name and address along the top. There were scores of others, all probably as touching and effective as this one, but my heart was too full at intervals, of one minute joy and the next minute emotion to notice the others and there were numbers of others present who were experiencing the same feeling.

Dear old Harry once placed his hand on my shoulder saying "Tom, old man, I don't think I have an enemy in the world." And I could readily believe him. But oh if only he could have seen the number of friends, sympathisers and others his doubts, if any, would have soon been set at rest. I could go on describing this interesting, beautiful and impressive ceremony to a considerable length further, but no doubt a full, detailed account will be found elsewhere in these pages. Anyhow, what a glorious feeling of satisfaction, gratification and consolation of knowing that such is the case of the life of him apart from death. He lived as he died, respected by all who knew him. May he rest in peace. Sleep on, dear Harry, sleep on!'

Funeral

'The funeral of the late Mr Henry Taylor of Feltham, Middlesex, took place at Hounslow cemetery on Monday amid scenes that were most impressive, for almost the whole of the route to the cemetery was lined with people, workmen on buildings stopped in their work, laid down their tools and uncovered their heads until the whole of the cortege had passed, for the grand old man was loved and respected by all, old and young.

The road leading to and from the cemetery was impassable, motor cars, pony traps and carts of every description, and the people present could be counted by thousands, and many had come many miles. The cream of Show life were at the grave, in fact everyone seemed to be present so great was the crowd. Also present were notable tradesmen of Hounslow and Feltham, men in every trade and calling known in every position in life. The floral tributes were most wonderful, flowers that were glorious. One that drew much attention was a set of swings in flowers.

The coffin was conveyed by open hearse, drawn by four horses and was covered with flowers. Eleven coaches filled with mourners followed. The principal mourners were: Amy Ott (daughter), Walter Taylor (son), Carrie Guess (daughter), Alice Daly (daughter), Albert Taylor (brother), Mrs E. Kefford (sister), Freddy Guess (grandson), Arthur Ott (grandson)'.

Other mourners included Louisa and Charles Thatcher (aka Lee) and J. Reynolds and family. Quite a few of the same people came to Charles Lee's funeral, including Henry's daughter's, Amy and Alice.

Elizabeth and Henry were buried in the same grave at Hounslow Cemetery along with the following

- Caroline Guess (daughter) died 1 June 1951 aged 63
- Walter (son) died 24 August 1938 aged 57
- Mary Ann (daughter in law, wife of Walter) died 22 December 1940 aged 60 formerly Mary Ann Thomas marriage Brentford 1902

Another family grave contains Henry and Elizabeth's daughter Alice and her husband David Daly together with their daughter Margaret and husband John Gratton. I believe Margaret was a writer.

Henry's sister Emma's (1858-1944) grave (Irene's great grandmother) has a new stone which was placed in 2010 and since Irene first visited with her mother as a young girl this is the third headstone to be place. Her memory lives on. Buried with her is her son Albert Smith died the year Irene was born 1949. Why he is not with his wife Emily (Pickett) I can only guess she outlived him by many years and Irene's mum says her Uncle Albert was a difficult man.... I think she was being polite.

Directly behind Emma and Albert's grave (old stone) is another son of her eldest child Edward born 1878 and his wife Annie (Wass).

There are many Taylor members buried in this cemetery which contains many Showmen / Gypsy / Traveller graves and some of them are very elaborate with pictures of roundabouts, etc:

- Elizabeth Clark (12 August 1923, aged 75), the sister of Henry Taylor. She was born in 1850 and married William Clark, a Hawker of Hampshire.
- Elizabeth's daughter, Mary Manning (November 1931, aged 58) and her son in law John Manning (1946, aged 71) are also in the family grave.

Irene contacted me again in July 2011: 'I have been loaned a box of documents, the property of Henry Taylor's daughter Amy who married Arthur Ott. The items belong to "young Arthur Ott" who asked me to archive and sort them for him. Lots of mice droppings and many in poor condition as they have been stored in "one of the loads". Mr Ott allowed me to take copies of anything of interest to me and gave permission for me to share these with you. There are many photos, unknown to the present owner. Amy had written on several, unfortunately in pencil. What I know I will send. I have scanned a great many in the hope someone, sometime, will know who they are.' These photos and documents included:

- Henry Taylor with his family
- Postcard to Mr Henry Taylor at Pleasure Fair Ground, High Barnet dated 4 September 1911 from the Royal London Opthalmic Hospital, (Moorfields Eye Hospital), City Road, EC: 'In patient Henry Taylor having been discharged by the Medical Staff it is desired that he be sent for on Tuesday the 5th of September at 2 o'clock.'
- Henry Taylor burial
- Henry & Elizabeth Taylor's grave
- From Amy Taylor (Ott) with love to Arthur
- Amy Taylor (Ott) in old age
- Alice Taylor Daly, daughter of Henry & Elizabeth Taylor, who married David P. Daly
- Betty & Margaret Daly, daughter of Alice Taylor & David P. Daly
- Margaret Daly & John Gratton on their wedding day
- Plans of the Royal Agricultural Hall, London for the New World's Fair 1935 – 'Your space is marked with a X.'
- Rules & Regulations for the New World's Fair, Royal Agricultural Hall, London, December 24th 1934 to January 18th 1935.

Irene also sent me some photos of 'Alice Elizabeth Ott daughter of Amy and Arthur granddaughter of Henry and Elizabeth. Alice is with her brother in law she married Henry Rowe. I am told the floods were at Billingham near Catford 1930s. The photograph appeared in a Daily Newspaper. I found old Pathe news for this if you go to web-site and search fairground flood you will see where this photo came from.

Alice Elizabeth and her husband Henry Rowe are also buried at Hounslow. Their grave is next to Albert Cooper and his sister Rosie who were children of Emma's daughter Jane Smith who married George Cooper (grandson of Matthias Cooper Royal Rat Catcher) so great niece and nephew of Henry and Elizabeth. Again Rosie and Albert both lived at Station Estate Feltham. Every time I go I find something new I must pitch a tent next time.

The Cooper connection to Matthias comes in yet again. Henry Taylor had another brother Elias born 1845 in Kent. Elias married Louisa Cooper daughter of another son of Matthias named Francis. The witness, Alfred Taylor was another brother of these two and the youngest. He married Jane Olive whose father was a London Gunsmith. The other witness to this marriage was I am sure the Genty Cooper who married yet another brother George Taylor although what happened to her I have yet to find out. George went on to live with a woman named Ellen and is buried with her in Hounslow. George, later in life, married Rebecca Stroud widow of John Stroud whose father was William Biddle of circus fame. Rebecca's brother used to tie her to a moving board, spin it around and throw knives at the board. It's very odd that no mention of this marriage appears in the Biddle Family History Book, I have the certificate. When George died Rebecca buried him in with Ellen. Perhaps this was one of those best kept secrets because I'm sure that the World's Fair funeral write up on George states that he had a widow with no mention of her name but the presence of other Biddles. Three of Elias's sons were known as the Wardrobe Boys and busked around London pubs. I am told this was because they sold wardrobes - I believe this was a term for a person selling second hand clothes. Elias and Louisa are buried close to Henry and Elizabeth in unmarked grave. Likewise George and Ellen are buried close to Henry and Elizabeth.

My greatest fear is water must be to do with x3 grandmother Sarah Taylor drowning in the Hartlake Bridge Disaster of 1853. The Green Silk Dress by Marie Cross lists those who were killed including Thomas Taylor (38), Sarah Taylor (55), and Thomas Taylor (4) who were killed and Emily & Nathaniel Taylor who were saved. The authors notes includes: 'Descendents of these Gypsies are still alive and there is a letter from the great, great granddaughter of Emily Taylor in the archives in Tonbridge library.'

Perhaps at the time you wrote of the Fatal Fight on Wimbledon Common in your book Hoo Hops and Hods you were not aware that Jeremiah was the husband of Sarah Fisher and they were both the grandparents of Henry Taylor. Sarah Thomas and son Thomas three generations of one family. In 1848 Jeremiah and Sarah's son Plato married at Hadlow Church - little did he know a few years later he would be burying his mother at the same church.'

Henry Pateman (1856-1858)

After the birth of Elizabeth, Robert Pateman headed north, to Frindsbury and the Hoo Peninsula, where Henry Pateman was born on 10 October 1856 in Snatts Lane. Robert's occupation was given as 'agricultural labourer' and it seems likely that he stayed in the area to pick fruit, vegetables and hops. Henry was baptized on 19 October at Frindsbury, and his father was a labourer.

Frindsbury

Hasted, in his *History of Kent* (1797), says of Frindsbury: 'The parish joins the River Medway from Strood, along the shore opposite Chatham Dock, where on a hill, is a house called Quarry House, having a beautiful view over the river, the Town, Dockyard and adjoining country.'

In 1840 the parish map was produced. The Tithe Assessment of the parish had been carried out the year before and no doubt the farmers thought a detailed map would allow them to check assessed acreages more accurately. The overall size of the parish was 3,600 acres of which 2,726 were subject to tithe. This was made up of 770 acres of pasture and meadow, 46 acres of private gardens, 140 acres of woodlands, 56 acres of hop gardens and market gardens, 34 acres of orchard and fruit plantations and 160 acres of building, public roads, river creeks, quarries, wharfs, canals, fortifications and wasteland.

Bagshaw's *History, Gazetteer and Directory of the County of Kent* (1847): 'Frindsbury in the south east corner of the Shamwell Hundred contains 3,549 acres, 125 of which are in hop cultivation with 140 acres of woodland. In 1831 there were 1856 people living in the parish and rateable value was £8,500.'

Kelly's Directory (1855): 'Anciently called Aeslingham, Frindsbury was given in the 8th century to Rochester Cathedral by Offa the Great, Kin of Mercia and Sigered, King of Kent. Frindsbury church, dedicated to all saints, is ancient, the chancel in particular. The living is a vicarage in the gift of the bishop of Rochester. The Strood terminus of the North Kent Railway is in this parish.'

The piece of land situated between All Saints Church and the River Medway, lately called the Frindsbury Peninsular, has an unusual and chequered history. When we look from Chatham and see wharves, industrial buildings and offices, all on a flat piece of ground edged in by chalk cliffs, it is difficult to imagine a gently sloping area where people would wish to live and walk amongst fields and orchards. The Romans occupied it and the Saxons were driven from it by the Danes who rowed their long ships up river to rob and pillage

All Saints Church represents different periods in the history of Frindsbury. The church was extensively repaired during the nineteenth century, including some major works which were carried out from June 1824 until March 1825: 'Repairs to Church and Walls by Order of George Gunning, Esq. and John Snatt, Esq., Churchwardens Parish of Frindsbury.' Was Snatt's Lane, where Henry Pateman was born, named after John Snatt?

Two brothers of Mary Ann Coulter (wife of William Bass Pateman) were married at All Saints, Frindsbury: William Coulter married Frances Hogwood on 29 July 1826; George Coulter married Frances Wickens on 29 January 1831. Charlotte Pateman married William Baldock at Frindsbury on 17 June 1822. Joseph Pattman married Eliza Fitch at nearby Gillingham on 10 September 1837.

All Saints Churchyard contains some interesting graves. Charles Roach Smith (1807-1890), a well known archaeologist died in 1890 and many distinguished people attended his funeral. Thomas Lear, a Medway waterman, is also buried here. He was killed on 13 September 1813 in an accident at Rochester Bridge, along with Thomas Gilbert, his two sisters, brother in law, three year old niece and nine girls aged between 6 and 13. Thomas Lear was honored with a public funeral by his fellow watermen. Another quite famous grave is that of John George Mount. His headstone states: '45 years in the R.N. many of which he was a gunner, and was with Lord Howe 1st June 1794, also with Admiral Lord Nelson at Trafalgar, 21 October 1805.'

Brickmaking

Frindsbury had a number of industries including ship building, the Thames and Medway Canal, barge building, brewing, windmills, cement manufacture and brick making. This takes us back to the Hods in our title and provides another link between the Pateman family and brick making.

The population of Frindsbury had grown between the census of 1801 and 1831 by about 80% and this latter shows that Frindsbury was one of the few Medway villages where agriculture had ceased to be the main employer. There were only 107 agricultural laborers out of a total population of 1,856 in 1831. Brick making was becoming a major source of employment in the area to which the increase in population is attributed. Of the 21 brickfields listed in 1847, scattered from Sheerness to Aylesford, the biggest concentration was at Frindsbury where there were six. Three of these were on Manor Farm, two of them at Whitewall Creek and one at Ten Gun Field, Upnor. The latter site had been in production since at least 1800.

For twenty years from 1828, one of the Whitewall fields leased by a Mr. Barton and then by a Mr. Everest, made almost one million bricks. The other under Hankey, Field and Larkin made three million over five years and the Ten Gun Field leased by Little, then Baker, produced 38.5 million over twenty years, averaging in the later years 2.5 million annually. The peak of production was in the year 1844 when just over 14 million bricks were made which equalled 1% of the country's total output.

In 1835, Henry Everest, probably the area's largest brick maker, contracted with a Mr. Nickolson to produce eight million bricks to be taken away by river. Mr. Everest proposed to dredge a creek at Whitewall to provide a second wharf at a cost of £30 and to spend £15 per year in maintaining this new wharf. Most brick makers were also farming the land, stripping the topsoil, removing the brick earth and then replacing the top soil to either continue farming or to plant orchards. Changes of levels can be seen in various places. In the tithe assessment Mr. Everest's brick field is listed as covering 26 acres.

Most of the bricks produced were the Yellow Stock Bricks which were much used locally and also sent to London to meet the increased demand for bricks as the city expanded and building regulations insisted on brick buildings. To give a stock brick its yellow hue, a small percentage of chalk is added during the slurrying in the wash mill.

In 1865 George Hankey of Mincing Lane in the City of London, took out a lease on Manor Farm. He also applied to the Dean and Chapter for permission to make bricks on two pieces of land he had leased. A license was granted for that piece of land called Beacon Hill situated at or near Upnor of 10 acres, 1 rood and 5 perches, and also Ten Gun Field of 14 acres, 31 perches, to make from the earth, bricks, and to carry away the same when made and burnt, and to build kilns and other erections to be used in the making and burning of the bricks.

He agreed to pay the Dean and Chapter one shilling for every 1000 bricks made and no earth was to be removed from the site except as bricks. He also gained permission to take brick earth from glebe land belonging to the Frindsbury Vicarage, called the Brickfield near Whitewall Creek but for these bricks he had only to pay three pence per 1000.

J. Foord and Sons, the Rochester builders, took over the brick works at Ten Gun Field to meet the requirements of the government departments with whom they had triennial contracts for maintenance. In 1855 they produced 2,163,027 bricks but by 1864 the production was down to 795,000.

A small farmer who went into brick production was Thomas Wickenden of Home Farm. In 1839 he owned Ten Acres Field, Four Elms Hill Wood, Cocked Hat Meadow, Ash Green Field, Green Gardens, Barn Meadow, Stable Field and Browning Field as well as the farm yard and barns. The farm was on Frindsbury Hill, then called Home Street and the farmhouse remains. In 1845 the six acre Barn Meadow was turned over to brick production. His son, also Thomas, joined him in both the farming and brick making and Thomas the elder died on 9 January 1875 in his 82nd year.

Wickenden's Brickfield and the others concentrated in the area bounded by Frindsbury and Cooling Roads have been well documented by the Kent Underground Research Group in *Chalk Mining and Associated Industries of Frindsbury* (1987). The area behind the *Royal Oak* public house was developed as a brick field in 1826. This was the scene of a fatal accident in November 1895. William Sayer, the landlord of the *Royal Oak* was at work with his father and brother in the chalk pit when nearly ten tons of earth fell and buried him alive. Further up Cooling Road was the Frindsbury Brickyard which was developed by the West family of Strood after 1842.

The Medway brick yards came under threat in the early 1880s when the clay at Fletton near Peterborough began to be exploited for brick making. Most of the Frindsbury yards, including the larger producers near the river, were running out of raw material anyway. Importation was a costly business and so they ceased to trade and the land went back to agricultural use, or just lay unused until the massive expansion of housing in the parish swallowed it up.

The Muddies

The 'muddies' earned their living digging out or excavating the blue/grey mud (clay) and chalk which were burned to produce cement. At first timber was used to produce the necessary heat, but coal in the form of coke, as soon as it became readily available, quickly superceded it. The process used by the Romans continued until the end of the eighteenth century when experiments with varying quantities of the main ingredients and with raw materials from differing sources produced the widely known Portland cement. The names of those who triggered the early development of the process for the production of Portland cement were Joseph Aspdin, L.C. Johnson, James Frost, and Sir C.W. Pasley. These men were all busy during the period 1825-1830. The last named produced cement by burning a mixture of chalk and river mud.

As far as Medway is concerned, chalk from the cliffs and quarries of Frindsbury and the mud of the river were readily available and in great demand by the many cement works on the banks of the Medway and the Thames. Transportation was by barge, and many were specially built with wide decks, but old 'dry-cargo' carriers would be pressed into service to help in maintaining uninterrupted supplies to the works. As London in particular and the overseas market grew, more factories were needed to meet the demand for the product.

By 1900 there were 152 chamber kilns in the Frindsbury area alone and about 30 tall brick chimneys all belching black smoke. The output of cement there was approximately 4,000 tons per week. The demand for mud increased in similar proportions and much of it was dug out of the marshes at Hoo. The Medway Conservancy Board estimated that between 1898 and 1908, over 289,000 tons of clay had been dug from Bishops, Barksore, Okeham, Hope, and Burntwick Marshes, an area of some 34 to 37 acres. Up to that date a total of 3,709,000 tons of clay had been excavated. In 1910 the Admiralty indicated its concern about the extent of the diggings, which were disrupting the course of the channel at Bishop's Marsh.

Henry died on 4 January 1858, aged 15 months, near Capstone, Gillingham. He was the son of Robert Pateman, licenced hawker, who was present at the death. The cause of death was 'intermittent fever and dysentery. We do not know where he is buried.

8. Notting Hill Potteries

- Anne Pateman (1858-?)
- Walter Pateman (1859-1943)
- Robert Pateman (1860-?)
- Louisa Pateman (1861-?)
- Thomas Pateman (1861)

In this chapter our family history moves from Kent to the Notting Hill Potteries, where Louisa and Thomas Pateman were born in 1861. London and the surrounding districts were the undisputed heart of the traveling population during the nineteenth century. Even when pushed from the central areas Gypsies continued to base their varied comings and goings from the fringes of the city into the surrounding counties. Thus it was in and around the metropolis that sizeable numbers of itinerants traveled, and their camps were to be found almost everywhere. When the season arrived for the commencement of traveling large numbers of Gypsies could be seen radiating from this centre, only for the direction to be reversed with the end of hop picking and the onset of wintry weather. London proved to be a convenient and large market for hawking and street trading, and a place where relative anonymity took precedence over conspicuousness. Vagrants, beggars and tramps were a common sight, and camps of people living in tents, in the open or under the arches of the London bridges were a regular feature of the landscape and environment. In London, then, was to be found the largest number of Gypsy travelers situated in a geographically limited area. The numbers would fluctuate with the seasons, and the types of travelers who camped here varied considerably in the nature and extent of their itinerancy and the permanency of their dwellings.

In the main the Gypsies camped, during the summer, on the edges of the metropolis in the forests, on the waste ground and on the commons. The winter months saw many of them migrate further inwards to seek alternative sites and lodgings in the mean streets of the city. Camp sites varied from the idyllic surroundings of the woodland and forest to the slum regions of the Notting Hill Potteries. They settled on waste land of every description, from yards belonging to public houses to pieces of common land over which no authority claimed any rights. The result was that they could be found in almost all areas of London. A London city missionary, writing in 1858, supported this picture of the widespread dispersal of the Gypsy encampments:

'The circuit of my district has necessarily been large, taking in Woodford, Loughton, Barkingside, Wanstead, Barking, Forest gate, Stratford, Barking road, Bow common, Hackney Wick, Holloway, Blackheath, Greenwich, Plumstead common, Streatham, Norwood, Wandsworth, Wimbledon, Putney and Barnes common, Hammersmith, Chiswick, Kensington, Potteries, Paddington, Battersea, Shoreditch and Borough. All these are regular stations, where I generally meet with Gypsies. In addition to these places I visit the hop gardens in Kent and Surrey during the hop picking season; also the fairs in the neighborhood of London, with Epsom races, in quest of Gypsies.'

The romanticism of the picture of the wild Gypsy, living al fresco in tents and shelters, applied in general only to the first part of the 19th century, and later only to a small section of the Gypsies. As the century progressed this image rapidly became part of the romantic myth that surrounded the Romany people. The reality of the situation in the metropolis, which was becoming increasingly apparent, was far less appetizing. The Gypsies pitched their tents and halted their vans in areas of transition, on brickfields and on waste ground, on sites of intended buildings and where buildings had been pulled down. They encamped in the midst of ruins, chaos and filth, and many of their camps were in such depressed areas that they were said to be satisfied to put up their tents 'where a Londoner would only accommodate his pig or his dog.'

Notting Hill Potteries

Such were the conditions which existed in Kensington, around the Notting Hill Potteries. Even the sites on the Thames mud flats and Plumstead Marshes were described as salubrious compared with those at Notting Hill. Whether from historical or geographical causes, tramps and travelers who entered London from the north and west had long used the district as a temporary halting place. Some stayed a night, some a week, maybe even months and years, but in general the travelers moved on, often to St Giles's or Whitechapel, only to return again on their later travels. Each time, though, some would have remained and Charles Booth commented that Gypsy blood was in evidence among the children in the schools, and was even 'noticeable in the streets.'

The area only became known as the Potteries from the 1830s onwards, about which time it also attracted a large colony of pig breeders. By 1849 the residents were living at a density of 130 to the acre, and the number of pigs was upwards of 3,000. Many of the residents lived in converted railway carriages and vans. During the years 1846-8 the living conditions had deteriorated rapidly, with vast quantities of semi liquid pig manure and other organic matter lingering in the cavities dug up by the potters and brick makers. These conditions contributed to the alarming statistic that the average age of death was just eleven years and three months compared to thirty seven years for London as a whole. Following the cholera epidemic of 1848-9 'the conditions of filth, disease and insanitation in which its inhabitants were found to be living and dying gave the area a notoriety perhaps unsurpassed by any other district in London'. It was not until the 1870s that conditions began to improve with the introduction of better systems of drainage, prosecution of pig owners and the decline of pig breeding as a regular business.

Yet despite the squalid environment, the Gypsies flocked to the area in large numbers, and those living in or near Latimer Road were estimated to comprise from forty to fifty families by 1862. It was about this time that missionary work in the area was thought to have led to some transformation in the Gypsy way of life. Many were said to have given up the traditional Gypsy 'vices' of drinking, swearing and fortune telling. Others had allegedly abandoned the Romany language and gone through Christian marriage services. A mission tent was erected in 1869, though the endeavors of the missionary worker were to be cut short by an outbreak of scarlet fever and the insistence of the local authority that the camp be broken up. As a result many took to living in 'melancholy looking cottages', in sheds and out houses, or in tenements, 'so closely packed together that little sun or air can penetrate.' Some, however, managed to evade the authorities and continued to live in dilapidated vans at the back of rows of houses and in 'narrow courts and dingy lanes'. Once settled in more permanent dwellings it was inevitable that traveling began to decline.

Other colonies of Gypsies, or van towns, similar to that described above, could be seen at Smethwick, between the railway arches at Clapham Junction, at Woodford, Wandsworth, Plaistow Marshes, and many other places besides. Of these, the camp on the borders of Wanstead Flats, in Cobbold Road, was a 'picture of order, cleanliness and industry'. This type of encampment remained exceptional, the majority being of the Notting Hill variety. They flourished mainly during the winter months, experiencing a steady outflow with the arrival of spring, but it was increasingly the case that a core stayed on the sites throughout the summer months. The main sites, at Notting Hill, Wandsworth and Battersea, all retained a small nucleus. With the return of bad weather over the winter months this core was added to. Grenwood:

'As soon as the cold weather sets in the members of the various Gypsy tribes whose headquarters are London and its suburbs, may be seen with their brown babies and their houses on wheels, the gay green and yellow paint with which their panels are bedecked, dulled and blistered by the son of a long summer, leisurely making their way to the winter settlements. These are not far. There are two or three at Camberwell, and one at a place called Pollard's Gardens, near the Waterloo Road. Peckham boasts several; they may be found at Homerton in the back slums of Lambeth, and among the potteries between Notting Hill and Shepherd's Bush. Lock's Fields, Walworth, is a favorite spot with the fraternity.'

Most of these colonies broke up with the onset of spring, and the months of April and May witnessed the beginning of the exodus of Gypsies from their winter camps. Some traveled far into Norfolk and the Midlands, others contented themselves by working in the market gardens of the London suburbs until July, when they crossed to Woolwich for fruiting, and then on to Sussex and Kent for the harvesting and hopping seasons. Seasonal employment of this kind was an essential ingredient of summer migration. The nearby fairs, seaside resorts and race meetings were also a major attraction, and Epsom during Derby week was overrun by Gypsies who either told fortunes, traded horses or set up coconut establishments. At the fairs they were the proprietors of 'Puff and Darts', 'Spin 'em Rounds', and other games. Sometimes they even created their own fairs and built primitive swings and roundabouts on plots of waste land, with the motive power being provided by 'ragged boys running around and pushing bars radiating from the centre pole'

Apart from the seasonal work of fruit, vegetable and hop picking, the usual occupations of the travelers were also practiced. The Gypsies who stayed at the Notting Hill Potteries carried on their trades of making clothes pegs and butchers' skewers, offering their services as tinkers and knife grinders, horse dealing and fortune telling. Hawking and tinkering thus remained as the mainstay of Gypsy employments. Yet their occupations were even more diverse than this picture allows. Hoyland's list of Gypsy lodgers in London at the beginning of the century shows that a great many trades were followed, including those of chair bottoming, basket making, rat catching, wire working, grinding, fiddling, selling fruit, fish and earthenware, and mending bellows. Although three were found to be employed on a regular basis, as a canal worker, lamplighter and journeyman saddler, the majority still relied on their own ability to maintain an existence and were dependent on selling their wares or skills directly rather than being employed as hired wage laborers. The variety of occupations and the dependence on self employment was a feature retained throughout the nineteenth century.

Thomas Herne, living in Gipsy Square in the Notting Hill Potteries, had a sign board on his cabin advertising his trade as a brush and cane chair bottomer in the 1860s. Although aged about ninety years he still walked the streets touting for business. These street menders were a common sight about London, carrying from house to house their bundles of canes and rushes and performing the necessary repairs on the doorsteps or in the gardens. They did not have the regular wages of those who worked for the dealers, but profits would generally compensate for this. The usual charge was from 8d. to 1s. per chair, according to the quality of cane, the size of the seat and the estimated wealth of the customer. The cost of the raw materials, the split and dressed cane, varied from 2s. 6d. to 4s. per pound weight, which covered from six to eight chairs. The work was precarious, though, and the profits were rarely sufficient to maintain a minimum standard of living on their own and needed to be supplemented by other work.

It was likely, therefore, that the Gypsy would be, variously, a basket maker, chair and sieve mender, tinker, horse dealer, peg and skewer maker. At times they would stay at home manufacturing small items for sale, and at others they would leave the camp to go tinkering old kettles and saucepans, grinding knives and scissors or selling oranges. The women usually left the camp to go out hawking and in south London were said to sell to the rich and poor alike. The major change that took place during the nineteenth century was that the items hawked were no longer primarily of their own manufacture. Even so it is still possible to find examples of Gypsies selling home made clothes pegs well into the twentieth century. The other major home craft was that of 'chinning the cost', or making butchers' skewers, sold directly to the butcher at around 1s. per stone.

But these were dying trades and by the end of the nineteenth century the items hawked were of greater variety and were generally bought from a wholesaler. These wares included small wool mats, vases, cheap ornaments, brooms, brushes, clothes props and pegs, fern roots, cottons, laces, and other odds and ends. All adult Gypsies, male and female, played crucial roles in the domestic economy. The importance of the children also should not be underestimated. While the girls traveled around with their mothers, the boys either assisted their fathers in the manufacture of various items at home or else went out hawking on their own.

Anne Pateman (1858-?)

After the birth of William at Rochester in 1857, Robert made a short journey to St Mary's, on the Hoo Peninsular, where Anne Pateman was born in 1858.

St Mary's

Kellys Directory (1855): 'The parish and village of. St Mary's, or Hoo St Mary's, is 8 miles north east of Rochester, 11 east of Gravesend, in the lathe of Aylesford, West Kent. The village lies high, but has a belt of marsh on the Thames. The population in 1851 was 320. The area is 2,196 acres of land and 670 of water.'

In the Middle Ages St Mary's Hoo was considerably larger, but the population has dwindled so that now it is no more than a hamlet. St Mary's Hoo is nicely secluded and were it not for the church its whereabouts would be even less noticeable. The church is thirteenth century and dominates a neat group of buildings: the village school (1868), the Hall, Red House, the Old Rectory and various farm buildings, including a large, typical barn.

St Mary's church welcomes visitors and is open daily. It is a retired church in the care of the Churches Conservation Trust, being 900 years old. Charles Dickens' daughter, Katie, was married at this church. Her brother in law was Wilkie Collins who wrote *Woman in White* and the *Moonstone*. St Mary's is located on a site overlooking the Hoo marshes with views on a clear day over the Thames to Essex. The exterior has horizontal bands of stone and flint. The south porch shelters a superb medieval door. It has traciered blind arches and is studded with flowers, animals and heads.

Two names are noted in the village: the Rev'd R. Burt and Henry Pye. Robert Burt performed the 'mixed' marriage of the Prince of Wales (later George IV) to Mrs Fitzherbert in 1785. He lived in the Old Rectory and was buried in the church. Henry Pye lived at St Mary's Hall and influenced farming techniques as to drainage, 'chalking', steam ploughing and threshing in the late nineteenth century.

Newlands to the west and Coombe to the East are within the Parish. There are footpaths leading to Egypt Bay and St Mary's Bay, old haunts of smugglers. When people talk about marshes in Kent they are usually referring to Romney Marsh in the south of the county. The marshes of the Hoo peninsula are no less impressive or mysterious. There are several marshes on the Hoo Peninsula: Hoo marshes, Stoke marshes, Cooling marshes, Cliffe marshes, Higham marshes, Halstow marshes, Grain marshes, Allhallows marshes and St Mary's marshes.

A walk across St Mary's marshes is both memorable and peaceful. The walk starts at St Mary's Hoo and passes by Moat Farm to Coombe Farm; the house, once a prominent farm and manor in the area and now a restaurant, stands on the site of a much older house. It was opened at the time of the Norman Conquest by Wilfred de Hou, until he became a monk at Rochester Priory. Sir William Wyatt, of nearby Allington Castle, acquired it after the reformation. A Bronze Age hoard of 28 objects was discovered on the site of the original farm, indicating that the site has been inhabited since ancient times.

The walk continues across the marshes, an important migratory point of international repute for wildfowl. A Site of Special Scientific Interest is located nearby at Cliffe, while at Halstow the Northward Hill Heronry, the largest in Britain, can be freely visited. Established since the Middle Ages and now providing a home to over 200 pairs, the sleek grey outlines of herons can often be seen overhead. Swans frequently haunt the inland creeks, especially Decoy Creek. Over wintering birds to be seen include Brent Geese, Plovers and, if you are lucky, Avocets, one of our rarest birds.

The footpath follows the sea wall for much of its length. The fascinating collection of roofless buildings standing just inland from the sea wall look for all the world like a deserted crofters' village. In fact they are the remains of an army ammunition dump.

A notice dated 1900 inside one of the buildings, which stand on private land, warns visitors to extinguish all lights.

The walk continues past West Point and around St Mary's Bay. Small oyster fisheries have existed along sheltered stretches of the north Kent coast since the Middle Ages. They operated on a commercial basis until the mid 19th century, after which they went into decline. Oysters are affected by the cold and water pollution, both of which were a particular problem on the Hoo Peninsula. Most of the beds were closed down under the Public Health Shellfish Regulations of 1934. Oysters can sometimes be seen near the old beds at Egypt Bay and St Mary's Bay.

Walking on to Egypt Bay, the desolation of the area made an ideal cover for the clandestine activities of smugglers, particularly in the eighteenth and nineteenth centuries. The notorious North Kent Gang centered their activities on the Hoo Peninsula. Sparsely populated and the haunt of malaria carrying anopheles mosquitoes, the lonely marshes frequently witnessed contraband, mostly tea, brandy and wool, being brought ashore. The two most favored landing places, because of their secluded beaches, were Egypt Bay and St Mary's Bay.

Turning back inland now, the footpath passes close to Halstow Marshes and leads to Swigshole. The name, sometimes spelt Snagshole, has an interesting derivation. The first element, 'snag', means 'snake infested hollow', while the second, 'sol', means 'muddy pool'. When put together we have the colorful, if somewhat disagreeable, combination of a 'snake infested muddy pool.' The walk concludes back at St Mary's Hoo.

This is the environment in which Anne Pateman was born. On 2 April1871, Anne (15, Kent, St Mary) was living with her family in an old barn on a brickfield at Becks Lane, Beckenham, Kent. After that we do not know what happened to Anne. We cannot find her in any later census records, and so we assume that she died some time between 1871 and 1881. We do not know where she is buried.

Walter Pateman (1859-1943)

After the birth of Anne in 1858, Robert left the Hoo Peninsula and traveled south-east, to Stockbury, Kent where Walter Pateman was born in 1859. You will recall that Robert's first child, Mary Ann, died at Stockbury in 1844 (chapter 4). Walter was baptized at Claygate on 3 July 1859 along with Elvey Pateman, daughter of John Pateman (Robert's brother) and Matilda Sherrif.

Stockbury

Kellys Directory (1859): 'Stockbury is a village in the lathe of Aylesford, 4 miles from Rainham, 8 from Chatham and 7 from Maidstone. The inhabitants are chiefly engaged in agriculture. The area of the parish is 2940 acres and its population in 1851 was 580.' Opposite the north side of St Mary Magdalene churchyard, across the road that leads westwards to the village, is a grass pasture known as Bell Meadow. I wonder if anyone has investigated below its surface ? If close to a church, areas with this name, Bell Field, or similar, often signify that it is the site where a bell or bells were cast for the church. In the days when rural highways were in poor condition for part of the year, instead of casting a bell in the nearest town or city and hauling it to the customer church, the bell founders would take their equipment and materials needed, find a suitable area nearest to the church, with a supply of timber in the vicinity, then cast the bell on this site. An example is that at Newchurch. During the digging of a grave there in 1973, a 'bell pit', believed to have been used for the casting of the church's original bells, was discovered.

In the church yard, near an old yew showing signs of having experienced many gales on this exposed hill top overlooking the Stockbury Valley, is a headstone that is possibly the oldest in a Kent church yard still legible. On the head stone the inscription, surmounted by a skull and cross bones, is all in capital letters. It reads 'Here Lieth the Body of Thomas, the Son of Thomas and Elizabeth Gover, who departed this life the Fifteenth of November, 1620, being aged 26 years and 3 months. This young man the people loved. He changed this Life for Heaven above.' Almost certainly the yew tree's cover has protected the lettering from erosion.

In the church if you stand high up close to and directly in front of the organ on its raised platform under the tower arch, by looking downwards and eastwards up the nave to the chancel it is possible to see how the tower and nave are not in alignment, but whether accidental or deliberate is unknown.

On 2 April 1871, Walter (12, Kent, Stockbury) was living with his family in an old barn on a brick field at Becks Lane, Beckenham, Kent.

On 3 April 1881, Walter (21, Skewer Maker) was living with his father in a tent on Mitcham Common, Surrey. Walter's younger sister, Louisa Lee (20, Notting Hill, skewer maker), was living in a neighbouring tent with her husband Charles Lee (21, Rochester, skewer maker). Also living on Mitcham Common with her father was Phoebe Diton (22, Bexley, hawker) who Walter married in August 1881.

Phoebe Dighton

On 22 August 1881 Walter Pateman (22, bachelor, hawker, Croydon, father – Robert Pateman, hawker) married Phoebe Diton (22, spinster, Croydon, father – James Diton, hawker) at Croydon parish church. The witnesses were Andrew Diton and Ebenezer Whittaker. Phoebe's brother, Solomon, was the great grandfather of Barry Dighton, who sent me the following information about Phoebe and her family:

'Phoebe was the sister to my great grandfather Solomon Dighton. Solomon was married to Patience (Mary) who was one of Rev Hall's chief informants. She in turn was the daughter of Samuel Roberts' (and George Borrow's) Clara Heron, wife of Cornelius Smith, and sister to the infamous Riley Bosvil. James Dighton Jnr., my 2 x Great grandfather was the sister of Justinia Dighton. Her son Levi Boswell was the husband of Gypsy Lee (Urania). They were from the same area in Tugmutton Common, Farnborough, as your ancestors (William and James Pateman).

Phoebe's father was James Dighton jnr, who, according to the 1851 census was born in Tonbridge, Kent and baptized there on 1 August 1824. But he may have been born in Hertfordshire, as his birth years suggested by census returns and death certificate are a little before his baptism, and his father, James snr, was described as 'tinker of Sawbridgeworth, Herts' on the baptism entry.

Phoebe's mother was Duanna Lee. According to census returns Duanna was born in either Hertfordshire or Worcestershire (two separate ones give conflicting birthplaces). Her baptism was actually recorded under the name "Pianna" daughter of "Righteous Lea and Pennee", in Shurdington, Gloucestershire on 14th March 1813. [perhaps the first initial P was a flowery version of a 'D' but I have a copy of the register and it doesn't appear so.]

Duanna must have married James Dighton jnr around the early 1840s. He also seems to have taken along Duanna's younger sister Elizabeth (alias Misel, Mizerotta, Mizerella) as well. Elizabeth (Misel) also gives her birthplace as 'Herefordshire' in 1881 and it may well have been. She was born on 27th January 1820 but was christened just over a month later at St Peter's, Carmarthen, Wales.

Duanna and James had several children together: (Baron) Nathan (1845), Solomon (1846), Eliza (christened 10 September, 1848 at Plaxtol, Kent), Elijah (1849), Oliver (1851), Deliah (1855), Noah (1858), Phoebe (born 1859, baptized on 15 March 1871, at Beckenham, Kent, when James and Duanna were still being reported as the parents), Walter (1861) and Priscilla (1866).

James and Elizabeth (Misel) had two children recorded in the 1881 Census: William (1862) and Andrick (1856). The *Journal of the Gypsy Lore Society* (1922 Volume V, page 28) has, in an article entitled 'Gypsy Marriage in England', the following extract: 'With regard to polygamy among the English Gypsies properly so-called … Borrow (Romano Lavo-Lil. Chapter on Ryley Bosvil) who was at some pains to describe Riley Boswell and his two co-wives; Groome, who has a passing reference to Riley ('Gypsy Folk Tales' – London 1899 – p. 23) …; and George Smith of Coalville ('Gypsy Life' – London 1880 – p.265; and 'I've Been A-Gypsying' – London 1883 – p.102), from whom we learn that a gypsy named D_____, a Dighton for certain, openly boasted that he had 'a brother not far from Mitcham Common, living with two sisters in an unlawful state'."

In the 1871 census Robert Pateman and his family were living in a caravan at Becks Lane, Beckenham. James Dighton and his family were living in a neighbouring van. The 1881 Census returns have their father's family caravans almost next to each other (only Solomon's is between) but James was now calling Misel 'wife', while Duanna was describing herself as 'widow': James Diton (head, 61, general dealer, Mitcham); Misel Diton (wife, 61, Hawker, Herefordshire); William Diton (19, general dealer, Beckenham); Andrick Diton (25, Labourer, N. Woolwich, Kent).

Duanna Diton (widow, 67, Hawker, Herefordshire); Noah Diton (23, general dealer, North Woolwich); Deliah Diton (26, Hawker, North Woolwich); Phoebe Diton (22, Hawker, Bexley, Kent); Walter Diton (20, Hawker, Streatham, Surrey); Priscilla Diton (15, Hawker, Wandsworth, Surrey).

Phoebe married Walter Pateman in Croydon in August 1881. Nathan, Solomon and Noah married three daughters of Cornelius and Clara Smith. There was an Eliza Dighton who died at Epsom in June 1852. If that was James's daughter she would have been about four years old. Walter Dighton, in 1891, was living with wife Fanny ('born Croydon') in a caravan at Epsom and describing himself as a Hawker. In 1901 he was living in a 'tent at Warlingham' and his occupation was a fruit picker. In both these censuses his birthplace was given as Streatham.

Given as 'Mizerotta' on the death certificate, Elizabeth (Misel) died at Mitcham Common on 4h September 1888. She was reported to be the wife of 'James Dighton, General Dealer'. Her death was reported in the *Croydon Times* in January 1897:

'DEATH OF AN OCTOGENARIAN. On Saturday Dr Jackson (the Borough Coroner) held an inquest upon the body of Johanna Diton, aged 85. The body was identified by Noah Diton, hawker, as that of his mother. She had been living in a tent in a field off Spring-gardens, Woodside. Recently she had suffered from a severe cold on her chest, but with the exception of that enjoyed good health. On Friday night she walked about the field until 11 o'clock, and then went to bed. In the morning the witness went to her tent, and found her lying in bed, dead, but in a natural position. Dr Green was called, and pronounced life extinct. He stated that there were no marks of violence upon the body, and death was due to failure of the heart's action. The jury returned a verdict accordingly.'

James Dighton Jnr seems to have had his travelling days somewhat tempered by moving into a more permanent home in his last years. However, his change of occupation to the fairground, perhaps balanced that innate desire to move around, with his great age's need for some permanence. He outlived both his wives and died on 6 April 1906 at 22 Queen's Road, Mitcham, aged 87. He was a cocoanut shy proprietor and died of senile decay. The informant was William Dighton, present at death.

We have not found Walter Pateman in the 1891 Census. On 31 March 1901, Walter (39, dealer in green vegetables, Kent, Stockbury) was living at Vinson's Cottages, St Mary Cray, with his wife, Phoebe (38, Kent, Bexleyheath).

In 1911 Walter Pateman (50, dealer, Maidstone) was living at 1 Vinsons Cottages, Hockenden with his wife Phoebe (50, work in the fields, Bexley). Also living with him were his nephew Noah Pateman (William's son) and his wife Annie and their children Nellie, May and Ivy.

Walter Pateman died on 5 April 1943 at Lewisham Hospital. He was an 84 year old retired jobbing gardener, living at 147 Kings Ground, Eltham, Woolwich. The cause of death was 'cardiac degeneration and senile decay'. The informant was 'Geo. E. Conolly, causing the body to be buried'. Walter was buried on 12 April 1943 in Star Lane Cemetery, St Mary Cray – the same cemetery where his sister, Alice, was buried in 1892 (see Chapter 4). We do not know when Phoebe Pateman died or where she was buried.

Robert Pateman (1860-?)

Sometime after Walter's birth in Kent, Robert moved to Surrey where his next son, Robert, was born in 1860.

Robert Pateman was baptized on 21 July 1861. His parents were Robert and Mary Bateman, Traveller, and their abode was Claygate, Surrey.

Robert was probably travelling with his brother John who also had a child at this time: Elvey was born at Claygate in 1860.

The only other reference to Robert is in the 1881 Census when he was living on Mitcham Common in a tent with his father and brother Walter.

We do not know if Robert got married and had children or when and where he died. We do not know where he is buried.

Louisa Pateman (1861-?)

Louisa Pateman (1861-?) = Charles Lee (1860-1928)
- Lavinia (Lovey)
- Albert
- Elizabeth (Betsy)
- Charles
- John (Jack)
- Mary Ann (Polly)

Sometime after Robert's birth in 1860, Robert senior moved from Claygate, through Surrey (via Wimbledon and Wandsworth?) and traveled into Middlesex, for the birth of Louisa and Thomas Pateman at the Notting Hill Potteries in 1861.

Contemporary maps show the close proximity between what George Borrow called the two 'grand Metropolitan Gypsyries' at Wandsworth and the Potteries. A map of Middlesex (1878) shows the road that Robert would have taken from Wimbledon (where Alice Pateman was born in 1842), over the bridge at Fulham, to Hammersmith. A series of ordnance survey maps show the development of Hammersmith from 1822 to 1861-1871 (published 1876-77).

Louisa Pateman was born on 8 February 1861 on the 'common, Latymer Road', Hammersmith, Middlesex. Her time of birth is recorded, '30 minutes after 11 am', which denotes a multiple birth, in this case twins: her brother, Thomas, was born at '15 minutes before noon'. Robert's occupation was given as general labourer.

<u>Hammersmith</u>

Kellys Directory (1852): 'Hammersmith, a part of London, which comprehends Brook Green and Shepherd's Bush, is situated on the Great Western Road, three and a half miles from Hyde Park Corner and contains 2140 acres. The population in 1801 was 5,000 and in 1841 it had grown to 13,453.' By 1861 the population was 24,519 and in 1871 it stood at 42, 691. Some of this increase was caused by the coming of the railways. *Post Office Directory* (1878): 'The Metropolitan Extension Railway has a terminal station here, the South Western Railway has a line from here to Richmond, and the District has a line to the Mansion House, via Earl's Court and Charing Cross, and is connected with the South Western Richmond line.

Hammersmith bridge was opened in 1827. Hammersmith was a part of Fulham parish until 1834, when it was formed into a separate parish by an Act of Parliament. The parish is divided into three wards (north, centre and south) and there are several churches: St Paul's (1629), St Peter's (1829), St John the Evangelist (1859), St Matthew's (1871). There are chapels for Methodists, Baptists and Congregationalists; a Weslyan chapel was erected in 1876 in the West End, it is a handsome stone building with spire and clock.

The Godolphin school was opened in 1862, in accordance with the will of William Godolphin. The buildings include a large schoolroom, capable of accommodating 200 boys, several class rooms, a dining hall, dormitories for several boarders, and an excellent residence for the head master. It is a public grammar school, in which, at the small capitation fee of ten pounds, boys residing in the neighborhood are instructed in classics, mathematics, French, chemistry, and all that is required for the universities.

Edward Latymer, in 1624, bequeathed 35 acres 1 rood of land (now very valuable), the rental to be appropriated in clothing poor men, and clothing and educating poor boys: the numbers until recently were thirty men and 100 boys; but by a scheme of the Charity Commission the number of pensioners is to be reduced to six, who are to receive £75 among them, and there are in future to be two schools, to be called respectively the Higher and the Lower Latymer Schools: the boys in the Lower School are to make small weekly payments, and the Upper School annual payments to be fixed by the Governors: the boys are to receive a sound English education, and in the Upper School Latin and one modern European language are to be taught.

The Institute is in King street west, and is well supplied with newspapers, periodicals and a library of upwards of 1,350 books. The Savings Bank has existed since 1816. In King street east is the West London Hospital, which is now (1878) being considerably enlarged. There is a Catholic church on Brook Green. There are many Catholic buildings in Hammersmith. The convent of the Good Shepherd has for its principal object the reformation of those unfortunate women who have lost their reputation: they are instructed in moral and religious duties, household, laundry and needle work. The Catholic Reformatory for boys is Blythe House, Blythe Lane, and contains about 160 boys under 16 years.

The West Middlesex Water Company have much enlarged their works here since 1852, and have also erected two large engines near the Thames, above Hampton, each capable of pumping 7,000 gallons per minute into the reservoirs at Barnes, Surrey: these reservoirs are duplicate, and are of 16 acres area: the water is filtered, after subsidence in the reservoirs, through a thick bed of fine sand, and passes under the bed of the river to the engine wells at Hammersmith, and is thence distributed by powerful engines, equal to 600 horse power, over the company's district, and also to their large covered reservoir near Primrose hill, 178 feet above Trinity high water mark; at this reservoir other pumping engines have been erected, and the filtered water is again pumped into their high level district, and raised an additional 150 feet – making the total lift 328 feet above the level of Trinity high water mark, and the water has to travel about 20 miles from the station at Hampton to reach the extremity of the district at present supplied by the company.'

The Potteries, 1864

The following description of the Potteries is taken from George Borrow's *Romano Lavo-Lil* (1874). The references to brickfields remind us, yet again, of the "Hods" in our title:

'The second great Gypsyry is on the Middlesex side of the river, and is distant about three miles, as the crow flies, from that of Wandsworth. Strange as it may seem, it is not far distant from the most fashionable part of London; from the beautiful squares, noble streets, and thousand palaces of Tyburnia, a region which, though only a small part of the enormous metropolis, can show more beautiful edifices, wealth, elegance, and luxury, than all foreign capitals put together. After passing Tyburnia, and going more than halfway down Notting Hill, you turn to the right, and proceed along a tolerably genteel street till it divides into two, one of which looks more like a lane than a street, and which is on the left hand, and bears the name of Pottery Lane. Go along this lane, and you will presently find yourself amongst a number of low, uncouth looking sheds, open at the sides, and containing an immense quantity of earthen chimney pots, pantiles, fancy bricks and similar articles. This place is called the Potteries, and gives the name of Pottery Lane to the lane through which you have just passed. A dirty little road goes through it, which you must follow, and presently turning to your left, you will enter a little, filthy street, and going some way down it, you will see, on your right hand, a little, open bit of ground, chock full of crazy, battered caravans of all colors – some yellow, some green, some red. Dark men, wild looking, witch like women, and yellow faced children are at the doors of the caravans, or wending their way through the narrow spaces left for transit between the vehicles. You have now arrived at the second great Gypsyry of London – you are amongst the Romany Chals of the Potteries, called in Gypsy the *Koromengreskoe Tan*, or the place of the fellows who make pots; in which place certain Gypsies have settled, not with the view of making pots, an employment which they utterly eschew, but simply because it is convenient to them, and suits their fancy.

A goodly collection of Gypsies you will find in that little nook, crowded with caravans. Most of them are Tatchey Romany, real Gypsies, 'long established people, of the old order'. Amongst them are *Ratzie-mescroes*, Hearnes, Herons, or duck people; *Chumo-mescroes* or Bosvils; a *Kaulo Camlo* (a Black Lovel) or two, and a Beshaley or Stanley. It is no easy thing to find a Stanley nowadays, even in the Baulo Tem, or Hampshire, which is the proper home of the Stanleys, for the Bugnior, pimples or small pox, has of late years made sad havoc amongst the Stanleys; but yonder tall old gentlewoman, descending the steps of a caravan, with a flaming red cloak and a large black beaver bonnet, and holding a traveling basket in her hand, is a *Tatchey Beshaley*, a 'genuine' Stanley. The generality, however, of 'them Gyptians' are *Ratzie-mescroes*, Hearnes, or duck people; and, speaking of the Hearnes, it is but right to say that he who may be called the Gypsy Father of London, old Thomas *Ratzie-mescroe*, or Hearne, though not exactly residing here, lives close by in a caravan, in a little bit of a yard over the way, where he can breathe more freely, and be less annoyed by the brats and the young fellows than he would be in yonder crowded place.

Though the spot which it has just been attempted to describe, may be considered as the head quarters of the London Gypsies, on the Middlesex side of the Thames, the whole neighborhood, for a mile to the north of it, may to a certain extent be considered a Gypsy region – that is, a district where Gypsies, or gentry whose habits very much resemble those of Gypsies, may at any time be found. No metropolitan district, indeed, could be more well suited for Gypsies to take up their abode in. It is a neighborhood of transition; of brickfields, open spaces, poor streets inhabited by low artisans, isolated houses, sites of intended tenements, or sites of tenements which have been pulled down; it is in fact a mere chaos, where there is nothing durable, or intended to be durable; though there can be little doubt that within a few years order and beauty itself will be found here, that the misery, squalidness, and meanness will have disappeared, and the whole district, up to the railroad arches which bound it on the west and the north, will be covered with palaces, like those of Tyburnia, or delightful villas, like those which decorate what is called Saint John's Wood. At present, however, it is quite the kind of place to please the Gypsies and wandering people, who find many places within its bounds where they can squat and settle, or take up their quarters for a night or two without much risk of being interfered with. Here their tents, cars, and caravans may be seen amidst ruins, half raised walls, and on patches of unenclosed ground; here their children may, throughout the day, be seen playing about, flinging up dust and dirt, some partly naked, and others entirely so; and here, at night, the different families, men, women, and children, may be seen seated around their fires and their kettles, taking their evening meal, and every now and then indulging in shouts of merriment, as much as to say:

What care we, though we be so small?
The tent shall stand when the palace shall fall.

Which is quite true. The Gypsy tent must make way for the palace, but after a millennium or two, the Gypsy tent is pitched on the ruins of the palace.

Latimer's Green

Of the open spaces above mentioned, the most considerable is one called Latimer's Green. It lies on the north western side of the district, and is not far from that place of old renown called the Shepherds Bush, where in the good ancient times highwaymen used to lurk for the purpose of pouncing upon the travelers of the Oxford Road. It may contain about five or six acres, and, though nominally under the control of trustees, is in reality little more than a 'no mans ground' where anybody may feed a horse, light a fire, and boil a kettle. It is a great resort of vagrant people, less of Gypsies than those who call themselves travelers, and are denominated by the Gypsies *Chorodies*, and who live for the most part in miserable caravans, though there is generally a Gypsy tent or two to be seen there, belonging to some Deighton or Shaw, or perhaps Petulengro, from the Lil-engro Tan, as the Romany call Cambridgeshire.

Amidst these *Chorody* caravans and Gypsy tents may frequently be seen the *ker-vardo*, the house on wheels, of one who, whenever he takes up his quarters here, is considered the cock of the walk, the king of the place. He is a little under 40 years of age, and somewhat under five feet ten inches in height. His face is wonderfully like that of a mastiff of the largest size, particularly in its jowls; his neck is short and very thick, and must be nearly as strong as that of a bull; his chest is so broad that one does not like to say how broad it is; and the voice which every now and then proceeds from it has much the sound of that of the mighty dog just mentioned; his arms are long and exceedingly muscular, and his fists huge and bony. He wears a low crowned, broad brimmed hat, a coarse blue coat with short skirts, leggings, and high lows. Such is the *kral o' the tan*, the *rex loci*, the cock of the green.

But what is he besides? Is he Gypsy, *Chorody*, or *Hindity mush*? I say, you had better not call him by any one of those names, for if you did he would perhaps hit you, and then, oh dear! That is Mr. G.A., a traveling horse dealer, who lives in a caravan, and finds it frequently convenient to take up his abode for weeks together on Latimer's Green. He is a thorough bred Englishman, though he is married to a daughter of one of the old, sacred, Gypsy families, a certain *Lurina Ratziemescri*, duck or heron female, who is a very handsome woman, and who has two brothers, dark, stealthy looking fellows, who serve with almost slavish obedience their sister's lord and husband, listening uncomplainingly to his abuse of Gypsies, whom, though he lives amongst them and is married to one by whom he has several children, he holds in supreme contempt, never speaking of them but as a lying, thievish, cowardly set, any three of whom he could beat with one hand; as perhaps he could, for he is a desperate pugilist, and has three times fought in 'the ring' with good men, whom, though not a scientific fighter, he beat with ease by dint of terrible blows, causing them to roar out.

He is very well to do in the world; his caravan, a rather stately affair, is splendidly furnished within; and it is a pleasure to see his wife, at Hampton Court races, dressed in Gypsy fashion, decked with real gems and jewels and rich gold chains, and waited upon by her dark brothers dressed like dandy pages. How is all this expense supported? Why, by horse dealing. Mr. G. is, then, up to all kinds of horse dealer's tricks no doubt. Aye, aye, he is up to them, but he doesn't practice them. He says it's of no use, and that honesty is the best policy, and he'll stick to it; and so he does, and finds the profit of it. His traffic in horses, though confined entirely to small people, such as market gardeners, travelers, show folks, and the like, is very great; every small person who wishes to buy a horse, or sell a horse, or swop a horse, goes to Mr. G., and has never reason to complain, for all acknowledge that he has done the fair thing by them; though all agree that there is no over reaching him, which indeed very few people try to do, deterred by the dread of his manual prowess, of which a Gypsy once gave to the writer the following *striking* illustration: '*He will jal oprey to a gry that's wafodu, prawla, and coure leste tuley with the courepen of his wast*' (He will go up to a vicious horse, brother, and knock him down with a blow of his fist).

The arches of the railroad which bounds this region on the west and north serve as a resort for Gypsies, who erect within them their tents, which are thus sheltered in summer from the scorching rays of the sun, and in winter from the drenching rain. In what close proximity we sometimes find emblems of what is most rude and simple, and what is most artificial and ingenious! For example, below the arch is the Gypsy donkey cart, whilst above it is thundering the chariot of fire which can run across a county in half an hour. The principal frequenters of these arches are Bosvils and Lees; the former are chiefly tinkers, and the latter *esconyemengres*, or skewer makers. The reason for this difference is that the Bosvils are chiefly immigrants from the country, where there is not much demand for skewers, whereas the Lees are natives of the metropolis or the neighborhood, where the demand for skewers has from time immemorial been enormously great. It was in the shelter of one of these arches that the celebrated Ryley Bosvil, the Gypsy king of Yorkshire, breathed his last a few years ago.'

Interior of van near Latimer Road Notting Hill

The Illustrated London News of 13 December 1879 contained an article on 'Gypsy Life Near London'. This article was illustrated with 'sketches of Gypsy life: interior of van near Latimer Road, Notting Hill'. The sketch shows the inside of a typical Gypsy van – a woman is on the floor, with a child on her lap, warming themselves by the fire. A young girl looks on while the father lies on a raised bunk at the back of the van. In the foreground there is a large kettle, a wicker basket and a chair. On the table there is a bowl and a candlestick. The window is open and there are curtains around the sleeping area:

'Another sketch of the singular habits and rather deplorable condition of these vagrant people, who hang about, as the parasites of civilisation, close on the suburban outskirts of our wealthy metropolis, is presented by our Artist, following those which have appeared in the last two weeks. Mr. G. Smith, of Coalville, Leicester, having taken in hand the question of providing due supervision and police regulation for the Gypsies, with compulsory education for their children, we readily dedicate these local Illustrations to the furtherance of his good work.

The ugliest place we know in the neighborhood of London, the most dismal and forlorn, is not Hackney Marshes or those of the Lea, beyond Old Ford, at the East End; but it is the tract of land, half torn up for brick field clay, half consisting of fields laid waste in expectation of the house builder, which lies just outside of Shepherd's Bush and Notting Hill.

There it is that the Gypsy encampment may be found, squatting within an hours walk of the Royal palaces and of the luxurious town mansions of our nobility and opulent classes, to the very west of the fashionable West end, beyond the gentility of Bayswater and Whiteley's avenue of universal shopping. It is a curious spectacle in that situation, and might suggest a few serious reflections upon social contrasts at the centre and capital of the mighty British nation, which takes upon itself the correction of every savage tribe in South and West Africa and Central Asia.

The encampment is usually formed of two or three vans and a rude cabin or a tent, placed on some piece of waste ground, for which the Gypsy party have to pay a few shillings a week of rent. This may be situated at the back of a row of respectable houses and in full view of their bedroom or parlor windows, not much to the satisfaction of the quiet inhabitants.

The interior of one of the vans, furnished as a dwelling room, which is shown in our Artist's sketch, does not look very miserable; but Mr. Smith informs us that these receptacles of vagabond humanity are often sadly over crowded. Besides a man and his wife and their own children, the little ones stowed in bunks or cupboards, there will be several adult persons taken in as lodger.

The total number of Gypsies now estimated to be living in the metropolitan district is not less than two thousand. Among these are doubtless not a small proportion of idle runaways or 'losels' from the more settled classes of our people. It would seem to be the duty of somebody at the Home Office for the sake of public health and good order, to call upon some local authorities of the county or the parish to look after these eccentricities of Gypsy life.'

Charles Lee

On 2 April 1871 Louisa (10, Middlesex, Hammermith) was living with her family, in an old barn, on a brick field, at Becks Lane, Beckenham, Kent. Louisa married Charles Lee (aka Charles Thatcher) some time before 1881, although we have not managed to trace any record of this event.

On 3 April 1881 Charles Lee (21, Skewer Maker, Rochester, Kent) was living with Louisa Lee (20, Skewer Maker, Notting Hill, Middlesex) in a tent on Mitcham Common.

The father of Charles Lee, Alfred (58, cutler, Gardner Street, Sussex) was living in a neighboring tent with his sons James (26, cutler, South Church, Essex), Alfred (17, cutler, Rochester, Kent) and Albert (14, cutler, Woolwich, Kent).

The brother of Charles Lee, William Thatcher (29, hawker, Gravesend, Kent) was also living in a tent on Mitcham Common with his wife, Lucy (27, Hawker, Brighton, Sussex) and their children Elizabeth (9, Gravesend, Kent), Lethy (7, Plumstead, Kent) and Moses (7 months, Beddington, Surrey).

Also living on Mitcham Common in 1881 were: Louisa's father, Robert Pateman, and her brother Walter; four groupings of the Diton family, including Duanna Diton and her daughter Phoebe, who married Walter Pateman in 1881; and four groupings of the Coates family, who had close connections with the Pateman family. Their son, Benjamin Coates (1885-1970) married Priscilla Pateman, widow of Walter Pateman (1886-1917).

Charles and Louisa went on to produce the following children, none of whom appear to be registered: Lavinia / Lovey (1881), Mary Ann /Polly (1883), Albert (1885), Elizabeth /Betsy (1881), Charles (1891) and John / Jack.

Elizabeth and Celia Lee were baptized at Christ Church East Grinstead on 26 May 1889. Bernice Thatcher was baptized at the same time. Her parents were William and Lucy Thatcher.

Charles Lee died on 12 May 1928, aged 68, at 181 West Street, Charlton. He was a Hawker and the cause of death was carcinoma of rectum. The informant was 'the mark of Lavinia Keen, daughter, present at the death, 6 North Street, Charlton.' Charles Lee was a Showman and a report of his funeral appeared in *The World's Fair*, on 2 June 1928:

'The internment of the late Mr. Charles Lee took place at Charlton Cemetery on Monday, May 21st, at 3pm. For many hours before the fixed time, friends and relatives were arriving from various parts, and numbers of local people, by whom he was liked and respected, collected along the road way. The oak coffin was borne to the cemetery by an open hearse drawn by four horses, and the inscription on the lid read: "Charles Lee, died May 12th, 1928, aged 68 years". He was a brother in law of the late Mr. Harry Taylor [husband of Elizabeth Pateman] whose funeral was reported in the 'World's Fair' some twelve months ago.

The mourners included: Mrs. M. Pateman (Mercy, wife of William Pateman) sister in law; Mrs. J. Pateman (Jane, wife of James Pateman) sister in law; Mr. and Mrs. G. Reynolds (George Reynolds and Mary Pateman), sister in law and brother in law; Amy Ott and Alice Daly (daughters of Henry Taylor and Elizabeth Pateman); Mr. William Thatcher (nephew); Mr. M. Thatcher, and Mrs. J Thatcher.

We do not know when or where Louisa Pateman died. Charles and Louisa Lee are buried at Charlton Cemetery, south east London, as are several of their children including Mary Ann and her husband Thomas Moses Crashley. Mary Ann and Thomas Moses had a son, Thomas John Crashley. The Crashley family were Watermen and Lightermen on the Thames for three generations. Before that they were shipwrights in the Royal Dockyard in Woolwich but the family originally came from Lincolnshire. Charles and Louisa Lee always went hopping in Kent, as did Mary Ann (who was baptized in Biddenden Church), Thomas Moses Crashley and Thomas John Crashley. The daughter of Thomas John Crashley, Linda Taylor, was also baptized in Biddenden Church when her parents were visiting Mary Ann and Thomas Moses.

Thomas Pateman (1861)

Thomas Pateman was born on 8 February 1861 at '15 minutes before noon' on the 'common, Latymer Road'. Unfortunately, Thomas only lived for 11 days and died on 18 February 1861 'in a van, common, Latymer road'. The cause of death was 'inanition from inability to suck'. Inanition is 'exhaustion from lack of nourishment'. Alice Pateman was in attendance, and Robert was described as a 'traveling clothes peg maker'. We do not know where Robert and his family were on 7 April 1861 when the Census was taken. We could not find them in the census for Hammersmith.

In a van

According to Thomas Pateman's death certificate, he died 'in a van'. This suggests that Robert and his family were living in a Gypsy van, wagon or *ker-vardo*, the house on wheels. John and James Pateman were both 'born in a tent' in 1844 and 1846 respectively. The fact that Robert was living in a van in 1861 suggests that he might have been a little better off than in previous years; or he could have been staying or lodging in someone else's van, or a railway carriage. The caravan was the most valuable possession of the Gypsy. It was home, and in it he carried his most treasured belongings – clothes, linen, china, a few photographs, perhaps medals won by himself or his family in the last war. But no true Gypsy ever talked of a caravan – he talked of a wagon or van. And the word *vardo* really means living wagon.

The typical *Romano vardo* is a comparatively recent introduction. Dickens, in *The Old Curiosity Shop*, was the first person to describe a wagon in England. He called it a caravan. That was in 1840, and there must have been wagons on the roads of Britain long before that. The typical living wagon wa a one roomed house on rather high wheels, with windows at the back and sides and a door and detachable steps at the front. There was a rack (*cratch*) at the back for carrying domestic articles of various kinds, and underneath the wagon at the back there was built a cupboard (pan box) which served both as larder and kitchen cupboard. Inside the wagon, behind the door, was a coal stove, with a chimney projecting through the roof, a cupboard and a locker seat. On the other side there was a corner cupboard for china, a chest of drawers in which was kept the family wardrobe and the family linen, and another locker. The whole of the back part was occupied by a two berth sleeping place.

We do not know what type of van Robert was living in 1861 but it could have been one of the following five types: the Reading wagon, the Leeds wagon, the Ledge wagon, the Burton or Showman's wagon, and the Fen or Brush wagon. The Reading wagon, so called because one of the best known builders lived in the Berkshire town, was a straight sided wagon with the wheels outside the body. Reading wagons were usually about 10 feet 6 inches in length, 6 feet wide at the bottom and 6 feet 6 inches at the eaves. The better and more expensive ones were fitted with a skylight.

The Leeds wagon was so called because the most famous builder of this type, one Bill Wright, lived near Leeds. It was also known as the bow or barrel topped wagon because of its shape. The usual length was about 9 feet 6 inches and the usual width at the widest part of the barrel was 6 feet to 6 feet 2 inches.

The Ledge wagon (sometimes called Cottage wagons) was the type most commonly seen on the roads, for these wagons were made by all the recognized builders, and were not connected with any particular place or any particular builder. In construction they came midway, as it were, between the Reading and the Leeds wagon. That is to say, they were not straight sided and did not have outside wheels, they were not barrel topped but had roofs very similar to those of the Reading wagon. The usual length was from 9 feet 6 inches to 10 feet, and the usual width 6 feet to 6 feet 2 inches at the widest part.

The Burton or Showman's wagon was a straight sided wagon like the Reading, but the wheels were placed underneath the body instead of outside it. All Burton wagons were made with a panelled or, less frequently, a rib and matchboard body, these latter sometimes with a panel about 4 inches wide running right round the centre of the body. The roof was much flatter than in the Reading wagon. All Burton wagons had pieces of carved wood attached to them somewhere or other. The usual length was 10 feet 6 inches and the usual width 6 feet.

The Fen or Brush wagon was by far the most picturesque of all wagons, but they were never popular with true Gypsies, and were used, as a rule, by people of dubious character who had taken to the roads to earn a yet more dubious living. The Brush wagon had external racks and cases for displaying wares for sale - brushes, baskets, pots and pans - and goods could be carried on the roof, for a rail ran all round to protect them.

Van Dwelling London

Living London was edited in 1901 by George R. Sims, who is credited as the pioneer of 'slum journalism'. Sims was one of the most famous journalists of the day. He made the transition from journalist to author by highlighting the plight of the urban working class in *How the Poor Live* (1883). *Living London* is a collection of essays on aspects of London life in 1901. One of these essays was *Van Dwelling London* by T.W. Wilkinson:

'Petulengro at the Agricultural Hall! The thing seems wildly incongruous; yet there he is, or somebody very much like him, during that rural carnival under cover, the World's Fair. Not that all, or even most, show people are Gypsies or of Gypsy descent. Let that be made perfectly clear. Still, a number of the van dwellers who congregate at Islington realize one of the finest characters immortalized by George Borrow.

The World's Fair is the greatest event in the showman's year. As Christmas draws nigh van dwellers come to town from east and west, north and south, and pitch their tents at Islington. In the yard of the Agricultural Hall their movable dwellings, a few of them exceptionally commodious and well furnished – low, ornate 'living wagons', having about double the cubic space of an ordinary caravan – are massed together, and life runs its course much as in other encampments. Though the owners of some betake themselves to fixed houses for the season, there are the usual scenes in the little colony, for all the world as if it were situated in the back woods of England. Children play about the 'living wagons'; out of business hours olive skinned, black haired men lounge against their caravans; and at meal times the air is laden with savory odors from sizzling frying pans, or seething pots perched on top of braziers that stand near the steps of some of the homes on wheels. Even in London in mid winter the open air has no terrors for most of the show folk.

Close by is another feature of the fair ground, though this is private – the clown's dressing room. And here, as the hour for opening approaches, you can watch the professional jesters perform the delicate operation of 'making up'. The paint is laid on with an uncommonly heavy hand; but then it has not to bear scrutiny through illusion dispelling opera glasses. It is, in fact, intended to be seen.
In the office there is a school for the show men's children, surely the only one in the wide world that is held in a company's board room. During the morning, and the morning only, about a score of swarthy youngsters bend over their lessons under the superintendence of one of the London School Board's mistresses. There is also a Sunday school, in connection with which a treat is given by Mr. Joseph Wright, of Glasgow, to all the children – and they number about sixty – in the fair. Naturally, the bairns look upon this as a most important function, more important by far than even the annual meeting of the Van Dweller's Association, though that body, with the show men, did have the honor of presenting a miniature carriage, a set of silver plated harness, and a well matched pair of Shetland ponies to the children of the Prince and Princess of Wales. The Agricultural Hall, however, is the van dwellers' Parliament.

To all seeming the show men are fixtures at Islington; but in reality their stay is short. Soon comes packing up time. Then for some days the hall has a peculiarly after the fair aspect. A ring is all that remains of the circus. Through the smoky air can be dimly seen the pole of a roundabout, sticking up without much visible support, like the mast of a partly submerged wreck. Cases, canvas, engines swathed in tarpaulins, bundles of sticks, odds and ends innumerable, lie scattered about everywhere. It is after the fair indeed! Some of the companies of itinerants have meanwhile departed, and a day or two later all have scattered – many not to meet again till Christmas comes round once more – and the hall is a waste land.

That is one side of Van Dwelling London. If you want to see another, you must travel further afield, to the ever extending outskirts of the Metropolis. Some morning you come on a regular encampment on a piece of waste ground well inside the county boundary. Last night it was bare; now a colony is spread over it. Sheeted vans are scattered about the plot, and among them rise bell shaped tents – the children's bedrooms. To each of the 'living wagons' a horse is tethered, while underneath it crouches the indispensable dog, one of the bread winners of the family. No need for him to see a game keeper; he can smell him a mile off. About the steps disheveled children, their toilet not yet made, play lightheartedly, indifferent to the curious gaze of the passers by; and here and there groups are gathered at breakfast – a vastly more substantial meal to these invaders than it is to most Londoners.

By and by the vans will crawl through suburban streets, and the brown-eyed syrens –greatest living exponents of the art of blarney – and the tall, lithe men will 'drop' a brush here, a basket there, a flower stand somewhere else. So they will pass away, and London may see them no more for years.

On the borders of Epping Forest, about the northern limits of Finchley and Hampstead, and round Wembley, there are numbers of more permanent and more squalid encampments. Pitiable indeed is the condition of some of the nomads in these settlements. When the air bites and stings, when there is a wind that you can lean against, whole families have no other home than the peculiar squat tent of the Gypsy or a wigwam formed of an old cart and a few yards of canvas.

In certain districts on the other side of the Thames, also, van dwellers' encampments last all through the winter. Though a good many of such colonies are situated in Wandsworth – where some of the hibernating nomads lay up their movable dwellings, go under a fixed roof, and become conventional, rent paying householders – Battersea contains more than any other metropolitan borough.

Donovan's Yard

Let us visit a typical specimen – Donovan's Yard. It is a plot of ground near the South Western line, commanding an unpicturesque prospect of palings, walls and arches, in one of which the Ragged School Union carries on a highly useful work, started by Mr. John Dyer, having for its aim the social and spiritual welfare of the van dwelling class. Two long lines of 'living wagons', broken here and there by a firewood dealer's hut, run the length of the yard. Instantly the eye travels along them you miss something. Ah! the horses! They have long since gone. The steps are down in the places they occupy while the movable houses are on the road. When the van dwellers come to town about October those who own steeds usually sell them, to save the cost of keeping them in idleness during the cold months, and purchase others just before taking to the road again.

On and between the lines there is a curious air of domesticity. Women, most of them stamped with their tribal characteristics, sit on the steps of the wagons, some at needlework, some merely gossiping. Other housewives are engaged on the family wash. Bent over tubs and buckets in close proximity to a fire, on which clothes are boiling briskly, they are rubbing and rinsing with a will, now and again going off for more water to a tap at one end of the ground. In a solitary instance a 'mother's girl' is engaged in this important household duty, while close by another child is scrubbing the chubby face of a sister not much younger than herself. The offspring of the poor seem to learn the domestic art in the cradle.

And now there is a diversion. Some half dozen youngsters come forward in a body and clamor for sweets, their healthy faces aglow with expectancy and their pinafores outstretched, lest their hands cannot hold enough! A moment later and they are happy!

Next, an interior. Go up the steps of a wagon, first noting that the ground rent for such caravans in Battersea is from 2s. to 3s. per week. The inside is a pocket edition of home as known to many thousands of house dwellers – the vast public of the one room tenement. On the left is a tiny fireplace, over which hangs a collection of brass and copper ornaments and utensils that glisten like burnished gold. The other side of the van is mostly taken up with a table placed underneath the neatly draped window. And, lastly, through some curtains at the far end of the van is a vista of a snowy white bed which extends across the whole width of the wagon.

Big as the bed is compared with the size of the little house on wheels, it does not seem sufficiently large to accommodate all the family. Nor, in fact, is it. The children sleep underneath when their home is in London, and in a tent when it is in the country. Sometimes a man owns two vans, and in that case his children, of course, occupy the extra bed. One feature of the van into which we have intruded must be emphasized – its spick and span condition. It would meet with the approbation of a 'house proud' Lancashire woman, who may be taken as an extreme representative of the slaves to cleanliness. Over the other encampments in Battersea we need not tarry. They are practically identical with the one in Donovan's Yard, though in some there are 'movable' homes which have been made fixtures. Shafts, wheels, and axles are gone. Only the bodies of the wagons remain, and these are numbered among London's myriad and strangely varied dwellings.

All the encampments exist for about six months of every year, from October till the flat race season begins. And it is not cold alone that drives van dwellers into town for the winter, but cold and 'nothing doing' combined. Many are in the cocoanut shy business, and may be seen on Hampstead Heath on Bank Holidays and at the various race meetings, chivalrously making a concession to one of woman's little weaknesses: 'Ladies half way!' A still larger section work in the fields at fruit picking, hopping, and harvesting generally. Dead, absolutely dead, of course, are these industries during the winter; so they come to London, and for the most part trust to hawking to carry them on till spring. And nobody welcomes it more heartily than they. Town is not their proper environment. They would rather hear the lark sing than the mouse cheep. But their spirits rise as the days grow longer, and when at last the Epsom meeting is at hand they rejoice at the glorious prospect that opens before them. Their period of hibernation is over. Sing hey! for the open road!"

9. Mitcham Common

- Noah Pateman (1866-?)

In this chapter our family history returns to Surrey and the London Commons, where Alice Pateman had been born in 1842. Robert had also passed through Surrey on his way to the Notting Hill Potteries in 1861.

Flora Thompson's trilogy *Lark Rise to Candleford* (1945) is one of the best loved of all books about the English countryside. It was published 60 years ago, and the past it describes is over a century away. Yet it remains perhaps the most vivid, detailed and immediate portrait of country life ever written.

Flora Thompson herself was a cottage child, born on 5 December 1876 and brought up in poverty in the tiny North Oxfordshire hamlet of Juniper Hill (which is renamed Lark Rise in the book; Candleford is Buckingham; Laura is Flora). From the age of five to when she left school at twelve, she and her brothers and sisters walked each day the three miles to Cottisford (Fordlow), where her teacher Miss Holmes used to say, 'Oh, Laura! What a dunce you are!' But Miss Holmes was wrong, for Flora possessed the literary gifts, the eye and memory for everyday detail and the intimacies of experience, which would one day combine to produce this gentle masterpiece.

In the 1870's and 1880's the countryside was on the brink of unalterable change, and the march of progress would soon wipe away the unique idiosyncracies of a centuries old way of life. But Flora Thompson was born in time to capture it before it vanished for ever, with her unforgettable gallery of characters – Old Sally, Miss Lane the post mistress, Sir Timothy, Miss Macey and the rest – and her unsentimental but deeply affectionate account of the humble details of the life she knew.

In *Lark Rise* especially we receive an unforgettable impression of the transitional state between the old stable, work pleasure England and the modern world. The different lives of the hamlet, village and market town are explored in rich detail. The parallels for Robert Pateman would have been the hamlet of Hollow Bottom (where Noah Pateman was born in 1866), the village of Beckenham and the market town of Bromley. Although they were geographically quite close they existed as separate worlds. Here is Thompson's description of Lark Rise:

'In the 1880's the hamlet consisted of about 30 cottages and an inn, not built in rows, but dotted down anywhere within a more or less circular group. A deeply rutted cart track surrounded the whole, and separate houses or groups of houses were connected by a network of pathways. The only shop was a small general one kept in the back kitchen of the inn. The church and school were in the mother village, a mile and a half away.'

Laura and her family never strayed far from the hamlet: 'A dell was the farthest point of their walk; after searching the long grass for mushrooms they turned back and never reached the second milestone. Once or twice when they reached the dell they got a greater thrill than even the discovery of a mushroom could give; for the Gypsies were there, their painted caravan drawn up, their poor old skeleton horse turned loose to graze, and their fire with a cooking pot over it, as though the whole road belonged to them. With men making pegs, women combing their hair or making cabbage nets, and boys and girls and dogs sprawling around, the dell was full of dark, wild life, foreign to the hamlet children and fascinating, yet terrifying.

When they saw the Gypsies they drew back behind their mother and the baby carriage, for there was a tradition that once, years before, a child from a neighboring village had been stolen by them. Even the cold ashes where a Gypsy's fire had been sent little squiggles of fear down Laura's spine, for how could she know that they were not still lurking near with designs upon her own person? Her mother laughed at her fears and said, 'Surely to goodness they've got children enough of their own,' but Laura would not be reassured. She never really enjoyed the game the hamlet children played going home from school, when one of them went on before to hide and the others followed slowly, hand in hand, singing:

'I hope we shan't meet any Gypsies tonight!
I hope we shan't meet any Gypsies tonight!'

And when the hiding place was reached and the supposed Gypsy sprung out and grabbed the nearest, she always shrieked, although she knew it was only a game.'

Callers

Callers made a pleasant diversion in the hamlet women's day, and there were more of these than might have been expected. There was old Jerry Parish with his cartload of fish and fruit. Mr. Wilkins, the baker, came three times a week. Many casual callers passed through the hamlet: 'Traveling tinkers with their barrows, braziers, and twirling grindstones turned aside from the main road and came singing:

'Any razors or scissors to grind?
Or anything else in the tinker's line?
Any old pots or kettles to mend?'

After squinting into any leaking vessel against the light, or trying the edges of razors or scissors upon the hard skin of their palms, they would squat by the side of the road to work, or start their emery wheel whizzing, to the delight of the hamlet children, who always formed a ring around any such operations.

Gypsy women with cabbage nets and clothes pegs to sell were more frequent callers for they had a camping place only a mile away and no place was too poor to yield them a harvest. When a door was opened to them, if the housewife appeared to be under forty, they would ask in a wheedling voice: 'Is your mother at home, my dear?' Then, when the position was explained, they would exclaim in astonished tones: 'You don't mean to tell me you be the mother? Look at that, now. I shouldn't have taken you to be a day over twenty.'

No matter how often repeated, this compliment was swallowed whole, and made a favourable opening for a long conversation, in the course of which the wily 'Egyptian' not only learned the full history of the woman's own family, but also a good deal about those of her neighbours, which was duly noted for future use. Then would come a request for a 'handful of little 'taters, or an onion or two for the pot', and, if these were given, as they usually were, 'My pretty lady' would be asked for an old shift of her own or an old shirt of her husband's, or anything that the children might have left off, and, poverty stricken though the hamlet was, a few worn out garments would be secured to swell the size of the bundle which, afterwards, would be sold to the rag merchant.

Sometimes the Gypsies would offer to tell fortunes; but this offer was always refused, not out of scepticism or lack of curiosity about the future, but because the necessary silver coin was not available. 'No, thank 'ee,' the women would say. 'I don't want nothink of that sort. My fortune's already told.'

'Ah, my lady! You med think so; but them as has got childern never knows. You be born, but you ain't dead yet, an' you may dress in silks and ride in your own carriage yet. You wait till that fine strappin' buy o' yourn get rich. He won't forget his mother, I'll bet!' and after this free prognostication, they would trail off to the next house, leaving behind a scent as strong as a vixen's.

The Gypsies paid in entertainment for what they received. Their calls made a welcome break in the day. Those of the tramps only harrowed the feelings and left the depressed in spirit even more depressed. There must have been hundreds of tramps on the roads at that time. It was a common sight, when out for a walk, to see a dirty, unshaven man, his rags topped with a battered bowler, lighting a fire of sticks by the roadside to boil his tea can.

The packman, or pedlar, once a familiar figure in that part of the country, was seldom seen in the 'eighties. People had taken to buying their clothes at the shops in the market town, where fashions were newer and prices lower. But one last survivor of the once numerous clan still visited the hamlet at long and irregular intervals. He would turn aside from the turnpike and come plodding down the narrow hamlet road, an old white-headed, white-bearded man, still hale and rosy, although almost bent double under the heavy, black canvas-covered pack he carried strapped on his shoulders.

'Anything out of the pack today?' he would ask at each house, and, at the least encouragement, fling down his load and open it on the door step. He carried a tempting variety of goods: dress lengths and shirt lengths and remnants to make up for the children; aprons and pinafores, plain and fancy; corduroys for the men, and coloured scarves and ribbons for Sunday wear. Few of the hamlet women could afford to test the quality of his piece goods; cottons or tapes, or a paper of pins, were their usual purchases; but his dress lengths and other fabrics were of excellent quality and wore much longer than any one would wish anything to wear in these days of rapidly changing fashions.

Other callers included a German band, a marionette show and a dancing bear. The greatest thrill of all and the one longest remembered in the hamlet, was provided by the visit of a cheap jack. One autumn evening, just before dusk, he arrived with his cartload of crockery and tin ware and set out his stock on the grass by the roadside before a back cloth painted with icebergs and penguins and polar bears. Soon he had his naptha lamps flaring and was clashing his basins together like bells and calling: 'Come buy! Come buy!'

Men, women and children rushed from the houses and crowded around in the circle of light to listen to his patter and admire his wares. And what bargains he had! The tea service decorated with fat, full blown pink roses: twenty one pieces and not a flaw in any of them. The Queen had purchased its fellow set for Buckingham Palace, it appeared. The teapots, the trays, the nests of dishes and basins, and the set of bedroom china which made everyone blush when he selected the most intimate utensil to rap with his knuckles to show it rang true.

'Two bob!' he shouted. 'Only two bob for this handsome set of jugs. Here's one for your beer and one for your milk and another in case you break one of the other two. Nobody willing to speculate? Then what about this here set of trays, straight from Japan and the peonies hand painted; or this lot of basins, exact replicas of the one the Princess of Wales supped her gruel from when Prince George was born. Why damme, they cost me more n'r that. I could get twice the price I'm asking in Banbury tomorrow; but I'll give 'em to you, for you can't call it selling, because I like your faces and me load's heavy for me 'oss. Alarming bargains! Tremendous sacrifices! Come buy! Come buy!'

Robert Pateman was neither a packman (although the similarity between packman and Pateman is interesting) nor a cheap jack. He was a licensed hawker. In the nineteenth century some 'travelling' trades were regulated by licence. Before 1870, these licences were issued by Quarter Sessions to pedlars (who travelled on foot), hawkers (who travelled by horse) and chimney sweeps – among others. From 1870, this licensing became the responsibility of local police forces. Most of the records relating to the licences are now held in County Record Offices. The information contained in them typically includes name, place of abode, age and date of issue.

Noah Pateman (1866-?)

Sometime after the birth of Louisa and Thomas at Hammersmith in 1861, Robert returned to Kent for the birth of his next child, Noah, in 1866. Given this five year gap between births, it is possible that Robert had more children in the interval who are unrecorded or who died in infancy.

Noah Pateman was born on 26 March 1866 at Hollowbottom, Bromley. Robert was described as a licensed hawker. Hollow Bottom, now Nichol Lane, is a fascinating spot which has almost, but not quite, changed out of all recognition. It is certainly one of the oldest residential streets in the parish of St Andrews. A 1723 map shows two houses on the site of the *Prince Frederick* pub, and two houses opposite. These were the only houses in Hollow Bottom, but there were other houses grouped around Plaistow Green. The hamlet was commonly known as Hollow Bottom until relatively recently, with the Ordnance Survey Map of 1863 identifying it as such. There are two houses of considerable interest in the lane; number 27 (in 1982 named Hollow Bottom Cottage) and *The Prince Frederick* itself.

The public house in Nichol Lane was named after Prince Frederick, Prince of Wales who lived from 1707 to 1751. The *Prince Frederick's Head* appears in a register of fire insurance policies of the Hand in Hand Fire and Life Insurance Society dated 28 January 1761. According to the 1841 Census in Hollow Bottom there were a total of 180 men, women and children, including about 30 laborers (general, builders' and agricultural) and others listed as carpenters, gardeners, grooms, blacksmiths, sailors, man servants, an army private, a meal man and a grocer (the publican). In 1861 the residents of Hollow Bottom included a general dealer, a dealer, three bricklayers and William Cooper, a basket maker.

In 1866, the year that Noah was born, John Wallis was the landlord of the *Prince Frederick*. According to *Strongs Directory of Bromley* (1866) the other residents of Hollow Bottom were Mr. Craker, Mr. J. Gould, Ezekiel Kelsey (brewer and coal merchant) and Mr. W. Morgrave. The area of Plaistow and Farwig in the 1860's was still rural. To the north of the parish were Plaistow Lodge, Plaistow Hall and Springhill whilst in Hollow Bottom a small group of cottages clustered around the *Prince Frederick*. One of these (number 27 Nichol Lane) is the oldest dwelling in the parish. Several bricks in the exterior walls bear the date 1739, almost certainly indicating the date of building.

Hosburgh, writing about Bromley in the 1860's said: 'To the north of the town there was practically open country beyond the College and from College Field an uninterrupted view, extending to the church in the distance, could be obtained of stiles and meadows, shrubs and trees.' This is a reference to St Mary's, Plaistow.

'Plaistow is a parish half a mile from Bromley and ten and a half miles from London. Formerly included in Bromley, it is now a separate ecclesiastical parish and consists of the two hamlets of Plaistow and Farwig, together with part of the London Road and also a portion of New Bromley. The population in 1861 was 2000; since then it has considerably increased owing to the rapid progress of buildings in this neighborhood". (*Kelly's Directory*, 1866).

The *Post Office Directory* (1878) noted that 'The Bromley cemetery (consecrated 19 September 1877) is pleasantly situated on the London Road in this district". The London Road Cemetery contains the graves of Elizabeth Pateman (19 December 1898, age 22) and, buried together, Noemie Pateman (26 August 1976, age 70) and Ernest Charles Pateman (13 September 1974, age 81).

An Ordnance Survey map of 1861 shows Bromley before it was developed; to the north and still separate from the town, stood Farwig, Bromley Hill and Plaistow, the latter dominated by Plaistow Lodge, with a 126 acre estate that stretched to London Road. Farwig, originally part of the Plaistow Lodge estate, was sold to Johann Farwig, an industrialist. Some small, artisans' houses were laid out here between 1825 and 1832, but wholesale development of the area did not come until the 1860's; the first signs of this are seen in the streets laid out between Farwig and Plaistow.

This map captures Bromley in its last years as a small country town. Perhaps the absolute moment of change came in 1863, in the Market Place, when the ramshackle old market hall was demolished and replaced by a Town Hall, which would dominate the square, and which led inexorably to the suppression of the old Bromley fairs. For a while even the market was discontinued. Within a few years the world of eating matches, roundabouts, of pigs and sheep in the High Street, of coaches outside the hotels, all this was gone as surely as if it belonged to the Middle Ages.

Bromley

Bromley developed as a suburb after 1858, new roads were built out from the centre and infilling took place. This was in addition to the development of hamlets such as Widmore, Sundridge, Plaistow and Elmstead. The new station at Bromley North in 1878 led to further building to the north linking up with Plaistow. As a suburb on the edge of London, Bromley was visited by Gypsies who wintered over there before returning to the home counties for fruit, vegetable and hop picking.

'Bromley is a market and union town and railway station and pulling place for the west division of the county, situated on the Hastings line of road, through Sevenoaks and Tonbridge, near the east bank of the Ravensbourne, in the Hundred of Ruxley. 10 miles from London, and the Chatham and Dover Railway, 14 miles from Sevenoaks, and 6 miles from Greenwich. Bromley is partially paved and well lighted with gas. The parish extends over 4,646 acres and had a population of 5,505 in 1861. Bromley New Town is half a mile east and is becoming a thickly populated place.'(*Kelly's Directory,* 1866).

Bromley was expanding rapidly and a local newspaper described it in 1866 as 'The town that was a village':

'The once quiet market town of Bromley (the glade among the broom) favorably situated on the London to Hastings turnpike road and always a busy and important coaching stop, is undergoing such an amazing metamorphosis that it now needs a Local Board to administer its affairs. The Board was elected this year to look after all the problems associated with progress – drainage, sewage disposal, water supply and the provision of new roads and schools.

Like most Kentish towns the change has been brought about by the arrival of the Iron Horse. When Bromley railway station was opened on Masons' Hill less than 10 years ago, the impact was immediate. New families arrived from London and some moved up from rural Kent. To them, the lure of residing in a small country town, surrounded by woods and fields, was far too compelling.

The population of Bromley is now approaching 7,000. Many are living in new homes built on the site of Bromley Palace and Bickley Park. Both estates were sold off for development. One man who has a small shop in Bromley High Street is the Kent cricketer Joseph Wells. It is a kind of pottery emporium and is called Atlas House. Wells is better known for a remarkable feat of bowling than the world of small time commerce. In his second county match against Hove five years ago he took four wickets in successive balls – all bowled. He became the first man in first class cricket to accomplish this feat.'

The population of Bromley virtually doubled from 5,505 in 1861 to 10,674 in 1871; and it subsequently grew by around 5,000 each decade, to 33,646 by 1911. The following items appeared in the *Bromley Record* in the months after Noah's birth:

'Within a radius of 15 miles around London there were 180 commons, covering 10,500 acres. A careful examination of these commons showed that great dissatisfaction existed with regard to the state of the commons, many of which were ill drained and cut up into gravel pits, frequented by tramps and disreputable people of all sorts and there was at present no means by which these commons could be kept in order' (1 April 1866).

'An easterly wind has prevailed the greater part of the month and with it we have had blights, a few frosts, great and ruinous bank failures and rumors of coming wars' (1 June 1866).

'The hop picking is nearly completed in Kent in spite of the fearful weather we have experienced and some strikes for higher pay the crop is estimated 7 cwt per acre, about half the yield of last year. It is estimated that about 18,000 hop pickers have been, by means of railways etc, imported into Kent and the previous fears that cholera might be thereby conveyed have been unhappily realised, a very serious outbreak of the disease has taken place in the Yalding district, the authorities are using the greatest exertions to diminish the effects of this dreadful scourge' (1 October 1866).

'The Black Illness is back in Kent. Despite the efforts of specially appointed inspectors to seize bad food from itinerant vendors, cholera has appeared in Mid Kent and is particularly rampant in the hopping villages of Yalding, Hunton, Nettlestead, Teston, Marden, Staplehurst, Otham, Bearsted and Barming. The disease was first reported in London and aboard the *Queen of the Colonials* at Gravesend. From London it was carried by barge to Faversham, Sittingbourne, Maidstone, Sheerness and Aylesford.

In Chatham, three dispensaries were opened and the roads watered with diluted carbolic acid. It was to no avail. In September the Maidstone guardians persuaded the South Eastern Railway to take as many hop pickers as possible directly to the hop gardens to protect the town. They did, but the workers were idle for some time because of heavy rains and spent many hours sitting in their hovels or old Crimean tents. The rain came in and so did the black illness' (October, 1866).

But this did not deter the 'dregs of London' from pouring back into Kent the following year, although the hopping was more regulated. 'No longer can hop pickers travel to Kent and hire themselves out to local farmers on a first come first served basis. In the last of many great reforms, introduced by the growers, London hiring agents will make a list of those who wish to register themselves for hopping. They will pass the information on to an agent in Maidstone and thus help to control the enormous burden on county services.

For many years now thousands of Londoners have come to Kent each year in search of work in the hop gardens and discovered they are not required. Hungry and destitute they have either thrown themselves on the mercy of the union house keepers or made their way home again on foot, with no money, no food and no lodgings. Last year thousands came from London, sleeping rough under hedges or in open fields. As they got nearer to the farms hundreds applied to the relieving officers for lodgings but others slept on the doorsteps in the towns of North and Mid Kent. The Coxheath Union, four miles from Maidstone, was taking 600-700 people every night but 1,200 slept rough in Gravesend town centre.

From now on each picker recruited will be given a Hopper's Letter which contains a registration number, the picker's destination, train times and the name of his employer. At the end of the picking season the farmer must endorse the letter with his comments about the suitability of the picker. This will be delivered to a London agent who will be in a position to draw up a black list of pickers. And there will be a black list because bad feeling has existed for many years. Militancy has been rife and it is not unknown for pickers, led by bully boys, to threaten farmers or set fire to their houses. Mob rioting has broken out frequently and local pickers have been terrorised by their visitors.

The Rev. J.J. Kendon from Curtisden Green, Goudhurst has been undertaking missionary work in an attempt to save the souls of the unsavoury characters and improve conditions for the hoppers. In his first report last year this is what he wrote: 'Here may be seen the dregs of many of our larger towns, and of London. They sleep in stables, lodges, barns, hoppers' houses, straw huts etc., almost like the cattle of the fields. To mingle among these poor creatures, to see their habits and hear their language, to witness the awful lengths in wickedness to which they go, makes it seem almost impossible that we can be living in England in the latter part of the nineteenth century.'

Mr Kendon intends to send missionaries into the hop gardens and hand out tickets for free teas at Curtisden Green. He wants to introduce prayer meetings and hymn singing, recognising they will 'probably hear more of the gospel during hop picking than they will during the rest of the year'. The Reverend J.Y. Stratton is also concerned about the seamier side of life in the Kentish farms during hop picking time and is delighted that the need for great improvement has been recognised by the growers themselves.

Two years ago a group of land owners and tenant hop farmers formed the Society for the Employment and Improved Lodgings of Hop Pickers. They said the huts should be wind and rain proof, that adequate latrines be provided and that an inspector be appointed by the Board of Guardians of each district to inspect food and water supplied to the hoppers. There must be sufficient floor space and screens between the beds. Even more revolutionary, they recommended that hopper huts should, in future, be brick built. With tighter controls over the numbers arriving in Kent it should be easier to provide better conditions when they arrive' (April 1867).

We do not know what effect these controls had, or how they affected Robert Pateman and other Gypsies who joined East Enders in the hop fields of Kent; in 1890 it was reported that 'more than 250,000 hoppers are now working in the Kentish hop gardens – about 70,000 of them come from London.'

Beckenham

Some time after the birth of Noah in 1866, Robert made the short journey from Bromley to Beckenham. At the time of the 1871 Census – held on 3 April - Robert and his family were living in 'an old stable' on a brick field at Arthur Road / Becks Lane, Beckenham. Robert was described as a Gypsy, his wife Mary was a Licensed Hawker and their children were Pedlars. It is interesting to note the brickfield connection and that they were living in a barn.

Another family of "Gipsys under the Pedlars Act" were living in a neighboring 'hut and van'. These were James Diton (30, Kent, Tunbridge), his wife Rahana (32, Worcs, Crapton) and their children: Baranathan (28, Kent, Farningham), Solomon (25, Kent, Plumstead), Noah (21, Kent, Plumstead), Dellia (16, Essex, Eastham), Noyou (15, Essex, Eastham), Phibea (11, Kent, Bexleyheath), Walter (7, Surrey, Streatham), Priscilla (6, Surrey, Battersea), Holly (20, Middlesex, Shepherds Bush), Abraham (15, Essex, East Ham), and William (11, Kent, Plaxtol). Also living with them was a sister, Nidella (40, Nothants, Peterboro).

Phibea (Phoebe) Dighton married Walter Pateman in 1881. It is interesting to note the Kent, Surrey and Middlesex connections with Robert Pateman and his family. Also living nearby on the brickfield was Joseph Hawkes, a brickmaker. There was an explosion at the Kent Brick Works in Worsley Bridge Road, Beckenham, in February 1885 when five men were killed while having their lunch in the engine shed. They were John Butler, John Poor, Frederick Edmeads and James Fisher and his son Daniel. A fund for their widows was opened by Albemarle Cator, one of the chief local landowners, who contributed £20 himself.

The 1871 census also notes the following people 'not in houses': Henry Ayres (21) and his daughter Betsy (1) were living in a 'traveling house or caravan in Croydon Road' and a 'girl about 10' was found 'singing in Beckenham village'.

Beckenham was 'a large parish and suburban village and railway station on the head of the Ravensbourne, 10 miles from London and 2 from Bromley. The London, Chatham and Dover and the Mid Kent Railways had stations here. The soil was sand and gravel, with clay on elevated spots. The crops were wheat, oats, barley and roots. The area was 3,875 acres and the population in 1861 was 2,124' (*Kelly's Directory*, 1866).

A concise portrait of Beckenham is given by *Ward's Directory* in the 1890's: 'The chief street of Beckenham is long and winding, and the houses are largely intermixed with fields and gardens, looking as if they were built at a time when space was plentiful. One or two old houses with timbered faces remain, especially an ancient one in the centre of the village, which bears on its face six panels carved with flowers – possibly the white and red roses. But modern grandeur is gradually driving away the air of quiet and homely respectability which has up to this time given a character to Beckenham.'

The village had become a town, but an Ordnance Survey Map of 1861 shows Beckenham at an earlier stage: still a country village but with the railways that would bring about its growth. Indeed, so new were the railways – and the map was revised in 1871 to include them all – that the census return probably included a number of railway navvies. The population increased from 2,124 in 1861 to 6,090 in 1871, 13,011 in 1881 and then progressively to 43,832 by 1931, after which the boundaries were extended. The fascination of this map, however, is that it captures a moment in time when a modern transport network had been imposed on an old Kentish village, but had not yet altered it.

The 1861 map shows Becks Lane and the brick field where Robert and his family were living, which was close to the London, Chatham and Dover Railway line.

Strong's Directory of 1879 notes three residences and two Mission Rooms in Arthur Road. By 1885 there were 63 addresses in Arthur Road and one of the Mission Rooms was also a reading room. The brickworks were still in evidence, between Sultan Road (let in small tenements) and the Arthur Road Mission Hall. By 1886 the brickworks had disappeared and more houses had been built, including Hope Terrace, where 'Bateman –' lived at number 18. A map of 1912 shows houses and schools on the brickfield site.

Beckenham has a number of churches including St George (1790), St Paul (1871), Christ Church (1876), St Michael and All Angels (1877), St Barnabas (1878) and Holy Trinity (1878). It was at Holy Trinity that Arthur Pateman (37, bachelor, coachman, 129 Victor Road, son of Joseph Pateman, brewer) married Sarah Frances Izzard (23, spinster, domestic servant, daughter of William Izzard, licenced victualler) on 28 September 1897.

One of the most remarkable people buried in Beckenham churchyard was probably Margaret Finch, a 'queen' of the Gypsies. She was a person of great notoriety and was said to have been 109 years old when she died in 1740. She had been accustomed to sitting on the ground with her chin on her knees and a pipe in her mouth. Eventually she could not rise from this position and when she died an ordinary coffin was of no use, and a deep square box was made in which she was placed and buried. A big crowd gathered in Beckenham on the occasion of her funeral and all the Gypsies for miles around attended.

On the subject of funerals, Arthur Road / Becks lane is almost opposite Beckenham crematorium, where a number of Pateman's were laid to rest: Arthur (1886), Claude (1897) and Gladys (1908) are in unmarked graves; James (1916), Elenor (1916) and Mary (1918) are all in plot L2 Row 5, which suggests they may have been related.

Members of my immediate family were also cremated or buried here, including Noah William (1967), Violet Nellie May (1974), Frank George (1977), Harry William (1979) and Robert Henry (1990). My grandmother, Ada Doris Poxon (1982) and my mother, Dorothy Florence May (1988), are also here, just a stones throw from where Robert Pateman and his family were living a century before.

Pedlars' Act 1871

Robert Pateman was described as a licensed hawker on Noah's birth certificate in 1866. Mary Pateman was described as a licensed hawker in the 1871 Census. All hawkers and pedlars were required by law to obtain and carry with them a hawker's licence / pedlar's certificate. In 1871, the issuing of these certificates became the responsibility of the Constabulary and every division was required to keep a record of all licences / certificates issued. Details recorded: surname, forename, abode, division in which issued, date of issue. Some registers also give a description of the pedlar / hawker, and sometimes cancellations on court convictions are recorded. Very often the certificate / licence holder was of no fixed abode but at least knowing the division of issue gives a place around which to locate a search.

At any time, a hawker or pedlar could be asked to produce his or her licence for inspection by the local police, wherever they happened to be. The licence would then be endorsed and details entered in the relevant register. Details recorded: name, address, police district in which certificate was granted, date granted, date endorsed. The individual's address, very often just the name of a town or village, and the place of endorsement provide the researcher with two possible areas in which to base a search. Pedlars returns (returns of Certificates Under Pedlars Act) were the forms which were completed by each division and returned to Divisional Headquarters. Details recorded: name of grantee of certificate, address, division, date of issue.

Mitcham

We do not know where Robert was between 1871 and 1881. He may have moved back down into Kent or travelled between Kent, Surrey, Middlesex and Bedfordshire. He was on one of these journeys at the time of the 1881 Census – the census was held on 3 April, but Mitcham Fair was not until August, so it seems unlikely that Robert was in Mitcham to do business at the fair. It is more likely that he was stopping at Mitcham on one of his regular journeys from Kent to Bedfordshire.

Mitcham was a parish and extensive village with two railway stations, 9 miles south west from Westminster Bridge, and 3 north west from Croydon, on the River Wandle, and the Reigate Road. 'The fair is held yearly, on the 12th, 13th and 14th August. The soil is a rich black mould; subsoil, gravel; laid out partly in market gardens, and partly for medicinal plants, such as roses, rhubarb, liquorice, lavender, mint, camomile, poppies, peppermint, wormwood, and aniseed; part of these are used for the manufacture of cordials and perfumes, particularly peppermint water, oil of lavender, and rose water. There are numerous mills on the river Wandle. The population in 1871 was 6,498.' (*Post Office Directory*, 1878)

By the end of the eighteenth century the sale of horses was an important activity at Mitcham Fair and trading, as well as the Fair itself, brought a large number of traveling people to the village. It was not only for the true Romanies that Mitcham provided the twin attractions of the chance of making a 'quid' or two and finding a temporary camping site. Travelers and tinkers of all kinds regularly camped on the Common, and the authorities seem always to have had difficulty in controlling the situation. In reminiscences of Mitcham around the middle of the nineteenth century it has been said that as many as 200 Gypsy tents and caravans were to be found on the Common in midsummer, and although many moved away at the end of Mitcham Fair, others remained until after Croydon Fair in October, taking seasonal work in the Mitcham herb fields harvesting lavender and camomile, or selling from door to door.

During the 1851 Census one enumerator, whose district included the Common, listed 35 poverty stricken Irish – men, women and children – sleeping rough in barns, fields, woodlands and on the Common itself. Many would have made their way to England after the outbreak of potato blight in Ireland, when families often had little choice but to emigrate or die in the ensuing famine. The fate of these tragic people is not known. Some probably moved on, but one imagines that others may eventually have found work and settled in Mitcham or the neighborhood. Some of the true Romany families certainly put down roots in Mitcham, for at this time many small yards and odd corners were to be found, particularly to the west of the village centre, where caravans could be tucked away and not be disturbed. Part of Mitcham was known as Redskin

Village because of the large numbers of Romanies who wintered in yards there while traveling to Kent for fieldwork in the summer.

A series of 'Sketches of Gipsy Life' appeared in the *Illustrated London News* in 1879/1880 (you will recall the sketch of a 'van near Latimer Road, Notting Hill', which we described in chapter seven). Another sketch depicts Gypsy life inside a tent on Mitcham Common:

'Another sketch of the wild and squalid habits of life still retained by vagrant parties or clans of this singular race of people, often met with in the neighbourhood of suburban villages and other places around London, will be found in our Journal. We may again direct the reader's attention to the account of them which was contributed by Mr George Smith, of Coalville, Leicester, to the late Social Science Congress at Manchester, and which was reprinted in our last week's publication. That well known advocate of social reform and legal protection for the neglected vagrant classes of our population reckons the total number of Gypsies in this country at three or four thousand men and women and ten thousand children.

He is now seeking to have all movable habitations – i.e. tents, vans, shows, etc – in which the families live who are earning a living by travelling from place to place, registered and numbered, as in cases of canal boats, and the parents compelled to send their children to school at the place wherever they may be temporarily located, be it National, British, or Board school. The following is Mr Smith's note upon what was to be seen in the Gypsies tent on Mitcham Common:

'Inside this tent – with no other home – there were two men, their wives, and about fourteen children of all ages: two or three of these were almost men and women. The wife of one of the men had been confined of a baby the day before I called – her bed consisting of a layer of straw upon the damp ground. Such was the wretched and miserable condition they were in that I could not do otherwise than help the poor woman, and gave her a little money. But in her feelings of gratitude to me for this simple act of kindness she said she would name the baby anything I would wish to choose; and, knowing that Gypsies are fond of outlandish names, I was in a difficulty. After turning the thing over in my mind for a few minutes, I could think of nothing but Deliverance. This seemed to please the poor woman very much; and the poor child is named Deliverance G------. Strange to say, the next older child is named Moses.'

1881 Census

On 3 April 1881 Robert Bateman (60, Hoo) was living in a tent on Mitcham Common with his two sons, Walter (21, Bembery) and Robert (13, Bearsted). They were all skewer makers. Walter was born at Stockbury in 1859. Robert junior was born at Claygate in 1860.

Also living in tents on Mitcham Common in 1881 were:

- Robert's daughter, Louisa Lee (20, Notting Hill) and her husband Charles Lee (aka Charles Thatcher, 21, Rochester), skewer makers

- Charles Lee's father, Alfred Lee (58, Gardner Stret), and his sons, James (26, South Church, Essex), Alfred (17, Rochester) and Albert (14, Woolwich), cutlers
- Charles Lee's brother, William Thatcher (29, Gravesend), his wife Lucy (27, Brighton) and their children Elizabeth (9, Gravesend), Lethy (7, Plumstead) and Moses (7 months, Beddington), hawkers
- James Diton (61, Mitcham) and his daughter Phoebe (22, Bexley) who married Walter Pateman in 1881.
- William Coates (27, Essex) and his children, who were later to have close connections with the Pateman family. Their son, Benjamin Coates (1885-1970) married Priscilla Pateman, widow of Walter Pateman (1886-1917).

The 1881 Census records that out of 231 people who were living on Mitcham Common in tents and caravans there were 106 adults who gave their occupations. The majority of them, numbering 68, described themselves as hawkers, pedlars or general dealers. Only two considered themselves to be laborers, the rest gave various itinerant trades and crafts including 16 basket makers, 5 tin men or tinkers, 4 cutlers, 4 chair makers and 3 peg makers. Those who described themselves as chair makers were probably weavers of cane and rush seats, the cutlers were most likely knife grinders and the tin men, or tinkers, repaired kettles and pots.

These tradesmen worked the suburban streets, calling from house to house to offer their services. Wooden clothes pegs were made in considerable quantities for sale from door to door along with other home made craft items such as primrose baskets and artificial wooden flowers. Most of these trades or odd jobs would not have been enough in themselves to provide a living, so most families would probably have had a mixed domestic economy which included the casual agricultural seasonal work. The occupations they gave for the purpose of the census might only have described what they were doing while actually in Mitcham.

Gypsy travelers didn't simply roam aimlessly around the countryside. Most families had a fairly regular annual circuit, by remaining within a locality they got to know at which farms they were most likely to get employment and which ones were best avoided, the landowners who tolerated Travelers and those who would have them moved on as quickly as possible. Local knowledge was important for survival, you needed to know where the stopping places were, where water could be obtained, whether the local residents were hostile and how tolerant the local constabulary were.

Of the 231 people living on Mitcham Common in 1881, eighty three of them gave their birth place as Surrey, 55 from neighboring Kent, 14 each from Sussex and Middlesex and 11 from Essex. The remaining 36 came from the rest of the country, just a few from each county. The majority of those from Surrey were actually born in Mitcham, the rest were mainly from neighboring areas including Epsom, Banstead, Croydon, etc. Although of no fixed abode, travelers were usually local people, although some did go further afield, most remained in fairly easy reach of work, family and friends.

The census also tells us that 196 of the travelers were living in tents and just 35 in caravans. In spite of the fact that the painted wooden horse drawn caravan is synonymous with the Gypsy traveler, it only became popular in the latter part of the nineteenth century. It was the traveling showmen who first really recognized the value of the specialist horse drawn vehicle when they began adapting carts and wagons to create mobile cages for their menageries in the early 1900s, soon after this some experimented with building living wagons.

On 11 July 1891 the newly formed Board of Conservators resolved that part of the Common should be set aside for an 18 hole golf course, 'providing none was enclosed and no one was prevented from walking or exercising commonable rights thereon.' Swamps were drained and filled in, large areas of gorse were grubbed out, tons of soil were carted to fill up the excavations left by the gravel diggers, and the further removal of gravel was stopped. The Gypsies who, it was alleged, had made the Common impossible for a woman to walk through alone, were pushed further afield.

Mitcham Fair

Although the custom of holding a fair on Mitcham Common is undoubtedly an old one, maybe even Elizabethan, the earliest known reference to a fair is in 1732 and concerned 'Christopher Halstead, a fiddler, that came to the Fair and died at Mr. Merrett's'. A hand drawn map of Mitcham Fair, dated August 12th, 13th, 14th 1882 depicts the various attractions at the fair including 'Our girls, a show of two fat girls' and a 'performing fish and seal'. In the last century the approach of the Fair was heralded by the arrival of large encampments of showmen and Gypsies on Mitcham Common.

Gypsy caravans were permitted to park on Three Kings Piece for some days before and after Mitcham Fair while it was still held on Upper Green. In the early days it was the Gypsies who supplied most of the dancing booths and stalls. They also took the opportunity to engage in some horse trading amongst themselves, using the road beside the Three Kings' Piece to show off the paces of the horses and ponies they were selling.

After the fair Gypsies moved on to casual work in the fields cutting lavender and harvesting other herbs for which the physic gardens at Mitcham are renowned. The women would work from door to door selling handmade clothes pegs, lavender bags, brushes and rush mats, together with besoms, or garden brooms, made of twigs bound together.

In past centuries most country towns and villages were too small to support permanent traders, apart from perhaps a black smith and a few other specialist craftsmen. Neither did most working people in rural areas have the means to go far to make purchases, only the better off could afford to own a horse so walking was the only option. They mainly relied instead on traveling pedlars and hawkers to come to them to supply their needs for the few material possessions that they required. These itinerant salesmen would trade as they traveled, dealing in all manner of essential domestic goods, and other less important but nevertheless desirable items like ornaments, trinkets and finery. As well as hawking their wares as they passed through towns and villages, there were the annual fair days when large numbers of traveling salesmen would arrive and set up shop. Most villages and towns had at least one or two fair days a year, but they were very different occasions to the fun fairs of today.

The first fairs to be granted charters by the King in the middle ages were primarily occasions for agricultural commerce, they were particular days of the year when farmers would bring their produce to town. Cattle and sheep were driven to the marketplace and produce brought by the cartload, these were times when wholesale and retail transactions took place. Naturally every other activity stopped, the local population would have a day off work to go to the fair, not only were there purchases to be made but friendships and acquaintances to be renewed. It was the one occasion when you could guarantee that everyone would be in town, including those from the far outlying areas, the town would be busy and the public houses and inns doing a good trade.

The presence of large, good humored crowds out for a spree attracted not only those with goods to sell but also the traveling entertainers who were always on the look out for a potential audience. Over the centuries the fairs evolved, eventually becoming as much a social event as an opportunity for business. By Victorian times all manner of showmen were traveling the circuit, actors playing on temporary stages, fighters sparring in boxing booths, dancing bears, acrobats, freak shows, musicians, quack doctors with dubious remedies all jostled for position to relieve the crowds of their money. The fairs at Mitcham, Cheam and Epsom Downs during race week all attracted large numbers of traveling people, some to buy and sell, others just to soak up the atmosphere and have a good time.

Because the local population were all enjoying a holiday, the fair days also became the time when local sports and competitions took place. Rival teams from different parts of town would compete in foot races and games of skill or strength including wrestling, tug of war or prize fighting. Even without the presence of the fair, Mitcham Common was an ideal venue for local sports and the popularity of horse racing on the common was noted in 1790 in *England's Gazeteer*. With the arrival of all manner of travelers on the common in the weeks preceding the fair these activities gradually increased, reaching a peak when the fair formally took place between the 12th and 14th of August.

A hundred years later trotting races were taking place along the mile between the Blue House and the Red House and there were prize fighting bouts taking place away from prying eyes in the quieter corners of the common. Fighting booths were an essential component of any fair as were the sale of horses which inevitably included the vendors showing of their wares by trotting and racing them.

Although Mitcham fair had been associated with periods of gambling and illegal tipping, by the middle of the nineteenth century the worst of the excesses had disappeared. Theatrical booths presented by Richardson became regular attendants and by the 1860's dancing booths were one of the most popular attractions. Until the advent of steam power the mechanical rides at fairs were few and limited to anything that could be driven by hand, swing boats and hand cranked roundabouts were about all that was possible until the advent of the first steam driven roundabout which made its debut in 1865.

From then on the nature of the fairs was to change dramatically, it was slow at first but very soon some showmen realized that the new latest high tech steam driven rides, with their dazzling paint work and mirrors reflecting the glow of napther lamps could make them very prosperous. And so it was that a new breed of showmen emerged, no longer spieling for punters at the entrance to his freak show, with a bank loan he could invest in a traction engine and mechanical ride that could make his fortune. The traveling general dealers and hawkers continued to ply their trades but now a greater distinction was emerging between them and the showmen who owned rides.

As well as being a special occasion for the sedentary population, fairs are important meeting points for people with a nomadic life style, they happen in certain places at fixed times of the year and form part of the annual cycle of life. They were, and still are in some places, times when large numbers of Gypsies and travelers congregate. When on the road and constantly moving from place to place, either following the work or being forcibly moved on, the fairs provide a fixed reference point in place and time. The extended family always traveled and worked together as one unit and may not have the opportunity to meet up with more distant parts of the family very often.

In any case communication was difficult between people who were constantly on the move and news could only be passed on by word of mouth via third parties. When visiting a fair, travelers knew that they would inevitably meet up with old acquaintances and that news and gossip would be shared. When most of the time is spent traveling through a world that is predominantly hostile, the gatherings at fairs reinforced your connections with other travelers and provided reassurance that you were not alone.

Epsom has long been a place at which Gypsy travelers have congregated. The Derby Oaks has been run since 1780 at the beginning of June and as an occasion attracted showmen and hawkers. The surrounding open downs and common land provided convenient stopping places and to this day there is still a large Gypsy market in the centre of the race course. The Epsom Derby and Mitcham Fair were both important events in the local Gypsy traveler calendar and extended visits to them were incorporated into the annual circuit of work. Once Mitcham fair was over many travelers moved on, some down into rural Surrey and neighboring Hampshire to be in good time for the start of hopping in early September, others remained to work the lavender and chamomile harvests on the herb farms that surrounded Mitcham and the adjoining areas.

Herbs

During the nineteenth century the areas surrounding Mitcham were an important centre for herb growing. A large number of medicinal and aromatic plants were in cultivation in the locality including rosebuds, hyssop, chamomile, elecampane, liquorice, angelica, peppermint and spearmint. But it was lavender for which Mitcham was particularly well known, the Yardley company were one of the major growers and operated a number of distilleries in Mitcham which produced the famous Yardley lavender oils.

In common with other crops, harvesting lavender in the nineteenth century was labor intensive, it was cut by hand with special small scythes before being bundled up to be sent for processing. Working on the harvest, the Gypsies could also buy directly from the growers and bunches of lavender were added to the stock of items that were hawked from door to door or sold to local greengrocers. Central London was only nine miles away and during Victorian times Gypsy lavender sellers were a common sight in town, advertising their wares by means of the traditional street cry:

'Will you buy my sweet lavender,
Sweet blooming lavender
Oh buy my pretty lavender
Sixteen bunches a penny'

Besides selling lavender in bunches, the Gypsies made up little bags of the flowers, which were bought by young middle class ladies to wear between their breasts, while larger sized bags were sold to be placed in wardrobes and chests of drawers. Flat, detachable sachets were also made for ladies to wear under the armpits, as substitutes for the effective but uncomfortable pieces of India-rubber which, sewn into the arm seams by dressmakers, prevented perspiration being absorbed by the material.

William Stewart described the Gypsy lavender sellers in his book, *Characters of Bygone London*: 'Sellers tended to be young women with sleeping infants bound to their side, leaving the right arm and hand entirely free. If a babe was not available, a small bundle of clothes might be used as a substitute; for Gypsies, being shrewd judges of human nature, knew how to arouse compassion. Using a small ragged boy was another ruse that seldom failed to attract a few sympathetic coppers, of which the urchin would no doubt be promptly relieved as soon as his benefactor turned the corner.'

One local resident recalled how in her childhood in the 1920's whole families went to work in the fields Camomiling, the schools having holidays at that time. Family working was also the norm for Gypsy travelers whose youngsters rarely went to school, learning everything that they needed to know about surviving directly by working alongside their parents. Knowledge was gained more by a process of osmosis than by formal education, a situation alluded to by Stewart in his description of the 'urchin' selling lavender.

There were also watercress beds alongside the river Wandle which also helped to provide a livelihood for local Gypsy travelers. As with the lavender not only was there work to be had by harvesting but also in sales of the produce, a romantic Victorian song illustrates how both crops were sold by street vendors.

'When Pol stays here and Jack goes there,
To earn their provinder
Her cries are all in Bethnal Green
Sweet lavender, sweet lavender
Who'll buy sweet lavender?
And oft wonders if her Jack
Enjoys a man's success
Who cries on top of Stamford Hill
Young watercress, young watercress
Who'll buy young watercress'

Constance Curry grew up in the 1920's and remembers well one Gypsy hawker who used to ply his trade along the suburban streets of Wimbledon:

'Of the many tradesmen in the area Mr. Jack Sparrowhawk is the one person I most remember. He arrived every Saturday by horse and cart to sell watercress which was grown by Mizens of Mitcham. His cry of 'lovely cresses' always puzzled me. On Sundays the small cart was filled with boxes of shrimps, cockles, whelks and mussels, which he measured from a pint pot.'

The herb industry served Gypsy travelers well for many decades but increasing urbanization would eventually put an end to this unique form of agriculture. It was pollution of the river Wandle that was suspected of causing an epidemic of typhoid that put an end to the growing of watercress and housing development that finally robbed the lavender growers of their land. The very last lavender fields were at Rose Hill, St Helier and were sold to the LCC for housing in the 1920's.

Galicians

The county of Surrey continued to host a very high Gypsy Traveler population throughout the nineteenth and twentieth centuries. In the more rural parts of the county further from London there were a number of areas in which particularly large numbers resided, around Chobham, Farnham, Hurtwood, Shere, West Horsely, Gomshall Marsh and along the north Downs. The census figures for 1911 records a total of 1,518 travelers in the county, making Surrey fifth in the league table behind Lancashire, Kent, West Yorkshire and Derbyshire. However, it covers a much smaller area and when the figures compared to the total acreage of the county, Surrey had the highest density of travelers of anywhere in the country. This number was added to by the occasional visits of Gypsies from overseas who also took advantage of the stopping places that the commons provided. They were generally en route, either on their way further into England or, as some believe, traveling west to eventually make the sea journey to the United States. All the English Gypsies were colorful and extravert, these visitors from Galicia and Hungary were altogether more exotic and excited a lot more attention. The women had large gold coins woven into their hair and strung about them, they wore brightly colored shawls, headscarves and full dresses.

The men wore equally brightly colored shirts with baggy trousers tucked into the top of tall leather boots, their jackets and waistcoats having big silver buttons. In 1911 some Galician Gypsies were stopping on Beddington Corner and one of their number, a girl called Sophie Karpath, fell sick with pneumonia and subsequently died. She was buried in Mitcham Old Churchyard on Saturday 14 October 1911 and according to contemporary accounts her funeral was predictably ostentatious: 'The female mourners seen, their faces smeared with mud, smoking cigarettes, performing quaint dances, and alternatively wailing and singing their weird native chants. The coffin bearing the remains being borne into the old church, where the lid was removed, and the men and women of the tribe took a farewell look at poor Sophie Karpath, with her hair beautifully dressed, robed as though for a festival in a scarlet frock, and adorned in valuable jewellery.'

The Galicians were Kalderash coppersmiths and the men looked for work by visiting local factories and businesses in the catering trade seeking copper vessels or pots and pans to repair. Whether any of them remained in the locality or had any interaction with the indigenous local Gypsies is very doubtful.

Merton

Mitcham Common and Wimbledon Common form part of the modern day London Borough of Merton. In *Some Memories of Merton* (1941) an anonymous author remembers what Merton was like in the 1880's: 'It was on a fine Sunday evening in the early autumn of 1884 that I first saw Merton. Stretching right ahead to the Morden Road, and away to Cannon Hill on the right was a breadth of open country where the Romany tribe halted their caravans, pitched their tents, and tethered their shaggy horses. I think there was some kind of restriction on the number that might encamp in the area, but when Epsom was calling the Gypsies from all over the country to come to the Derby hordes of swarthy men, dark eyed women, and shoeless children would hawk their baskets and besoms from door to door in the daytime, and fill the air with the savoury smell of frying rashers and strange brews when evening came down and called the wanderers back to camp. It must be more than forty years since the last Gypsy camp of any size was struck in Merton, and so one of the choicest entertainments enjoyed by the boys of the neighbourhood was robbed of some of its charm.

I do not know where they found a market, or whether the soil of Cannon Hill was specially suited to the manufacture of bricks, but it is quite certain that the grunts and groans of the primitive machinery used in their making, and the rancid pungency emitted by the smoking kiln were never ending fascinations. Boys who penetrated to the forbidden 'Brickie' in the broad light of day were looked upon as bold adventurers by their sisters and the smaller fry; but those who ran the gauntlet of the Gypsy peril when the white mists of evening were stealing through the camp and giving a ghostly quality to the flitting forms were counted thrice valiant heroes.'

This provides yet another connection between Robert Pateman, Gypsies and brick making. As well as the 'charms of the Brickfields' the author goes on to describe some other visitors to Merton including 'the little Swiss with his huge dancing bear', 'all kinds of travelling showmen and German bands' and May Day 1887. These memories of Merton are very similar to the callers and events in *Lark Rise to Candleford* remembered by Flora Thompson.

Farnborough

On 3 April 1881 three of Robert's sons were living in Farborough, Kent. James Pateman (29, bricklayers labourer) was living with his wife, Jane Reynolds (20, St Mary Cray) and their daughter Betsy (4 months, St Mary Cray), on Bastard Green; John Pateman (34, agricultural labourer) was lodging in Orpington Lane; William Pateman (22, Beehive maker) was living with his wife, Mercy Reynolds (25, Crockenhill) and their two children, Mary (5, Crockenhill) and Henry (1, Crockenhill), in a 'van on side of Orpington Lane'. Jane and Mercy Reynolds were sisters. Their brothers John (and his family) and George (married to Mary Pateman) were also living in Farnborough.

'Farnborough is a large village and parish, pleasantly situated on the high road from London to Sevenoaks, 4 miles south from Bromley, 14 from London, and one and a half south west from Orpington station. The church of St Giles has a register dating from 1558. The soil is mostly gravel; subsoil chalk. The chief crops are wheat, barley, and oats, and there are a great number of fruit gardens. 200 acres of land are planted with strawberries. The population in 1871 was 1,086' (*Post Office Directory* 1878).

It was here that Robert Pateman spent his final days. He moved to Farnborough from Mitcham some time between 1881 and 1890. Following the death of his wife he lived with his children: the 1890 *Strong Directory of Farnborough* records that William Pateman was living in Stow Cottages (Farnborough Village) and James Pateman was living at Tugmutton (Locks Bottom).

Robert Pateman died of 'pleurisy, bronchitis' on 15 June 1890 at Farnborough. The age and occupation given on his death certificate were '77 years, greengrocer'. The informant was 'J. Pateman, son, present at the death'. So it seems likely that Robert was living with James Pateman and his family at Tugmutton.

Robert was buried on 19 June 1890 at St Giles, Farnborough. He is in the same grave as his son James (1926) and his grandson George (1921). There are several other members of Robert's family buried at St Giles including his son John (1883) and six grandchildren (children of James Pateman and Jane Reynolds): Betsy (1881), Celia (1894), Mary (1900), John (1900), Phyllis (1902) and Robert (1960).

Robert's funeral was attended by many of the Gypsy families living at Tugmutton Common, which is named after the English village green game of tying a leg of mutton on a high branch or pole, and getting contestants to jump to try and tug it down. The area of Tugmutton was named on old maps as either Brasted Green or Broad Street Green, also known as Broad Green or Bastard Green. The famous Gypsy residents of Tugmutton Common included Levi and Urania Boswell, 'King and Queen' of the Kent Romanies. The story of the Tugmutton Gypsies is told in the next volume of this family history – *Tugmutton Common: the life and times of William Pateman and his family*.

10. Chronology

1742 – John Pateman born
1772 – John Pateman moved from Bobbing to Borden
1772 – 12 April: John Pateman married Catherine Becon at Borden
1772 – 2 August: John Pateman baptized at Borden
1778 – 3 May: Theophilus Pateman born at Bobbing
1778 – 14 October: Theophilus Pateman baptised at Bobbing
1799 – 11 October: John Pateman married Sarah Cook at Bredgar
1800 – 7 September: Theophilus Pateman married Mary Agar at Bobbing
1801 – 12 April: William Bass Pateman baptized at Bobbing
1802 – 4 February: John Pateman moved from Bobbing to Bredgar
1802 – 4 February: Theophilus Pateman moved from Bobbing to Borden
1803 – 18 August: John Pateman buried in Borden
1807 – George Pateman born at Bredgar
1807 – 10 January: Catherine Becon died at Bobbing
1807 – 18 January: Catherine Becon buried in Borden
1816 – 15 December: Jessie Pateman baptised at St Mary Hoo
1816 – 22 December: Jessie Pateman buried at St Mary Hoo
1817 – 5 February: John Pateman moved from Hoo to Bredgar
1821 – Robert Pateman born at Hoo, Kent
1821 – John Pateman born at Hoo, Kent
1821 – 18 February: John Pateman married Charlotte Mirtle at Chatham
1823 – 7 October: Mary Patenman died at Borden
1824 – 19 July: William Bass Pateman married Mary Ann Coulter at Gillingham
1825 – 24 July: Harriett Pateman born at Borden
1826 – 9 December: William Bass Pateman removed from Borden to Bobbing
1827 – 3 June: Mary Ann Pateman baptized at Borden
1828 – 7 December: George Pateman married Frances Clarke at Newington
1829 – 19 July: William Pateman baptized at Borden
1830 – 18 April: Charles Pateman baptized at St Mary Hoo
1831 – George Pateman baptized at St Mary Hoo
1831 – 9 October: James Edward Pateman baptized at Borden
1832 – 20 February: Sarah Ann Pateman baptized at St Mary Hoo
1833 – 18 April: Theophilus Pateman married Mary Pain at Milton
1833 – 22 September: Ellen Ann Marie Pateman baptized at Borden
1834 – 6 November: Sarah Ann Pateman buried at St Mary Hoo
1835 - 11 October: Sarah Ann Pateman baptized at Borden
1835 – 26 February: William George Pateman baptized at St Mary Hoo
1837 – 6 August: William Pateman baptized at St Mary Hoo
1837 – 2 September: Ellen Ann Marie Pateman died at Chalkwell
1837 – 10 September: Ellen Ann Marie Pateman buried at Newington.
1838 – 2 May: George Henry Pateman born at Borden
1839 – 5 September: Thomas Pateman born at St Mary's, Hoo.
1839 – 18 October: Thomas Pateman baptized at St Mary's Hoo
1840 – 3 February: Elizabeth Ann Pateman born at Milton
1840 – 12 February: George Pateman died at Stoke Hoo
1840 – 9 April: Thomas Pateman died at Newington
1840 – 9 May: George Pateman died at Newington
1840 – 19 May: Mary Ann Pateman born at Chelmsford,

1841 – 6 June: John Pateman at Bredgar on census day
1841 – 6 June: Theophilus Pateman at Borden on census day
1841 – 6 June: William Bass Pateman at Milton on census day
1842 – Alice Pateman born at Wimbledon
1842 – 24 January: John Henry Pateman born at Milton
1844 – Esther Pateman born at Wimbledon
1844 – 23 June: John Pateman born at Cliffe
1844 – 26 July: Henry George Pateman born at Milton
1844 – 13 October: Mary Ann Pateman died at Stockbury
1845 – 26 January: William Pateman died at St Mary Hoo
1845 – 13 April: Harriett Pateman married Thomas Wood at Milton
1846 – 17 July: James Pateman born at Cooling
1846 – 23 July: Mary Ann Pateman married Thomas Pearce at Frinstead
1846 – 26 July: James and John Pateman baptized at St Helen's Church, Cliffe.
1846 – 23 October: Esther Mole Pateman born at Milton
1848 – John Pateman born at Hoo
1849 – 26 January: James Coulter Pateman born at Milton
1849 – 11 October: Esther Mole Pateman died at Sittingbourne
1849 – 14 October: Esther Mole Pateman buried at Newington
1849 – 28 December: John Pateman died at Bredgar
1850 – 3 January: John Pateman buried in Bredgar.
1850 – William Bass Pateman moved to Bermondsey
1851 - Mary Ann Pateman born in Westwood
1851 – 30 March: William Bass Pateman at Bermondsey on census day
1851 – 30 March: Theophilus Pateman at Borden on census day
1852 – 18 March: Charlotte Pateman died at Maidstone.
1852 - 23 March: Charlotte Pateman buried at Bredgar
1852 – 13 November: Elizabeth Pateman born at Burham
1855 – William Pateman born at Redlynch
1856 – 10 October: Henry Pateman born at Frindsbury
1857 – William Pateman born at Rochester
1857 – Alice Pateman born at Bearsted
1857 – 19 November: James Edward Pateman married Mary Bray at St Marylebone
1858 – Ann Pateman born at Hoo St Mary
1858 – 4 January: Henry Pateman died near Capstone, Gillingham, aged 15 months
1858 – 14 October: Matilda Elizabeth Pateman born at Milton
1859 – Walter Pateman born at Stockbury
1859 – 1 March: James Edward Pateman went to New Zealand
1859 – 7 April: Matilda Elizabeth Pateman died at Milton
1859 - 11 April: Matilda Elizabeth Pateman buried at Bobbing.
1859 – 23 November: Sarah Ann Pateman married Edward Hill at Stepney
1860 – Alva Pateman born at Ciligate
1861 – 8 February: Louisa Pateman born at Hammersmith
1861 – 8 February: Thomas Pateman born at Hammersmith
1861 – 18 February: Thomas Pateman died at Hammersmith
1861 – 7 April: Theophilus Pateman at Borden on census day
1861 – 7 April: William Bass Pateman at Bermondsey on census day
1861 – 7 April: John Pateman at Stanbrook, Thaxstead, Essex, on census day
1862 – 27 April: Thomas and Annie Pateman born at Great Maplestead, Essex
1862 – 18 September: Mary Pateman died in New Zealand

1863 – 15 March: James Edward Pateman married Charlotte Smith in New Zealand
1863 – 21 June: Mary Pateman died at Borden
1864 – 11 February: Theophilus Pateman died at Borden
1865 – 10 July: Henry George Pateman married Elizabeth Fagg at Bermondsey
1866 – 26 March: Noah Pateman born at Bromley
1867 – Ruth Pateman born at Crayford
1869 – 11 April: John Henry Pateman married Elizabeth Bennett at Twickenham
1870 – 29 October: James Coulter Pateman married Mary Ann Price at Bethnal Green
1871 – 2 April: William Bass Pateman at Bermondsey on census day
1871 – 2 April: Robert Pateman at Beckenham on census day
1872 – 17 April: Mary Ann Pateman died at Bermondsey
1874 – 17 April: James Coulter Pateman went to New Zealand
1879 – 18 August: James Coulter Pateman died in New Zealand
1879 - 20 August: James Coulter Pateman buried at Christchurch
1880 – 22 November: Betsy Pateman born at St Mary Cray
1881 – 3 April: John Henry Pateman at Bermondsey on census day
1881 – 3 April: William Bass Pateman at Bermondsey on census day
1881 – 3 April: Robert Pateman at Mitcham on census day
1881 – 3 April John Pateman at Woodford on census day
1881 – 3 April: Alice Pateman at St Mary Cray on census day
1881 – 3 April: John Pateman at Farnborough on census day
1881 – 3 April: James Pateman at Farnborough on census day
1881 – 3 April: Mary Ann Pateman at Farnborough on census day
1881 – 3 April: Elizabeth Pateman at Kingston on Thames on census day
1881 – 3 April: William Pateman at Farnborough on census day
1881 – 3 April: Louisa Pateman at Mitcham on census day
1881 - 22 August: Walter Pateman married Phoebe Dighton at Croydon
1883 – 26 June: John Pateman died at Farnborugh
1884 – 11 June: Mary Ann Pateman married Job Cartwright in New Zealand.
1885 – 22 January: William Bass Pateman died at Milton
1886 – 30 June: John Henry Pateman died at Bermondsey
1890 – 15 June: Robert Pateman died at Farnborough
1890 – 19 June: Robert Pateman buried at St Giles
1891 – 5 April: James Pateman at Farnborough on census day
1891 – 5 April: Mary Ann Pateman at Farnborough on census day
1891 – 5 April: William Pateman at Farnborough on census day
1892 – 22 January: Alice Pateman died at St Mary Cray
1892 – 29 January: Alice Pateman buried in Star Lane Cemetery, St Mary Cray.
1893 – 11 December: Henry George Pateman died at Edmonton
1894 – 27 January: Harriett Pateman died at Sittingbourne
1897 – 2 September: Charlotte Pateman died in New Zealand
1897 – 13 September: Sarah Ann Pateman died at Lambeth
1899 – 1 May: Mary Ann Pateman died at Lewisham
1901 - James Edward Pateman married Eliza Witte in New Zealand
1901 – 31 March: James Pateman at Farnborough on census day
1901 – 31 March: Mary Ann Pateman at Farnborough on census day
1901 – 31 March: William Pateman at Farnborough on census day
1901 – 31 March: Walter Pateman at St Mary Cray on census day
1905 – 27 May: James Edward Pateman died in New Zealand
1916 – 10 March: Elizabeth Pateman died

1921 – 24 October: William Pateman died at Orpington
1921 – 29 October: William Pateman buried at All Saints churchyard, Orpington
1926 – 29 May: James Pateman died at Farnborough
1926 – 5 June: James Pateman buried at St Giles Churchyard, Farnborough
1927 – 12 February: Henry Taylor died at Hounslow
1928 – 12 May: Charles Lee died at Charlton
1929 – 14 May: Mary Ann Pateman died at Farnborough
1937 – 28 October: George Reynolds died at Farnborough
1939 – 25 March: Jane Pateman died at Farnborough
1939 – 1 April: Jane Pateman buried at St Giles Churchyard, Farnborough
1940 – William Pateman died
1940 – 3 January: Mercy Pateman died at Orpington
1940 – 9 January: Mercy Pateman buried at All Saints Churchyard, Orpington
1940 – 3 March: Eliza Pateman died in New Zealand
1943 – 5 April: Walter Pateman died at Lewisham
1943 – 12 April: Walter Pateman buried in Star Lane Cemetery, St Mary Cray

11. Family Trees

John Pateman (1742-1803) = Catherine Becon (1732-1807)
- John Pateman (1772-1849)
- Theophilus Pateman (1778-1864)

John Pateman (1772-1849) = Sarah Cook (m. 1799) = Charlotte Mirtle (m.1821)
- George Pateman (1807-1840)
- Jesse Pateman (1816)
- Robert Pateman (c. 1821-1890)
- John Pateman (1821-?)

Theophilus Pateman (1778-1864) = Mary Agar (m. 1800) = Mary Pain (m. 1833)
- William Bass Pateman (1801-1885)

William Bass Pateman (1801-1885) = Mary Ann Coulter (1807-1872)
- Harriett Pateman (1825-1894)
- Mary Ann Pateman (1827-1899)
- William Pateman (1829-?)
- James Edward Pateman (1831-1905)
- Ellen Ann Maria Pateman (1833-1837)
- Sarah Ann Pateman (1835-1897)
- George Henry Pateman (1838-?)
- Elizabeth Ann Pateman (1840-?)
- John Henry Pateman (1842-1886)
- James Henry (Henry George) Pateman (1844-1893)
- Hester Mole Pateman (1846-1849)
- James Coulter Pateman (1849-1879)

George Pateman (1807-1840) = Frances Clarke (c.1813)
- Charles Pateman (1830-?)
- George Pateman (1831-1840)
- Sarah Ann Pateman (1832 -1834)
- William George Pateman (1835-?)
- William Pateman (1837-1845)
- Thomas Pateman (1839-1840)

John Pateman (1821-?) = Matilda Sheriff (1830-1908)
- Esther Pateman (1844-?)
- John Pateman (1848-?)
- Matilda Pateman (1851-?)
- William Pateman (1855-1940)
- Alice Pateman (1857-?)
- Elvey Pateman (1860-?)
- Thomas Pateman (1862-1902)
- Annie Pateman (1862-?)
- Ruth Pateman (1867-?)

Robert Pateman (c.1821-1890) = Mary Ann Enis (c.1819-?)
- Mary Ann Pateman (1840-1844)
- Alice Pateman (1842-1892)
- John Pateman (1844-1883)
- James Pateman (1846-1926)
- Mary Ann Pateman (1851-1929)
- Elizabeth Pateman (1852-1916)
- Henry Pateman (1856-1858)
- William Pateman (1857-1921)
- Anne Pateman (1858-?)
- Walter Pateman (1859-1943)
- Robert Pateman (1860-?)
- Louisa Pateman (1861-?)
- Thomas Pateman (1861)
- Noah Pateman (1866-?)

12. Census

John Pateman (1772-1849)

1841

Bredgar Street, Bredgar, Kent

Name	Sex	Age	Birth Year	Where Born
PATEMAN, John	M	60	1781	Kent
PATEMAN, Charlott	F	55	1786	Kent

Theophilus Pateman (1778-1864)

1841

Chesnut Street, Borden, Kent

Name	Sex	Age	Birth Year	Where Born
PATEMAN, Theophilas	M	60	1781	Kent
PATEMAN, Mary	F	50	1791	Kent
PAIN, David	M	20	1821	Kent

1851

Chesnut Pound Wood Cottages, Borden, Kent

Name	Relation	Condition	Sex	Age	Birth Year	Occupation Disability	Where Born
PATEMAN, Theophilus	Head	Married	M	74	1777	Ag Lab	N K
PATEMAN, Mary	Wife	Married	F	65	1786		Ware Hertfordshire
GOODHEW, Sarah	Lodger	Widow	F	43	1808		Hartlip Kent
GOODHEW, Elizabeth	Daughter	Unmarried	F	5	1846	Ag Lab	Borden Kent

1861

Chesnut Street, Borden, Kent

Name	Relation	Condition	Sex	Age	Birth Year	Occupation Disability	Where Born

PATERSON, Theophilus	Head	Married	M	85	1776	Agricultural Labourer	Bobbing Kent
PATERSON, Mary	Wife	Married	F	75	1786		Ware Hertfordshire

William Pateman (1801-1885)

1841

Crown Lane, Milton, Kent

Name	Sex	Age	Birth Year	Where Born
PATEMAN, William	M	40	1801	Kent
PATEMAN, Mary	F	30	1811	Kent
PATEMAN, Harriot	F	15	1826	Kent
PATEMAN, William	M	12	1829	Kent
PATEMAN, Edward	M	10	1831	Kent
PATEMAN, Sarah	F	5	1836	
PATEMAN, George	M	3	1838	Kent
PATEMAN, Elizabeth	F	1	1840	Kent

1851

12 Wright Buildings, Bermondsey, Southwark, Surrey

Name	Relation	Condition	Sex	Age	Birth Year	Occupation Disability	Where Born
PATEMAN, William	Head	Married	M	50	1801	Tanner	Babbacombe Kent
PATEMAN, Mary A	Wife	Married	F	44	1807		Barnwell Kent
PATEMAN, William	Son	Unmarried	M	22	1829	Tanner	Berden Kent
PATEMAN, George	Son	Unmarried	M	18	1833		Berden Kent
PATEMAN, Elizabeth	Daughter	Unmarried	F	10	1841		Wootton Kent
PATEMAN, John	Son		M	7	1844		Sittingbourne Kent
PATEMAN, Henry	Son		M	6	1845		Sittingbourne Kent
PATEMAN, James	Son		M	2	1849		Sittingbourne Kent
MILINER, Ralph	Visitor	Unmarried	M	22	1829	Tanner	Sutton Kent

1861

12 Wright Buildings, Bermondsey, Southwark, Surrey

Name	Relation	Condition	Sex	Age	Birth Year	Occupation Disability	Where Born
PATRIARCA, Willms	Head	Married	M	61	1800	Farmer	Bordon Kent
PATRIARCA, Mary A	Wife	Married	F	53	1808		... Kent
PATRIARCA, Henry	Son		M	16	1845	...	... Kent
PATRIARCA, James	Son		M	12	1849	Errand Boy	... Kent

1871

Wright's Buildings, St Mary Magdalene

Name	Relation	Sex	Age	Birth Year	Where Born
PATEMAN, Wm Boss	Head	M	70	1801	Kent
PATEMAN, Mary Ann	Wife	F	64	1807	Kent
PATEMAN, James Coulter	Head	M	21	1850	Kent
PATEMAN, Mary Ann	Wife	F	22	1849	Warwickshire

1881

56, Ambrose St, Bermondsey

Name	Relation	Condition	Sex	Age	Birth Year	Occupation Disability	Where Born
PATEMAN, William	Head	Widower	M	80	1801	Tanner	Babbing Kent
HILL, Sarah Ann	Daughter	Widow	F	46	1835	Charwoman	Bording Kent
HILL, Rebecca	Grand Daughter	Single	F	8	1873	Scholar	Bermondsey Surrey
GREGG, Ellen	Boarder	Single	F	8	1873	Scholar	Middlesex
HILL, Minnie	Grand Daughter	Single	F	13	1868	Scholar	Middlesex

John Pateman (1821-?)

1861

Travellers..., Fish Street Hill, Thaxted

Name	Relation	Condition	Sex	Age	Birth Year	Occupation Disability	Where Born
PATERMAN, John	Head	Married	M	40	1821	... Mat Maker	... Kent
PATERMAN, Matilda	Wife	Married	F	36	1825	... Mat Maker Wife	... Buckinghamshire
PATERMAN, Esther	Daughter	Unmarried	F	15	1846	... Mat Makers Daughter	... Kent
PATERMAN, John	Son	Unmarried	M	13	1848	... Mat Makers Son	Exeter Kent
PATERMAN, William	Son	Unmarried	M	10	1851	... Mat Makers Son	Doulting Wiltshire
PATERMAN, Mathilda	Daughter	Unmarried	F	10	1851	... Mat Makers Daughter	Doulting Wiltshire
PATERMAN, Alice	Daughter	Unmarried	F	6	1855	... Mat Makers Daughter	Banstead Kent
PATERMAN, Elroy	Daughter	Unmarried	F	2	1859	... Mat Makers Daughter	Claygate Surrey

1881

In A Caravan Peel Road, Woodford, Essex

Name	Relation	Condition	Sex	Age	Birth Year	Occupation Disability	Where Born
BATEMAN, John	Head	Married	M	60	1821	Licensed Hawker	Luton Bedfordshire
BATEMAN, Matilda	Wife	Married	F	57	1824	Licensed Hawker	Kingsey Buckinghamshire
BATEMAN, Esther	Daughter	Single	F	37	1844	Licensed Hawker	Wimbledon Essex
BATEMAN, John	Son	Single	M	33	1848	Tinman & Brassier	Hundreds of Hoe Kent
BATEMAN, William	Son	Married	M	30	1851	Labourer	Red Lynch Wiltshire
BATEMAN, Alice	Daughter	Single	F	24	1857	License Hawker	Birstead Kent
BATEMAN, Alva	Daughter	Single	F	21	1860	License Hawker Lunatic	Ciligate Surrey
BATEMAN, Thomas	Son	Single	M	18	1863	License Hawker	Maplestead Essex
BATEMAN, Ruth	Daughter	Single	F	14	1867	Scholar	Crayford Kent
BATEMAN,	Daughter	Single	F	20	1861		Peckham

| Rose Ann | In Law | | | | | | Kent |

1891

Caravan Forest, Chigwell Mow, Chigwell, Essex

Name	Relation	Condition	Sex	Age	Birth Year	Occupation Disability	Where Born
BATEMAN, John	Head	Married	M	72	1819	Travelling Hawker	Huntingdonshire
BATEMAN, Matildia	Wife		F	67	1824		Buckinghamshire
BATEMAN, Clara	Daughter		F	32	1859	Dumb From Childhood	Surrey
BATEMAN, Thomas	Son	Single	M	29	1862	Cripple From Childhood	Maplestead Essex
BATEMAN, Marth	Daughter		F	23	1868		Crayford Kent

1901

2, Suttons Cottages, North Cray, Kent

Name	Relation	Condition	Sex	Age	Birth Year	Occupation Disability	Where Born
PATEMAN, Matilda	Head	Married	F	78	1823		Kingsey Buckinghamshire
PATEMAN, Thomas	Son	Single	M	39	1862	Cripple From Birth	Maplestead Essex
PATEMAN, Ruth	Daughter	Single	F	34	1867	Field Worker On Farm	Crayford Kent

Robert Pateman (1821-1890)

1871

Arthur Road An Old Stable, Beckenham, Kent

Name	Relation	Sex	Age	Birth Year	Where Born
PATEMAN, Robert	Head	M	55	1816	Hertfordshire
PATEMAN, Mary	Wife	F	52	1819	Somerset
PATEMAN, Alice	Daughter	F	27	1844	Surrey

PATEMAN, John	Son	M	23	1848	Kent
PATEMAN, James	Son	M	21	1850	Kent
PATEMAN, Mary Ann	Daughter	F	20	1851	Kent
PATEMAN, William	Son	M	19	1852	Kent
PATEMAN, Elizabeth	Daughter	F	16	1855	Kent
PATEMAN, Anne	Daughter	F	15	1856	Kent
PATEMAN, Walter	Son	M	12	1859	Kent
PATEMAN, Louisa	Daughter	F	10	1861	Middlesex

1881

Mitcham Common (Tent), Mitcham, Surrey

Name	Relation	Condition	Sex	Age	Birth Year	Occupation Disability	Where Born
BATEMAN, Robert	Head	Married	M	60	1821	Skewer Maker	Hoo Kent
BATEMAN, Walter	Son	Single	M	21	1860	Skewer Maker	Bembery Kent
BATEMAN, Robert	Son	Single	M	13	1868	Skewer Maker	Bearstead Kent

John Pateman (1844-1883)

1881

Orpington Lane, Farnborough, Kent

Name	Relation	Condition	Sex	Age	Birth Year	Occupation Disability	Where Born
RUDD, Robert	Head	Married	M	56	1825	Beerhouse Keeper	Swinton Norfolk
RUDD, Sharlott	Wife	Married	F	54	1827		
RUDD, Edward	Son	Single	M	30	1851	Lab	
RUDD, Cristifer	Son	Single	M	20	1861	Lab	London, London Middlesex
PATEMAN, John	Lodger		M	34	1847	Ag Lab	Rochester Kent
GAUN, John	Lodger Head	Married	M	49	1832	Taylor	Bromley Kent
GAUN, Matilda	Wife	Married	F	36	1845		Walton Wolds Leicestershire
GAUN, Willen	Son	Single	M	10	1871	Scholar	

| CHESTOR, James | Lodger | Single | M | 30 | 1851 | Bricklayer | Bromley Kent |

James Pateman (1846-1926)

1881

Bastard Green, Farnborough, Kent

Name	Relation	Condition	Sex	Age	Birth Year	Occupation Disability	Where Born
PATEMAN, James	Head	Married	M	29	1852	Bricklayers Lab	Clist Kent
PATEMAN, Jane	Wife	Married	F	20	1861		St Mary Gray Kent
PATEMAN, Betsy	Daughter	Single	F	0	1881		St Mary Gray Kent

1891

Trymutton, Farnborough, Kent

Name	Relation	Condition	Sex	Age	Birth Year	Occupation Disability	Where Born
PATEMAN, James	Head	Married	M	45	1846	Potato Dealer	Cliffe Rochester Kent
PATEMAN, Jane	Wife	Married	F	35	1856		Sittingbourne Kent
PATEMAN, Groven	Daughter	Single	F	8	1883		Farnborough Kent
PATEMAN, Phyllis	Daughter	Single	F	7	1884		Farnborough Kent
PATEMAN, Robert	Son	Single	M	6	1885		Farnborough Kent
PATEMAN, Mary A	Daughter	Single	F	5	1886		Farnborough Kent
PATEMAN, Charlotte	Daughter	Single	F	3	1888		Farnborough Kent
PATEMAN, Phebes	Daughter	Single	F	2	1889		Farnborough Kent
PATEMAN, Jane	Daughter	Single	F	0 (8M)	1891		Farnborough Kent

1901

Tugmutton Green, Farnborough, Kent

Name	Relation	Condition	Sex	Age	Birth Year	Occupation Disability	Where Born
PATEMAN, James	Head	Married	M	48	1853	Green Grocer	Glift Kent
PATEMAN, Jane	Wife	Married	F	42	1859		Sidden Kent
PATEMAN, Robert	Son	Single	M	16	1885	Green Grocers Apprentice	Farnborough Kent
PATEMAN, Mary A	Daughter		F	15	1886		Farnborough Kent
PATEMAN, Charlotte	Daughter		F	14	1887		Farnborough Kent
PATEMAN, Phebie	Daughter		F	13	1888		Farnborough Kent
PATEMAN, Janey	Daughter		F	11	1890		Farnborough Kent
PATEMAN, Eliz	Daughter		F	3	1898		Farnborough Kent
PATEMAN, Georgy	Son		M	2	1899		Farnborough Kent

1911

5 Willow Walk Farnborough Kent

Name	Relation	Condition/ Yrs married	Sex	Age	Birth Year	Occupation	Where Born
PATEMAN, James	Head	Married	M	60	1851	Greengrocer	Kent Clift
PATEMAN, Jane	Wife	Married 32 years	F	51	1860	Assisting In The Business	Kent Sittinbourne
PATEMAN, Emily	Daughter		F	14	1897	School	Kent Farnborough
PATEMAN, George	Son		M	13	1898	School	Kent Farnborough
PATEMAN, Daisy	Daughter		F	10	1901		Kent Farnborough
PATEMAN, Rose	Daughter		F	8	1903		Kent Farnborough
PATEMAN, William	Son		M	6	1905		Kent Farnborough

Mary Ann Pateman (1851-1929)

1881

Van In Piggendens Lane, Farnborough, Kent

Name	Relation	Condition	Sex	Age	Birth Year	Where Born
REYNOLDS, George	Head	Married	M	25	1856	Highton Kent
REYNOLDS, ?	Wife	Married	F	28	1853	Honden Hooe
REYNOLDS, John	Son	Single	M	6	1875	Farnborough, Kent
REYNOLDS, George	Son	Single	M	4	1877	Bromley Kent
REYNOLDS, James	Son	Single	M	2	1879	Farnborough Kent
REYNOLDS, Thomas	Son	Single	M	0	1881	Sidcup Kent

1891

Trymutton, Farnborough, Kent

Name	Relation	Condition	Sex	Age	Birth Year	Occupation Disability	Where Born
REYNOLDS, George	Head	Married	M	36	1855	Labourer	Farnborough Kent
REYNOLDS, Mary	Wife	Married	F	40	1851		Farnborough Kent
REYNOLDS, John	Son	Single	M	17	1874	Labourer	Farnborough Kent
REYNOLDS, George	Son	Single	M	15	1876	Labourer	Farnborough Kent
REYNOLDS, James	Son	Single	M	12	1879		Farnborough Kent
REYNOLDS, Thomas	Son	Single	M	10	1881		Farnborough Kent
REYNOLDS, Elvy	Daughter	Single	F	4	1887		Farnborough Kent

1901

Tugmutton Green, Farnborough, Kent

Name	Relation	Condition	Sex	Age	Birth Year	Occupation Disability	Where Born
REYNOLDS, George	Head	Married	M	51	1850	Agricultural Labourer	Hoo Kent
REYNOLDS, Mary A	Wife	Married	F	50	1851		Hoo Kent

Name	Relation	Condition	Sex	Age	Birth Year	Occupation	Where Born
REYNOLDS, James	Son	Single	M	21	1880		Farnborough Kent
REYNOLDS, Eliz	Daughter		F	13	1888		Hoo Kent

1911

4 Willow Walk Farnborough, Kent

Name	Relation	Sex	Age	Birth Year	Occupation	Where Born
REYNOLDS, George	Head	M	64	1847	General Labourer Farm	Kent Farnborough
REYNOLDS, Mary Ann	Wife	F	65	1846	Home	Kent Farnborough

Elizabeth Pateman (1852-1916)

1881

Acre Road, Kingston, Surrey

Name	Relation	Condition	Sex	Age	Birth Year	Occupation Disability	Where Born
TAYLOR, Henry	Head	Married	M	27	1854	Hawker	Malden Surrey
TAYLOR, Elizabeth	Wife	Married	F	26	1855	Hawker	Maidstone Kent
TAYLOR, Henry	Son	Single	M	1	1880		Oakingham Surrey

1891

2, Quinions Ground Caravan And Tent, Inwood Road, Isleworth, Hounslow, Middlesex

Name	Relation	Condition	Sex	Age	Birth Year	Occupation Disability	Where Born
TAYLOR, Henry	Head	Married	M	37	1854	General Dealer	Malling Surrey
TAYLOR, Elizabeth	Wife	Married	F	37	1854		Gravesend Kent
TAYLOR, Walter	Son		M	9	1882		Egham Surrey
TAYLOR, Amy	Daughter		F	7	1884		Wanstead Essex
TAYLOR, Caroline	Daughter		F	5	1886		Islington

Name	Relation	Condition	Sex	Age	Birth Year	Occupation	Where Born
							London
DARNBOROUGH, Arthur	Lodger	Single	M	31	1860	General Dealers Assistant	London
HIZZE, James	Lodger	Single	M	20	1871	General Dealers Assistant	Fulham London

1911

Caravan White Bear Field Hounslow, Middlesex

Name	Relation	Condition/ Yrs married	Sex	Age	Birth Year	Occupation	Where Born
TAYLOR, Henry	Head	Married	M	59	1852	Showmen	Malden Surrey
TAYLOR, Betsy	Wife	Married 32 years	F	59	1852	Assisting In The Business	Dartford Hunt
TAYLOR, Alice	Daughter	Single	F	19	1892	Assisting In The Business	Hounslow
PYER, Sidney	Servant	Single	M	25	1886	Travellers Servant	Lanark Near Paddington
PEREY, Edward	Servant	Single	M	30	1881	Travellers Servant	Hammersmith

William Pateman (1856-1921)

1881

Van On Side Of Orpington Lane, Kent

Name	Relation	Condition	Sex	Age	Birth Year	Occupation, Disability	Where Born
PATEMAN, William	Head	Married	M	22	1859	Beehive Maker	Dartford Kent
PATEMAN, Mary	Wife	Married	F	25	1856		Crockenhill Kent
PATEMAN, Mary	Daughter	Single	F	5	1876		Crockenhill Kent
PATEMAN, Henry	Son	Single	M	1	1880		Crockenhill Kent

1891

Church Road, Farnborough, Kent

Name	Relation	Condition	Sex	Age	Birth Year	Occupation, Disability	Where Born
PATERMAN, Willm	Head	Married	M	38	1853	Labourer	Rochester Kent
PATERMAN, Mercy	Wife	Married	F	35	1856		Crocken Hill Kent
PATERMAN, Mary	Daughter	Single	F	15	1876	Scholar	Crocken Hill Kent
PATERMAN, Henry	Son	Single	M	13	1878	Scholar	Crocken Hill Kent
PATERMAN, Noah	Son	Single	M	8	1883	Scholar	Farnborough Kent
PATERMAN, Walter	Son	Single	M	5	1886	Scholar	Farnborough Kent
PATERMAN, Alice	Daughter	Single	F	1	1890		Farnborough Kent

1901

Cobden Road, Farnborough

Name	Relation	Condition	Sex	Age	Birth Year	Occupation, Disability	Where Born
PATEMAN, William	Head	Married	M	50	1851	Farm Labourer	Farnborough Kent
PATEMAN, Mercy	Wife	Married	F	50	1851		Farnborough Kent
PATEMAN, Mary	Daughter	Married	F	25	1876		Farnborough Kent
PATEMAN, Alice	Daughter		F	15	1886		Farnborough Kent
PATEMAN, Walter	Son	Single	M	17	1884	Farm Labourer	Farnborough Kent
PATEMAN, Poebe	Daughter		F	13	1888		Farnborough Kent
PATEMAN, Amy	Daughter		F	5	1896		Farnborough Kent
LEWIS, Elias	Son-In-Law	Married	M	25	1876	Builders Labourer	Farnborough Kent
LEWIS, Charles	Grand Son		M	4	1897		Farnborough Kent

1911

6 Epsom Cottages Fordcroft St Mary Cray

Name	Relation	Condition	Sex	Age	Birth Year	Occupation, Disability	Where Born
PATEMAN, William	Head	Married 35 years	M	60	1851	Farm Laborer	Croydon Surrey
PATEMAN, Mercy	Wife	Married	F	55	1856	Flower Seller Hawker	Orpington Kent
PATEMAN, Mary	Daughter	Single	F	23	1888	Dealer Flowers	Farnboro Kent
PATEMAN, Amy	Daughter	Single	F	15	1896		Farnboro Kent

Walter Pateman (1859-1943)

1901

Vinsons Cottages, Hockenden, St Mary Cray

Name	Relation	Condition	Sex	Age	Birth Year	Occupation, Disability	Where Born
PALEMAN, Walter	Head	Married	M	39	1862	Dealer In Vegetables	Stockbury Kent
PALEMAN, Phoebe	Wife	Married	F	38	1863	Field Work On Farm	Bexley Heath Kent

1911

1 Vinson's Cottages Hockenden

Name	Relation	Condition/ Yrs married	Sex	Age	Birth Year	Occupation	Where Born
PATEMAN, Walter	Head	Married	M	50	1861	Dealer Vegetables And Firewood	Maidstone Kent
PATEMAN, Phoebe	Wife	Married 30 years	F	50	1861	Work In The Fields	Bexley Kent
PATEMAN, Noah	Nephew	Married	M	27	1884	Bricklayers Labourer	Farnborough Kent
PATEMAN, Annie	Niece	Married 9 years	F	29	1882	Domestic Duties	Portsmouth Hants
PATEMAN, Nellie	Niece		F	8	1903	School	Crofton Kent
PATEMAN, May	Niece		F	5	1906	School	Portsmouth Hants
PATEMAN,	Niece		F	3	1908	School	Portsmouth

								Hants
Ivy								

Louisa Pateman (1861-?)

1881

Tent on Mitcham Common, Surrey

Name	Relation	Condition/ Yrs married	Sex	Age	Birth Year	Occupation	Where Born
LEE, Charles	Head	Married	M	21	1860	Skewer maker	Rochester, Kent
LEE, Louisa	Wife	Married	F	20	1861	Skewer maker	Notting Hill, Middlesex

1911

174 Wornington Road No Kensington W

Name	Relation	Condition/ Yrs married	Sex	Age	Birth Year	Occupation	Where Born
LEE, Louisa	Head	Widow	F	60	1851		Sarratt Hertfordshire
LEE, Charles	Son	Single	M	32	1879	Labourer	North Kensington Midd EX
LEE, Frederick	Son	Single	M	20	1891	Labourer	Chelsea Middlesex

13. Sources

Helen Allinson, *Bredgar: the history of a Kentish parish* (1997)

Ralph Arnold, *The Hundred of Hoo* (1947)

Derek Barnard, *Merrily to Frindsbury* (1996)

Daniel Beagles, *The Middlesex Sessions Vagrancy Records*

Beckenham 1861-71, (Ordnance Survey Map)

Alan Bignell, *The Kent Village Book*, (1986)

John Blundell, *An Illustrated Guide to St Mary Cray and the Upper Cray Valley* (1999)

George Borrow, *Romano Lavo-Lil: a book of the Gypsy* (1874)

C. Brigden, *Dickens Country Sketchbook* (1987)

Bromley 1861, (Ordnance Survey Map)

Frances Brown, *Fairground Strollers and Showfolk* (2001)

Robert Dawson, *British Gypsy Slavery* (2001)

Robert Dawson, *The Genealogy of the Romany Boswells* (2004)

W. Desmond, *Tanning Hides and Skins* (1801)

Charles Dickens, *Christmas Stories* (1871)

Charles Dickens, *Great Expectations* (1861)

Charles Dickens, *The Uncommercial Traveller* (1860)

Geoffrey Dudley, *The Victorian Agricultural Labourer*

Simon Evans, *Surrey and the London Commons* (unpublished)

Sally Festing, *The Story of Lavender* (1982)

Keith Fielding, *History of England*

Filmer, *Kentish Rural Crafts and Industries* (1981)

Sharon Floate, *My ancestors were Gypsies* (1999)

Sharon Floate, *Starting Out in Family History* (Romany Routes, Vol 3, No. 6)

Funeral of the late Mr. Charles Lee, (The World's Fair 2 June 1928)

Funeral of the Late Mr Henry Taylor at Feltham, (The World's Fair, February 1927)

Gipsy Life Near London, (The Illustrated London News, 13 December 1879)

James Greenwood, "Some Secrets of Gipsy Life" in *Low Life Deeps* (1881)

John Guy, *The forgotten landscape of the Hoo Peninsula* (Byegone Kent, Vol 23, No.10)

Hammond, *All Hallows, Hoo, Kent* (1928)

Martin Hammond, *Bricks and Brickmaking* (2001)

Katherine Harding & Denise Baldwin, *Along the River Cray: a pictorial history of the Cray Valley* (2003)

Shirley Harrison and Sally Evemy, *Dickens in Rochester* (1997)

Edward Hasted, *Kent*

Alastair Heseltine, *Baskets and basket making* (1996)

Hoo St Werburgh's Women's Institute, *A Village Scrapbook – Hoo St Werburgh*

E.L.S. Horsburgh, *Bromley* (1928)

Howell, *The Kentish Notebook Volume 2* (1894)

William Howitt, *The Rural Life of England* (1844)

Frank E Huggett, *A day in the life of a Victorian Farm Worker*

Eric Inman, *Beckenham* (2002)

Kelly's Directory of Kent (1845)

Kellys Directory of the Home Counties (1852)

Kent County Record Office, *Kent Settlement Indexes*

David Lazell, *Fast fingers in the hop fields – Romanis and itinerants at the magic lantern show* (Family Tree Magazine, December 2000)

London Borough of Southwark, *Charles Dickens & Southwark*

London Borough of Southwark, *The Story of Bermondsey*

Pat Loveridge, *A Calendar of Fairs and Markets held in the nineteenth century* (2003)

Philip MacDougall, *The Book of Medway: the story of Rochester, Chatham and Strood* (1989)

Philip MacDougall, *The Hoo Peninsula* (1980)

Philip MacDougall, *The Prison Ship Hero*

Alan McGowan, *On the Gypsy Trail* (1998)

Alan Major, *Hidden Kent,* (1994)

Andrew Martin, *Not a Mile from Milk Street* (1982)

David Mayall, *Gypsy-travellers in nineteenth century society* (1988)

Merton Historical Society, *Some Memories of Merton* (1983)

Richard Milward, *A New Short History of Wimbledon* (1989):

Richard Milward, *Wimbledon Past* (1998)

Mitcham - a historical glimpse (1988)

Mitcham Fair (1991)

Eric Montague, *Mitcham Common* (2001)

Vernon Morwood, *Our Gipies in City, Tent and Van* (1885)

W. Nichols, *Cooling, Kent and its Castle*

W. Nichols, *A History of the North Kent Marshes in the Area of Cliffe*

Monica North, *Dickens Country: a literary guide to the Medway area* (2002)

Bob Ogley, *Kent 1800-1899: a chronicle of the 19th century* (2003)

Norman Plastow, *A History of Wimbledon and Putney Commons* (1986)

Pigot's Directory (1840)

Post Office Directory (1878)

Henry R Procter, *The text book of tanning* (1885)

Doris Pullen, *Beckenham – towards township*

Michael Rawcliffe, *Bromley Market Square and High Street in 1900*

Gillian Rickard, *Vagrants, Gypsies and Travellers in Kent 1572-1948* (1995)

Carson Ritchie, *Gypsies of Kent* (Byegone Kent, Vol. 12, No. 3)

The Riverside Story, 1900-1965

Margaret Smith, *Cooling: A Dickens of a Village* (1998)

South London Record No. 1 - 1985

Dorothy Thompson, *The British People*

E.P. Thompson, *The Making of the English Working Class* (1963)

Flora Thompson, *Lark Rise to Candleford* (1945)

Roy Tricker, *St James's Church, Cooling, Kent*

Brian Vesey-Fitzgerald, *Gypsies of Britain* (1973)

Alan Watts, *Dickens at Gad's Hill* (1989)

T.W. Wilkinson, *Van Dwelling London*, (Living London, 1861)

Nerissa Wilson, *Gypsies and Gentlemen*

Clive Whichelow, *Secrets of Wimbledon Common and Putney Heath* (2000)

Wimbledon – a historical glimpse (1985)

Winifred Whitehead, *Wimbledon 1885-1965*

Des Worsdale, *Hoo St Werburgh in old picture postcards* (1984)

Des Worsdale, *Peninsula Round: The Hoo Peninsula, Kent* (1982)

Des Worsdale, *The Times of Hoo St Werburgh* (1997)

Other Books by John Pateman

Bren Gunner on Manoeuvres: Arthur Pateman Goes To War: The story of Arthur Pateman and his time in the Royal West Kent Regiment in Palestine, Malta, Samos, Leros and a POW camp.

Canadian Corner: The story of the Canadian Corps in the Great War and the Commonwealth War Graves Commission cemetery at All Saints churchyard, Orpington, Kent.

Charles Dickens and Travellers: Extracts from the works of Charles Dickens concerning Gypsies and Travellers.

Dippers Slip: the life and times of Noah Pateman: The story of Noah Pateman and his family and their life in Orpington and the Crays.

Fordcroft: The story of a small working class community in St Mary Cray, their lives and living conditions.

Hoo, Hops and Hods: the life and times of Robert Pateman: The story of Robert Pateman and his family and their life on the Hoo Peninsula.

Lincolnshire Asylums: The story of The Lawn (1820), St John's (1852), Rauceby (1902) and Harmston Hall (1930).

The Ontario Military Hospital: The story of how the Great War hospital was built in Orpington in 1916 by the Government of Ontario.

Orpington at War: The story of the War Shrines, War Memorials and War Graves at All Saints Church and the men of Orpington who died in the Great War, between the Wars and in the Second World War.

Orpington Man: the life and times of John Pateman, Volume One 1956-74: The story of John Pateman and his family and their life at Oakdene Road and the Ramsden Estate.

Orpington Man: the life and times of John Pateman, Volume Three 1997-: The story of John Pateman and his family and their life in Lincolnshire.

Patemans By Census: The story of the Pateman family as recorded in the national census between 1841 – 1911.

Patemans By County: The story of the Pateman family as recorded in the births, marriages and deaths registers for England from 1837.

Patemans in Kent: The story of the Pateman family in Kent as recorded in the births, marriages and deaths registers for England from 1837 and the national census 1841-1911

Petten Grove: The story of a street on the Ramsden Estate in south London and the people who lived in it from 1956 – 2003.

The Ramsden Estate: The story of how the Ramsden area of Orpington was developed from open farmland into a large post-war council housing estate.

St Mary Cray Cemetery: The story of a Victorian cemetery in Star Lane and the fallen from RAF from Biggin Hill who were buried there in World War Two.

Seven Steps to Glory: Private Pateman Goes to War: The story of Walter Pateman, a Kent Gypsy who fought and died in the Great War.

Strewing the Pateran: the Gypsies of Thorney Hill: The story of the Pateman family of Gypsies who lived in the New Forest.

Ten Pound Pom: the life and times of Victor Poxon: The story of Victor Poxon and his life in the Royal Navy and Australia.

Three Years on the Western Front: Gunner Rodbourne Goes to War: The story of Albert Rodbourne, one of the first men in St Mary Cray to volunteer to fight in the Great War.

Tugmutton Common: the life and times of William Pateman: The story of William Pateman and his family and their life at Locksbottom, Farnborough.

What Dark History is This? William Pateman and the Gordon Riots: The story of William Pateman, a ringleader in the Gordon riots which rocked Georgian London.

Copies of these titles can be purchased from Lulu.com or 11 Windsor Close, Sleaford, Lincolnshire, NG34 7NL. Please make cheques payable to John Pateman.